D1711480

MASOCHISM
The Treatment of
Self-Inflicted Suffering

MASOCHISM
The Treatment of
Self-Inflicted Suffering

Edited by
Jill D. Montgomery, Ph.D.
Ann C. Greif, Ph.D.

Austen Riggs Center
Stockbridge, Massachusetts

International Universities Press, Inc.
Madison   Connecticut

Library of Congress Cataloging-in-Publication Data

Masochism: the treatment of self-inflicted suffering / edited by Jill D. Montgomery, Ann C. Greif.
     p. cm.
    Includes bibliographies and index.
    ISBN 0-8236-3145-1
    1. Masochism—Treatment. 2. Psychoanalysis. I. Montgomery, Jill D. II. Greif, Ann C.
    [DNLM: 1. Masochism. WM 610 M3982]
RC553.M36M38 1989
616.85'835—dc19
DNLM/DLC
for Library of Congress   88-13669
                                              CIP

Manufactured in the United States of America

To our patients for all their patience and courage in the shared enterprise of the analytic situation.

Contents

Preface

Jill D. Montgomery, Ph.D.

Dawn

Cold rapid hands
Draw back one by one
The bandages of dark
I open my eyes
                    Still
I am living
                    At the center
Of a wound still fresh

Octavio Paz, "Salamandra"

There are individuals who organize experience masochistically. Each morning they awaken to rediscover themselves by the familiar contours of a reality resurrected out of memory and constructed out of pain. These are the individuals we will refer to as masochistic. They have come to organize their world by way of a particular, stable pattern through which they know and maintain themselves. The aim of this book is to delineate a point of view about masochism through clinical narrative, a study of these lives as we came to know them within the psychoanalytic situation. In the process we would like to reclaim the clinical usefulness of the term "masochism," which has become theoretically weak, although it has remained experientially powerful and alive in psychoanalytic discourse. For as we have worked to mitigate suffering it has been impossible to ignore the fact that lives can be captivated by it, that self-torture is one possible construction for a life, and that the slave clings to its master with as much force as the master clings to its slave. Apparently there is something at the heart of what is human that perversely refuses the possibility offered by our insight. Thus we have kept the term masochism alive as if in its naming this something would be accounted for.

Psychoanalysis has addressed the existence of self-inflicted pain throughout the historical evolution of its theory building. Philosophy and religion have long observed that humanity seems trapped in structures of self-generated suffering, and that freedom is obstructed by self-imposed obstacles. Freud by way of the natural sciences corporealized the idea: Man became man with a biology that anchored the irrationality and the perversity in the body. Mind was connected to body through metapsychological pathways that allowed the unconscious out of sight to pursue its own plans for its own reasons. These unconscious plans and these unconscious reasons existed in their own time, an archaic time that persisted alongside the present. Human actions were understood as divided — body to mind, unconscious to conscious, past to present — the outcome of a history, a biology, and the civilizing pressures brought to bear by the attachment to others. Sexuality became the unignorable manifestation of this confluence. Its appetitive force became a powerful explanatory principle, and its manifestations became paradigmatic of the hidden perversity at the heart of what was human. Human behavior was now treatable as biology, and nameable as distinct diagnostic entities. This is where masochism begins as a clinical term.

Kraft-Ebbing (1931) named a particular form of human behavior masochism. That this relational activity was sexual gave rise to what is now known as the narrow (i.e., manifestly sexual) definition of masochism. Naming a clinical entity is an act of creation that seems to give birth to a new phenomenon separate from the activity that inspired and predated the naming. Kraft-Ebbing in his sexual research described a behavior involving sexual excitement accompanying subjugation to the tyranny of the sexual object. Pain was not the essential factor; it was a component of the tyranny of the relationship. Pain and the aroused body formed the field upon which the dyadic drama was enacted. What he named was a sexual deviancy. What we believe he in fact saw was a particular structure, in this instance concretized (Atwood and Stolorow, 1984) through interpersonal sexual enactment. What he gave us was an enlightened description of a particular form of human experience.

The term masochism became linked to biology through the body, pain, and sexuality. It was a compelling example of self-generated suffering, since pain was perversely sought over pleasure and subjugation over freedom. As sexuality masochism could be subjectively felt as a force that could irresistibly grip mental life. Its tie to biology gave it scientific veracity, and with Freud's conception of masochism as an instinctual component of mental life it gave a depressive inevitability to suffering that reflected the intellectual climate of the late nineteenth century. But it was never a theoretically powerful explanatory term, either as psychoanalytic biology (erotogenic masochism or primary masochism) or as psychoanalytic materialist philosophy (death instinct). It was preeminently a descriptive term, a word linked to its referent descriptively. The term masochism could not easily be severed from the phenomenon it described to stand behind it deterministically as an explanatory, metapsychological principle, and as such, over the history of its usage in psychoanalysis, it was pulled toward its referent behavior in an ever broadening descriptive use of the term. Masochism came to be used, even by Freud, to describe manifestly nonsexual intrapsychic and interpersonal relational patterns (e.g., moral masochism) that required complicated metapsychological transformations to be related back to their sexual, erotogenic masochistic underpinnings.

There is no historical development of a theory per se of masochism in psychoanalysis. We believe that the term masochism has had a fascinating history within psychoanalysis and that the recent, impressive reviews of the literature on the subject (Maleson, 1984; Grossman, 1986) actually give us a historical account of the progress of psychoanalysis as an intellectual and political movement, but add little to an understanding of masochism as a phenomenon. The attempts have been to clarify the use of the *term* within psychoanalysis, to recommend the use of either the narrow (manifestly sexual) or broad (manifestly nonsexual) definition. There seems to be an implicit acceptance of the fact that the theory of the observer shapes the understanding of the phenomenon. Masochism understood by the drive theorists will be different from that of the ego psychologists or the object-relations theorists. The phenomenon disappears inevitably in the theory of the examiner. And so the history of masochism within psychoanalytic discourse has been the history of a word, and the history of overlapping, often contradictory, theoretical schools. Clinical observation conforms to theoretical expectations to greater and lesser degrees, and to greater and lesser degrees the theories themselves appear through the elimination of information.

We believe that the clinical usefulness of the term masochism will not depend on its theoretical elegance, or even on the clarity of its definition. If the term is to be useful — and certainly, if the literature is any indication, we keep using it — then it will be because it is trying to describe something that is, that has a meaning and a shape within human experience. The word is moving toward its referent descriptively, and as such stands in relation to it not as an explanatory principle, not as "electricity" to "lightbulb," but more as "map" to "landscape." If we then regard the existing analytic accounts of masochism as attempts at portraiture and disregard the intent, the level of abstraction, the degree of inference, and the differences in theoretical language, the broad outlines of a structure begin to appear. This structure delineates the stable patterns and shapes that organize and give meaning to lives we can term masochistic. It is a structure informed by relational patterns involving subjugation, pain, and the disavowal of activity within a context of captivity and stagnation. This structure is the manifestation of personal meaning, and as such its particulars are overdetermined and serve multiple functions, the outcome of a history, a biology, and a culture of necessary attachments, and the repeated syntheses involved in the construction of a life.

The intent of this book is clinical, and by that we mean several things. It was conceived within a unique clinical context, the Austen Riggs Center, which in a sense forced the project on us out of the intensity of the clinical work. The center is a small, psychoanalytic, teaching and research hospital located in the Berkshire Mountains of western Massachusetts. It provides an open setting for the long-term psychoanalytic treatment of troubled individuals. This type of treatment is a luxury and a rare opportunity for patient and analyst. The winters are long, the center is isolated, and the work is concentrated, problematic, and exposed. Our patients presented us with the extremes of human behavior and the opportunity to learn from it. The treatments were turbulent, marked by a starkness of suffering, rapidly fluctuating transference and countertransference responses, impasse, and vivid enactments within the psychoanalytic dyad and the institution. Our research questions were pressed on us by our clinical work, and by the need to address personal issues raised by our involvement with human suffering. We were forced to work beyond our theories and training, and in the process began to articulate theories and methods of our own.

We wanted to write a book in which we could speak personally and clinically about our work. We wanted the analysis to remain experience-near, the descriptions to be clinical, and the details to be personal, and in this way present the reader with a truthful portrayal of an ongoing process rather than the crystallization of a finished theory. We wanted to include data rather than eliminate it, even when it revealed the ragged edge or the unfinished seam. We wanted to talk to the reader about what we actually did in a way that would remain recognizable and thereby useful, and invite the reader to join our discussion, to examine our clinical data critically, and to participate in the theory-building process.

Our focus on masochism and the gradual development of our belief in its usefulness as a clinical term began with the unavoidable observation that despite our best efforts, and the efforts of a talented staff, a group of our patients continued to suffer. They suffered by their own actions and by the actions of others. They suffered our interpretations of their suffering, and they suffered the humiliation of their patient status while simultaneously clinging to it, repetitively presenting us with their suffering in desperation and in hopelessness. Impasse and a deadening stagnation alternated with problematic acts of destruction and intense countertransferential reactions. We had, after all, wished to release our patients from their pain and captivity and could not comfortably sit in the role of torturer or impotent healer. These patients seemed locked within their self-generated masochistic configurations, ones that appeared to unavoidably dominate their treatments in uninterpretable ways. Experience seemed monothematically organized into rigid subsuming dyadic configurations of master–slave — self to other, self to body, self to self — that efficiently functioned to resist change.

As a group of colleagues working in such a setting we had the opportunity to work collaboratively over a long period of time. We were familiar with each other, with each other's patients, and with the progress of the individual treatments, since all clinical staff were responsible for regularly presenting their work in detail for staff discussion. Further, we had complete psychological test data and evaluations, and repeat evaluations as additional data on each patient. We began to develop a growing dissatisfaction with the standard interpretation of these patients and their behaviors. Based on our clinical experience and understanding of our patients and their development we found formulations that typically stressed the aggressive component of this behavior, or instinctual gratification and superego retribution, as the primary level of interpretation to be useless if not actually destructive.

We began an ongoing collaborative study and a series of symposia. What slowly evolved out of this work was the description of a particular type of patient we came to understand as embedded within a masochistic way of life. These individuals suffered in order to stay alive and attached. For them pain was their other half, a maternally toned self-constituting context (Montgomery, Chapter 2). For some individuals it appeared that a masochistic life, however costly, represented their best possible effort at creating and maintaining a separate and autonomous sense of self. Their suffering salvaged for them a modicum of satisfaction, security, and self-esteem and thereby staved off the pull toward identity diffusion, psychotic regression, or suicide (Sacksteder, Chapter 8).

The perspective of this book is developmental in that it comes out of a clinical point of view that greets the troubled patient with the active acknowledgment that they were not always so. Psychoanalysis then as the explication of personal meaning seeks to find a path back through the creative syntheses necessitated in the construction of this troubled life. We have organized the chapters in this book to emphasize shared solutions and historical similarities rather than traditional diagnostic categories. Traditional diagnosis is insufficient and fragmenting in that the available diagnoses do not always represent information that is organized at the same level of abstraction. Are the diagnoses meant as mutually exclusive entities, developmental lines, stable levels of organization, or descriptive complexes of behavior? We are in a sense choosing to avoid this issue, at least for the time being, by speaking of a masochistic way of life, a masochistic organization of experience that crosses diagnostic groups and includes behavioral manifestations traditionally spoken of in other ways.

Chapters cover patients diagnosed as neurotic, character disordered, borderline, narcissistic, and schizophrenic. As individuals they presented with histrionic, impulsive, obsessive, schizoid, or paranoid defensive styles. Their behaviors included self-starvation, self-mutilation, chronic depression, sexual perversion, suicidal gestures and attempts, repetitive involvement in situations of victimization and abuse, and chronic failure. Their subjective experience was one of subjugation, pain, and passivity within an overall context of captivity and stagnation. The underlying masochistic structure and the developmental path seemed to be the same. What differed was the degree, manner, and field of enactment for the dyadic intrapsychic relational pattern of master–slave.

These patients existed in a paradoxical dreamlike representational world built from a history of pain and surrender. We have rather loosely divided the chapters into parts highlighting the major developmental issues involved in these histories — separation, pain, and the body; identity and the construction of the self; absence, the father, and recognition. In this way we hope to suggest commonalities in the ongoing process of living a life rather than impose an abstracted clinical homogeneity. We want to present a mosaic of lives, narratives that will leave the reader with an overall sense of the enormous complexity of the developmental layering that informs the isolated symptom and behavioral pathology.

Although all of the chapters are actually clinical, in the final part, "Transference, Countertransference, and the Holding Environment," we will address problems of treatment and change more specifically. The problem of enactment, repetition, and impasse was the motivating concern behind this study. We could not then be content with a developmental understanding — no matter how informed — if it would just support an appreciation of the status quo. As clinicians we are manifestly involved in change, and all of the chapters address this issue. In the course of this study we were forced to confront the obvious failure of interpretation, our own masochism, repeated crises, our role within institutions, and the easy disintegration of our treatments into empty discourse.

Masochism has a shape and a meaning in certain lives that we are called on to treat. The question in these cases is always how to gain entry into a masochistically constructed subjectivity without being caught up in the aggressivity of the struggle of the master–slave relationship (Gorney and Muller, Chapter 10). Since we were a group of individual clinicians, men and women, of different ages, styles, and histories, we answered this question in characteristic ways. We have not tried to disguise our differences in the presentations that follow. We report clinical examples that demonstrate that long-standing masochistic patterns can change, and also present those in which we have failed. We believe that we have evolved useful methods for the treatment of self-inflicted suffering that address the interpersonal origins and creative functions of the behavior, and respect the humanity in seemingly entrenched psychopathology.

References

Atwood, G., & Stolorow, R. (1984), *Structure of Subjectivity: Explorations in Psychoanalytic Phenomenology*. Hillsdale, NJ: Analytic Press.

Grossman, W. (1986), Notes on masochism: A discussion of the history and development of a psychoanalytic concept. *Psychoanal. Quart.*, 55(3): 379–413.

Kraft-Ebbing, R. (1931), *Psychopathia Sexualis*. Brooklyn: Physicians & Surgeons Book Co.

Maleson, F. G. (1984), The multiple meanings of masochism in psychoanalytic discourse. *J. Amer. Psychoanal. Assn.*, 32(2): 325–356.

Acknowledgments

Behind each chapter in this volume, there lies the influence of many supervisors, teachers, and analysts, whose names often do not appear overtly, but whose wisdom, vitality, and integrity have nonetheless contributed immeasurably to what has been articulated. These more personal connections have fostered the development of the authors. These individuals have lent their vitality generously and freely. In this spirit, we would like to thank all the staff of the Austen Riggs Center. In this unique setting, scholarship and careful clinical work have flourished over the years, and we have felt privileged to participate in this tradition.

In particular, we wish to thank Dr. Daniel Schwartz, Medical Director of the Center, who encouraged his staff members to risk thinking seriously about themselves and their work, and to write as an avenue for discovery and communication. Not only did he lend moral support to our efforts, but he recognized the need for practical support in the form of time to study and reflect, and much needed secretarial help. For all these considerations, we are most grateful. Beyond his role as an institutional advocate and wise teacher, Dr. Schwartz and, before him, Drs. Otto Will and Robert Knight, the former Medical Directors of the Center, have by their own creative energy and original insights stimulated the thinking of their staff, and thereby generated an atmosphere of inquiry, in which truth is valued and knowledge accrued.

We also wish to thank Drs. Martin Cooperman, Ess A. White, Jr., Margaret Brenman-Gibson, Anne F. deGersdorff, Paul Seton, and Paul Lippmann. In particular, we want to thank Dr. Cooperman for his honest, sympathetic, and above all else human approach to psychoanalytic treatment. We thank Dr. Brenman-Gibson for her "radical" perspective of placing the person of the patient uppermost in one's concern before any "objects" or objectives, whether they be in the form of theory or other unholy allegiances. We thank Drs. White and Seton for their sympathetic support and guidance, and thoughtful insights. Of course, the other staff members of the Center have contributed to our understanding of masochism in the many forums of daily intellectual exchange, case conferences, and staff meetings, and have given generously of both their encouragement and helpful criticism.

Dr. Margaret Emery, Editor-in-Chief, International Universities Press, has helped us turn our clinical experiences into a book. For this we gratefully thank her.

For secretarial help, which has maintained a tradition of excellence at Riggs, we wish to thank Ms. Betsy Cobb, Jeanne Herrick, Virginia Fenn, and Liz Thomson for their invaluable assistance and patience in the careful preparation of this manuscript.

We would like to thank our husbands, Robert Montgomery and Randall Howe, the hidden partners for each of us in this enterprise.

And lastly, we wish to thank Dr. Leo Goldberger, without whose firm insistence on the value of the project none of this would have been possible.

Introduction: Historical Synthesis

Ann C. Greif, Ph.D.

The term masochism has gone through multiple transformations of meaning since it first entered the arena of psychoanalytic discourse through Freud's contribution (1919). Even this early psychoanalytic exposition on the concept of masochism entailed the reframing of an earlier conceptualization as laid out by Kraft-Ebbing (1931). Each transformation, beginning with Freud and extending on to other theorists such as Menaker (1942), Brenman (1952), Berlinger (1958), Brenner (1959), Eisenbud (1967), and Grossman (1986), has resulted in increased richness and depth to our understanding, and at the same time added to our confusion and uncertainty both in our theory and our clinical practice. One answer to this dilemma lies in appreciating the essential complexity of the phenomenon itself. As Grossman (1986) has recently articulated, reductionism is at the heart of our conceptual confusion with this concept. For example, to turn masochism into a phenomenon solely of sexual perversion does not do justice to the object relation factor nor to developmental issues. Masochism is a multifaceted metaconcept involving the complex intermeshing of defenses, drives, character structure, and object relations.

Another way to organize the apparent disparity which exists in the literature is to place each revision within its proper historical context. The meaning of masochism and our understanding of it as a clinical phenomenon has shifted and been reconstructed along with the growth of our theory and clinical expertise in general. Just as our theory moved beyond drive-related conceptualizations into ego psychology, so did this concept. Much like the concept of narcissism, masochism as a concept dealing with a hierarchically organized, multifaceted, multidetermined symptom constellation is most sensitive to these theoretical shifts, each redefinition revealing some new facet and simultaneously constructing a new gestalt mirroring the overall permutations of our theory.

Understanding masochism may be of historical significance today beyond the confines of our theory or of our practice. In a world troubled by the prospect of nuclear war and global destruction, the issue of humankind's troubled self at odds with its own vitality and integrity, is even more important today than in earlier times. Much like Lasch's (1984) "minimal self" the masochistically disordered person lives in an experiential world of misery, humiliation, and anxiety, primarily constituted for self-protection against harsh emotional and interpersonal realities that threaten the self with painful fragmentation.

The Real, the Imaginary, and the Symbolic

This book works from three seemingly contradictory premises about masochism. The first of these is most apparent in the clinical chapters, and it has to do with the extent to which masochism is viewed as real. Masochism as embodying an apparent determination to castrate, punish, or annihilate the self has real effects in interpersonal relationships, including the therapeutic one; has real precipitants specifically in the parents' early, persistent acts of commission and omission to curtail and sabotage the self and the body of the child; and has real consequences such as depression, sexual dysfunction, interpersonal withdrawal, self-mutilation, and suicide. These real events and effects are clearly and undeniably interrelated and connected. Patients with either a masochistic perversion or a masochistic life-style in which suffering has permeated all avenues of expression and activity, are viewed as living out a truth that was once real, palpable, and intensely felt between them and their caretakers.

The second premise from which this book operates has to do with the extent to which each of us exists in a world of subjectivity (Atwood and Stolorow, 1984). From the first moments of life, and throughout life, we are each shaped by experiences that occur in relation to others. We exist within a psychosomatic matrix constituted of several realities — our own developing selfhood intersecting and interpenetrating the "selves" of those significant others who are at first literally ensuring our survival and then later, perhaps less pointedly but still critically, enriching and deepening our awareness of our own personal identity. So to begin with, our awareness of who we are comes from this "mix-up" (Balint, l968), and constitutes the subjective vantage point, which, like an ever-receding and -advancing tide, defines and delimits our insights and understanding of ourselves and others, while simultaneously it is being recreated and transformed with each new encounter between the self and others. The masochistic individual is seen then as someone who has been embedded in a subjective world of pain and suffering. For these individuals, the sexual masochists whose perversions link them to their partners through mock acts of torture and defilement and the moral masochists whose suffering emanates more from their own personal sense of wretchedness and inadequacy, the very fiber of their identity has been constituted developmentally around such experiences of shame, guilt, and punishment. As Menaker (1942) noted, masochistic individuals lack a clear sense of their own power or initiative, and thus they repetitively hand over control of their lives to others in the hopes that someone else will compensate for their ego deficiencies. The boundaries defining self and others are thereby repetitively blurred, perpetuating the entrapment of the self by the other. The masochist exists in a peculiar subjective universe in which the oppressive presence of the other is required for any experience of vitality and wholeness. A sense of self is never truly established, and what little has been acquired is always coupled with a sense of pain and oppression.

The third and final premise of the book has to do with the centrality of symbolic activity in the search for "creative living" (Winnicott, 1971). Symbol formation, in essence, is the mediating process between those real, palpable events and the images of self and others that define our intrapsychic life. Symbolic activity is creative activity at its most basic. From the two-month-old infant who suddenly recognizes the face of humanity in his mother's countenance and who registers his sense of awe and adoration with a beaming smile, to the adolescent transforming a myriad of conflicting familial identifications into a coherent and original identity, each of us must create in order to survive, in order to forestall fragmentation and annihilation by the multiplicity of forces continually acting upon us. We must create in order to live, we must synthesize and integrate, and arrive at new breakthroughs of meaning. Dysfunctions in living are conceptualized as failures of creativity and as the inability to transform events into personal experiences (Winnicott, 1963).

Masochism like other psychopathological phenomena is a compromise between forces of fragmentation and synthesis. It represents the best approximation to creative living for that person. Why it becomes an approximation rather than an actual expression of creativity has to do with the as yet immutable tie to early traumata that has forestalled a free exchange with the present and the possibility for transmutative experiences. Said differently, at the core of the masochistic, perversion or the masochistic character is a reification of early trauma in which pain becomes associated with pleasure in all its forms, from sexual pleasure to romantic love.

The Question of Passivity and Femininity in their Relation to Masochism: Freud's Legacy

The work of Masud Khan (1979) has contributed significantly to an understanding of the link between thwarted self-definition and perversion, and since his early work in this area many others followed to document the importance of preoedipal experiences on later perverse behavior and character difficulties. The seeds of this understanding were first sown by Freud (1924) when he noted that sexual arousal is highly pliable in terms not only of object and aim in the very young child or even the infant, but also in terms of specific affective coloring. Sexual arousal can easily transform itself into rage or sadness or laughter, and vice versa. Thus, sexual excitation, as he saw it, could easily become paired with other emotional states, much like a conditioned response. It does not seem too great a leap then to postulate that the "arousal" of a sense of selfhood might become associated with feelings of pain and suffering, as well as with erotic feelings. Similarly, Freud (1920) also came to understand something of the importance of early object relations on sexual adjustment: in this case, latent and overt female homosexuality being cited as the result of developmental arrests involving an intense preoedipal attachment to the mother.

The clinical reality of masochism is that it is almost invariably tied to disillusionment with parental figures on whom the self has been passively dependent. Masochism is by definition the consequence of thwarted passivity rather than the cause or the inversion of passivity, feminine or otherwise. Masochism contains often, if not always, a mocking transformation of passivity into something deadly, grasping, and noxious, something hardly passive at all. What has come to replace the need of the child is the assertion of paralysis by an enfeebled self, a self both dynamically clinging and dependent for reasons of displaced aggression and also, for some individuals, authentically underdeveloped to the tasks of love and work.

Why then are women so much more frequently than men seen and understood to be masochistic in their character style? Likewise, both sexual masochism and moral masochism are understood clinically as predominantly feminine in orientation; that is, as being rooted in feminine identifications, again predominantly with a preoedipal maternal figure. Freud (1924) certainly believed that some degree of masochism was integral to heterosexual adjustment in women, for example, in tolerating the pain of coitus and childbirth. Deutsch (1944) reiterated this point and even exaggerated its importance for the mental life of women. The reasons for this apparent feminization of masochism may lie not so much in sociological explanations related to the politics of gender nor in recourse to explanations based on sex-role socialization and stereotyping, but may be better understood in examination of parent–

child interactions from the neonatal period through adolescence. Clearly it is in the nitty-gritty of moment-to-moment interactional patterns that cultural and social attitudes toward sex and gender are transmitted to the young of our species; the younger the age of the child the smaller the unit of time required for observation. Recent observational research (Lewis, 1972) comparing mother–child dyads shows rather dramatic differences according to the gender of the child. Little girls, for example, are more often and more easily soothed by their mothers. The bond between mother and daughter intensifies from the first moments of life by the temperamental availability of the daughter as well as by the mother's earliest recognition that the child will grow into a woman like herself. The vicissitudes of this bonding — for example, if the daughter does not mold, is not easily soothed, does not feel to the mother as if she is like herself in some important respect — may complicate the bond, but does not alter usually the initial experience of mirroring and identification between mother and daughter. Likewise, it is now recognized that mothers and their very young infants are exquisitely synchronized in their interactions, and that the rhythmic patterns of their movements can be organized around avoidance as well as contact. This means that even if a conflictual relationship develops both partners are mutually regulating the behavior of the other, and an underlying attachment exists.

Such ideas about mothers and their babies are certainly not new to psychoanalysis. Maternal ambivalence, identification, and capacity for nurturance have been seen as central to the child's developmental progress or failure. To take only one example, Lichtenstein (1961) describes the process as "imprinting," whereby the mother's script for the child is communicated and sets the basic pattern for the child's emergent identity. Long before the child is able consciously to symbolize his experiences with the mother, he is both being treated as a unique human being and at the same time is being acculturated and molded by the image the mother holds of what that child will become.

What is it about this maternal image, though, that can make it so noxious, particularly to the female child or to the exceptional male child in terms of lending a masochistic cast to the character or, at the most extreme, promoting the formation of a perversion or serious character pathology? It is the mother's own life experiences of shame, regret, and disillusionment shaped and sanctioned by cultural norms, as well as heightened by biological givens, that foster the same depressive and masochistic vulnerabilities, usually in her more socially responsive daughter. In an ironic twist of our contemporary view of equality between the sexes, biology still seems to be destiny in terms of both the mother's identificatory inclination toward the daughter and the female child's proportionately greater socializability. As some have said, woman's greatest tragedy is not the lack of the penis but her overwhelming desire to be loved.

In an effort to redress the paternalistic laments of Freud (1924) and other male analysts who have seen only the limitations and propensity for psychopathology in the woman's more profound and lasting loyalty and attachment to the preoedipal mother, certain woman analysts such as Helen Block Lewis (1976) and Carol Gilligan (1982), to name only two, have attempted to reframe our view of women as social and moral beings. Specifically, they have challenged the belief that differences between women and men, whether they be anatomical or psychological, do not justify the conclusion that women are inferior to men. Why not even regard women's greater social tendency as superior given that civilization is by definition founded on social order and cohesiveness? H.B. Lewis has written extensively on how the propensity for shame in women is grounded not so much in penis envy nor in the little girl's recognition of her organ inferiority but more on the readiness for anaclitic identification and attachment between mother and daughter. Shame, the feeling of humiliation and inferiority in the eyes of the other, is an affect based on an interpersonal transaction, whereas guilt is an introspective, self-delimiting affect having the effect of accentuating the distance between self and other. It is in the woman's propensity to experience shame that one can also see the seeds of her masochism. In masochism the self is handed over to the other for judgment, ownership, and possible punishment. Masochism provides an affective release from shame because the other is endowed with total power, responsibility, and insight, while the self is left depleted but nonculpable.

The devaluation of the self is at the heart of both the propensity for shame and the masochistic surrender to others so often seen in women. Likewise, men who are primarily identified with their mothers show similar patterning to their personalities. The devaluation of womankind extends beyond the boundaries of western culture, and can be seen in the pervasive tendency to regard the work of women as inferior and as less important than the work done by men. Many feminist writers (Rich, 1976) and, from a very different perspective, many analysts (Mahler, 1968) recognize in such devaluation the defensive denial of the power held by women, especially the mother, during early childhood. All children, male and female, are faced with the task of negotiating their way outside the symbiotic orbit, and of individuating along with their mothers into a more autonomous coexistence. One reason the feminine imago seems to be devalued intrapsychically is because of the actual mother's inevitable fall from grace in her children's eyes. As the child matures, the limitations and flaws of the mother are exaggerated, it would seem, not so much because of her lack of the penis but by comparison with the revered position she initially held for the child. It is curious that the defensive nature of viewing women as inferior is not more vigorously explored by the analytic literature, especially given their fundamental concern with unconscious transformations of early experiences. Perhaps again it is the defensive flight from the image of woman that explains why our theory shies away from such conceptualizations. It is true that the concept of womb envy has held a place in psychoanalytic theory, but it has been mostly of historical significance, and rarely is referred to as a primary dynamic in either normal development or in the formation of psychopathology. Likewise, our theoretical references to woman as castrated man, as genitally inferior, as "gaping wound," only reinforce the cultural stereotypes and do nothing to further our understanding of why a biological given becomes psychosocial destiny. The inseparable meshing of subjectivities between mother and child explains why, in looking for reasons behind the feminization of masochism, one comes full circle, from the mother's image of the child, to the child's responsiveness to the mother, from the mother's image of herself to the child's image of the mother, as once loved and valued to devalued and emptied. The reciprocal action of envy cannot be overestimated in its effect on both partners' capacity to appraise realistically the parameters of their affection for one another and the goodness contained within the self and the other. It is the very envy the daughter feels toward her mother that thwarts her positive identification and limits her own self-esteem.

Masochism is a shortcut to true intimacy. It is full of denials, evasions, fractured meanings, and lost hopes for love and meaningful communication. Masochism becomes the alternative to genuine loving when anger and disappointments are suppressed but not forgotten, when an attachment is betrayed, and when the pain is disowned and displaced. What more profound disappointment is there than the disillusionment in the once all-important mother to whom the child first invests their total being for confirmation and nurturance. Perhaps this is yet another reason why the roots of masochism always appear to extend back to the preoedipal attachment to the mother.

Beating Fantasies and the Paternal Influence: The Confusion of Love with Powerlessness

Unlike the devaluation of women, which has seemingly been accepted at face value, the meaning of beating fantasies in the psychology of both men and women have been understood in a highly abstracted fashion to represent the distortion of the child's incestuous wish to have sex with the father. The fact that the actual father or father surrogate is portrayed as injuring, punitive, and belittling is overlooked. The presence of the father's sadism is secondary presumably to the victim's wish to be beaten for both sexual gratification and the relief from guilt. Why not interpret these fantasies more literally and in concert perhaps with the masochistic identification with the mother, which usually is present as well in individuals with masturbatory beating fantasies? That is, why not interpret beating fantasies as metaphors for the cruelty of the father, whether it was in the form of deadening indifference to the child's need to individuate from the mother or in the form of direct assaults to the child's self-esteem. These fantasies, which usually emerge in childhood and are then developed in adolescence and held onto during adulthood, reflect the individual's best effort to represent the difficult process of extracting love from the paternal figure either because of the father's emotional unavailability or because of their own inability to free themselves sufficiently from the early preoedipal attachment to the mother and their feelings of helplessness at her hands.

Recent research (Brazelton, Yogman, Als, and Tronick, 1979) has shown that children form very particular relationships with their fathers quite different from the nature of their relationships with their mothers. Fathers seem to be recognized as different-from-mother yet important figures from the very start. These findings, it would seem, support even more the contention that individuals with preoedipally fixated disorders such as masochism have specific types of troubles with fathers as well as with their mothers, which are reflected in deficiencies in early developmental milestones such as self-object differentiation, the fusion of instincts, and reality testing.

Needless to say, the father's role in the family cannot be understood apart from the mother's and vice versa. Typically, there is a sadomasochistic quality to the marriage as whole, with the wife most often assuming the role of victim to the husband's more aggressive stance. The family structure becomes the medium in which masochism develops in the child. Love is confused by the power inequalities between the parents, and becomes equated with the giving over of autonomy and control. Cultural stereotypes encourage this distortion, especially in little girls who come to feel themselves unlovable, unfeminine, and untouchable if they assert themselves and compete with their peers, siblings, and/or parents for recognition and narcissistic supplies. In addition, the children are faced repeatedly with the inequality of their own position within the family, their extreme dependence on the parents for love, and their frequent inability to extract love (Miller, 1981). To be seen and not heard, to be nearly invisible as a whole person, and to submit one's will to the parent (Menaker, 1953) become adaptations to these harsh realities that the person is not yet equipped to understand or accept.

Fathers, as potential rescuers from the seductive and frustrating presence of the mother, all too frequently disappoint their children by failing to meet the developmental need with candor and love. Instead, the child's longing to rediscover intimacy with a new partner on new terms is disillusioned, compounding the original trauma. Beating fantasies express this reality metaphorically — the longing for contact, the pain of disillusionment, as well as the guilt over both libidinal and aggressive wishes.

An Alternate Vision: Masochism as Virtue

Despite the effort to purge our theory of moralistic attitudes, it is impossible to do so. For example, we can hardly forswear any knowledge of or interest in humanistic values and the evaluation of our own and others' conduct if we are to talk about the human condition, much less to treat other human beings who bring us their pain and suffering. On the other hand, it is certainly possible to limit the excesses of our consciences as they affect our clinical work and theoretical speculations. It has from the beginning been a hallmark of psychoanalysis to attempt to shun puritanical attitudes toward instinctual life. A phenomenon such as masochism poses a curious problem then because it challenges our capacity to think in complex terms about human behavior and to recognize the paradoxical in our development. Masochism is most obviously a disorder in living that inhibits the full flowering of the person's potential. Nevertheless, it is a vehicle for the expression of many positive virtues in the personality. Virtues such as discipline, humor, playfulness, loyalty, selflessness, and humility can all be recognized in the individual's yielding up of the self to the other (Cowan, 1982).

Winnicott (1975) has addressed the issue of paradox in human experience. He saw the appreciation of paradox as a cognitive–affective–social achievement related to the negotiation of separation–individuation, and the use of transitional phenomena. Perhaps masochism is best seen as simultaneously a virtue and a vice. Each of the positive qualities listed above has its negative, life-negating counterpart. Hypocrisy, rigidity, morbidity, narcissistic regression, alienation, and vengeful self-satisfaction all are present and operative in the masochistic individual. In a similar vein, Andre Green (1980-1981) calls for a renaming of moral masochism and refers to it instead as moral narcissism. His paper addresses the dialectical nature of this phenomenon. For Green, the self-denial of the moral narcissist is symptomatic of a pervasive arrogance and self-satisfaction that shuns the usual social norms and values.

In clinical work, it is particularly incumbent on the analyst to avoid a unidimensional view of masochistic behavior and attitudes. Too easily reduced to an equation in which masochism is seen as illness or undesirable symptom, the richness of the person's experience can be lost to exploration and understanding. Much like Erikson's (1959) concept of dynamic polarities at each psychosocial stage, masochism, like other psychopathological syndromes or character styles, is comprised of inseparably linked identity fragments, forged into a unified schema, and supported within a particular social context.

The Curative Matrix of the Masochistic Patient and Psychoanalyst

An introduction to this book would not be complete without acknowledging the indebtedness to the work of Winnicott whose writings on the holding environment, good-enough mothering, hate in the countertransference, and transitional phenomena have proved seminal to several of the chapters. Certainly, the work of others such as Hermann, Balint, Erikson, Kohut, and Stolorow have contributed deeply as well, but even when not directly influenced by Winnicott's writings the chapters reflect the sensitivity and thoughtfulness to interpersonal processes and to the full range of human potentials that are the hallmarks of Winnicott's thinking about clinical work.

The idea of a therapeutic alliance between the masochistic patient and the psychoanalyst is almost by definition contradictory. Negative therapeutic reactions have been nearly synonymous with the term masochism. One might say the masochist experiences a negative therapeutic reaction to life in general. Freud (1916) referred to such individuals as being ''wrecked by success.'' The authors of the chapters to follow, however, have not found the technical problems of these treatments to be insurmountable. Like Winnicott (1963) and others (Balint, 1952) they seem more attuned to the hope for a new beginning, for the birth of a new self into a good-enough relationship with the analyst, than to the restrictions imposed on the relationship by early traumata. These authors share a common vision of their role as curative agents: this vision entails a keen appreciation for developmental processes, an intense interest in and curiosity about the vagaries of regression in the transference, and a commitment to seeing the psychoanalytic situation as an arena not only for an intrapsychic drama but also for an interpersonal drama involving two participants, each effecting the other's growth and understanding. However, such acceptance of the inevitable struggle involved for the patient and the analyst does not entirely exclude problematic countertransferential responses. Mirroring the appreciation of the patient's dilemma, these clinical–theoretical papers seek to clarify the position of the analyst and to illuminate the genuine intersubjectivity of the analytic situation.

These patients pose specific treatment problems for the analyst. To begin with, they challenge the analyst's capacity to endure and to survive with integrity, as a person and as a healer. Winnicott (1975) once said somewhat facetiously that he aimed in an analysis at keeping alive, keeping well, and keeping awake. In facing the masochistic patient's insistence on suffering and their eschewing of pleasure, the analyst experiences a real threat to the very essence of what he or she hopes to be. These patients unconsciously, and sometimes consciously, attack that inner sense of goodness and potency that the analyst requires in order to continue the treatment of the patient. The analyst's ego ideal of being someone who lends himself to another's development is severely taxed, and in an ironic twist, pits the "normal masochism" (DeMonchy, 1950) of the analyst (who hopes to achieve a desired goal through self-denial) against the perverse, rigid, and entrenched masochism of the patient. The analyst as a sentient being, alive, perceptive, and feeling must stand witness to these attempts by patients to render themselves, and their treatments, lifeless, inert, and empty, and thereby give claim to something other than what has been known by the patient up until that time. Given these patients' life histories and consequent sensitivity to being controlled and manipulated, however, the analyst must avoid an attitude of martyrlike submission to the patient's symptoms, which will all too easily feel like an effort at guilt induction. At the same time, such a countertransference reaction would intensify the depressive leanings in these patients who are looking to the analyst for a different solution to the seemingly impossible dilemmas of their lives. The absolute intersubjectivity of the analytic situation can be seen no more clearly than in this mirroring of the patient's lifelong experience of oppression in the analyst's complementary experience of burden, heavy-heartedness, and discouragement in the treatment.

Alongside the capacity to endure, the analyst must find a means to communicate with the patient in a way that offers the possibility of change. What the contributors to this book understand is that the establishment of a dialogue leading to change does not rely solely on insight via interpretation but more often than not on a shared experience of empathy, which entails both patient and analyst feeling empathically understood and held by the other and by their shared work together. As Greenacre (1968) and others (Robbins, 1981) have recognized, the therapeutic relationship, like any intimate relationship, attempts to achieve a level of communication that has its origins in the child's original "interpenetrating mix-up" (Balint, 1968) with the mother.* By this it is meant not that the therapist shares confidences with the patient but rather that they meet and recognize each other in their joint effort to understand the patient's life. The analyst, like the patient, needs to see himself in how he is being seen just as the patient needs to experience his own image

---

*Terms such as "symbiosis," "enmeshment," and even "dependence" are avoided here because the author wishes to stress the complementarity and interdependence found in the early mother-child dyad, and thereby to stress the importance for the analytic situation of rekindling such a state of deep communication.

reflected in a form he can himself recognize, sometimes lovingly and sometimes hatefully. Kohut's (1977) concept of self-object transference has
helped clarify the centrality of empathy in working with an individual whose
self identity is fractured or incomplete. What Kohut did not stress, which the
authors in this book seem to have found repeatedly on their own, is the reciprocal nature of empathy between the participants, the dialectic of truth and
recognition between analyst and patient, if you will.

Recognizing the intersubjectivity of the psychoanalytic relationship helps
orient the analyst to his or her task, but falls short of addressing how something new can be entered into the "system," to borrow a term from cybernet-
ics. If the participants' self-awareness as well as actions within the treatment
are regulated by the relationship, this still leaves unanswered how new intrapsychic and interpersonal patterns are established beyond the initial engagement
in a new relationship. Traditionally, the literature has assumed the superior
capacity of the analyst to formulate insights and to lend these to the patient,
with different affects attached. Thus, sometimes with caution or force, or with
kindness or frustration, the insights can be said to be given, and the patient
is seen then as the more or less passive recipient of the decisive action taken
by the analyst. What is stressed in the chapters to follow is not only the legitimate authority of the analyst as an objectively perceived other whom the
patient looks to for new information about the self, but also the facilitating
role of the analyst freeing the thwarted initiative of the patient who becomes
gradually but progressively an agent in his or her own curative process.

Winnicott (1963) felt that the capacity to not communicate was equal in
importance to the capacity to communicate directly. This book reflects a respect for the processes set in motion by a treatment, and for the needed autonomy of masochistic patients struggling to rediscover their thwarted initiative.
Not every thought need be analyzed, nor every feeling disentangled; much
more critical is the coming together with the patient to make a new beginning.
These patients are in desperate need of having their boundaries affirmed and
promoted (Menaker, 1942). As has already been stated, the masochist all too
readily seeks to be dominated and penetrated: handing themselves over to the
analyst is one more replication of the early object relations in which their separateness was denied, mistrusted, and perhaps even condemned. These chapters suggest that the analyst must allow himself not only to be used as a container for the patient's forbidden impulses, thoughts, feelings, and mental representations, but must also accept and own the patient's projections and thus
allow himself to be defined by the patient. By accepting the projections the
analyst also then has an opportunity to "play" with the transference. Much
like in play therapy with children, the analyst is thereby afforded an opportunity to embellish, modify, partially discard, and in subtle ways redefine the
fixed self and other schemata that have underlain the life of the masochist.

Several of the chapters to follow look at the problem of engagement, finding not surprisingly that the analyst's own counteridentification with the patient can provide an opening for communication. The success or failure of the treatment seems to hinge on the creation of such a shared reality.

Masochistic individuals impress us alternately with their arrogance and their poor self-esteem. Like the good parent, the analyst has to promote and appreciate the patient's strengths, without seductively holding out an image of perfection and completion, and at the same time acknowledge deficits, without being punitive and demeaning. Holding out hope for a new beginning establishes an ideal for the self, implying both the potentials of the future and the triumphs and defeats of the past. Through identification with the analyst who tolerates both failure and success in the treatment, the patient learns to appreciate their own flawed existence, accepting his limited desirability and bounded perfection, and no longer has to search for a parasitic relationship with another human being in which, as master–slave, he longs to have his needs totally gratified and his identity totally defined.

In the clinical work to be reported, one can sense the uniqueness of each dyad. In seeming contradiction to what has just been said, these relationships are intense, problematic, and often exist as if nothing else in the world mattered to the two participants. Interpretative statements take on meaning in this context, especially when they are passionately felt or at least when each person feels passionately about what is taking place in the treatment. This is no more true than at the time when both participants are considering terminating the treatment, and reflect on the impact they have had on one another. Whether the patient managed to organize a new type of life that does not hold suffering at its core, or whether the patient has simply been able to feel more intensely or to not feel bad so often, the treatment has effected a change that has shifted the life course of the patient. The analyst, it seems, often learns the degree of his or her attachment as the separation is anticipated: again, this is not unlike the patient whose underlying positive transference is now open for scrutiny and interpretation.

For masochistic individuals who come to treatment because of their failures in separation–individuation, the termination phase is particularly critical. At this time suicide is a real risk for the patient while the analyst may find unexpectedly that he or she feels depressed by the anticipated loss of the patient. Often the termination phase will be extremely protracted, or may never truly occur, as the patient needs to return to the analyst for occasional "refuelings" (Mahler, 1968). Like the transitional object, the analytic relationship fades in importance but is never totally lost as it hovers at the edges of consciousness for each participant, lending meaningful memories to new relationships, providing valuable lessons about life, and enriching the psychic reserves that add depth to other creative encounters.

References

Atwood, G., & Stolorow, R. (1984), *Structures of Subjectivity: Explorations in Psychoanalytic Phenomenology*. Hillsdale, NJ: Analytic Press.

Balint, M. (1952), New beginning and the paranoid and depressive syndromes. In: *Primary Love and Psychoanalytic Technique*. New York: Liveright Publishing, pp. 230–249.

——— (1968), *The Basic Fault: Therapeutic Aspects of Regression*. New York: Brunner/Mazel.

Berlinger, B. (1958), The role of object relations in moral masochism. *Psychoanal. Quart.*, 27:27–38.

Brazelton, T. B., Yogman, M. S., Als, H., & Tronick, E. (1979), The infant as a focus for family reciprocity. In: *Social Network of the Developing Child*, eds. M. Lewis & L. Rosenblum. New York: Wiley, pp. 29–43.

Brenman, M. (1952), On teasing and being teased: And the problem of "moral masochism." *The Psychoanalytic Study of the Child*, 7:264–285. New York: International Universities Press.

Brenner, C. (1959), The masochistic character: Genesis and treatment. *J. Amer. Psychoanal. Assn.*, 7:197–226.

Cowan, L. (1982), *Masochism: A Jungian View*. Dallas, TX: Spring Publishers.

DeMonchy, R. (1950), Masochism as a pathological and as a normal phenomenon in the human mind. *Internat. J. Psycho-Anal.*, 31:95–97.

Deutsch, H. (1944), *The Psychology of Women*. New York: Grune & Stratton.

Eisenbud, R. (1967), Masochism revisited. *Psychoanal. Rev.*, 54:561–582.

Erikson, E. H. (1959), Identity and the Life Cycle. *Psychological Issues*, Monograph 1, Vol.1, No.1. New York: International Universities Press.

Freud, S. (1916), Some character types met with in psychoanalytic work. *Standard Edition*, 14:311–331. London: Hogarth Press, 1957.

——— (1919), A child is being beaten: A contribution to the study of the origin of sexual perversions. *Standard Edition*, 17:179–204. London: Hogarth Press, 1955.

——— (1920), The psychogenesis of a case of homosexuality in a woman. *Standard Edition*, 180:149–172. London: Hogarth Press, 1955.

——— (1924), The economic problem of masochism. *Standard Edition*, 19:159–170. London: Hogarth Press, 1961.

Gilligan, C. (1982), *In a Different Voice: Psychological Theory and Women's Development*. Cambridge, MA: Harvard University Press.

Green, A. (1980-1981), Moral narcissism. *Internat. J. Psychoanal. Psychother.*, 8:243–270.

Greenacre, P. (1968), The psychoanalytic process, transference and acting out. In: *Emotional Growth: Psychoanalytic Studies of the Gifted and a Great Variety of Other Individuals*, Vol. 2, ed. P. Greenacre. New York: International Universities Press, 1971.

Grossman, W. I. (1986), Notes on masochism: A discussion of the history and development of a psychoanalytic concept. *Psychoanal. Quart.*, 55(3):379–413.

Khan, M. (1979), *Alienation in Perversions*. London: Hogarth Press.

Kohut, H. (1977), *The Restoration of the Self*. New York: International Universities Press.

Kraft-Ebbing, R. (1931), *Psychopathia Sexualis*. Brooklyn, NY: Physicians & Surgeons Book Co.

Lasch, C. (1984), *The Minimal Self: Psychic Survival in Troubled Times*. New York: W.W. Norton.

Lewis, H. B. (1976), *Psychic War Between Men and Women*. New York: New York University Press.

Lewis, M. (1972), State as an infant-environment interaction: An analysis of mother-infant interaction as a function of sex. *Merrill-Palmer Quart.*, 18:95–121.

Lichtenstein, H. (1961). Identity and sexuality: A study of their interrelationships in man. *J. Amer. Psychoanal. Assn.*, 9:179–260.

Mahler, M. (1968), On Human Symbiosis and the Vicissitudes of Individuation. New York: International Universities Press.

Menaker, E. (1942), The masochistic factor in the psychoanalytic situation. *Psychoanal. Quart.*, 11:171–186.

———— (1953), Masochism as a defense reaction of the ego. *Psychoanal. Quart.*, 22:205–220.

Miller, H. (1981), *Prisoners of Childhood*. New York: Basic Books.

Rich, A. (1976), *Of Woman Born: Motherhood as Experience and Institution*. New York: W.W. Norton.

Robbins, M. D. (1981), The symbiosis concept and the commencement of normal and pathological ego functioning and object relations: II Developments subsequent to infancy and pathological processes. *Internat. Psycho-Anal.*, 8:379–391.

Winnicott, D. W. (1963), Communicating and not communicating leading to a study of certain opposites. In: *The Maturational Processes and the Facilitating Environment*. New York: International Universities Press, 1965, pp. 179–192.

———— (1971), *Playing and Reality*. New York: Basic Books.

———— (1975), *Through Paediatrics to Psychoanalysis*. New York: Basic Books.

I

Separation, Pain, and the Body

1

Problems of Separation and Clinging in Masochism

Cecilia Jones, Ph.D.

In talking about any aspect of masochism, I think it is important to begin by restating the warning that Margaret Brenman (1952) made so usefully thirty years ago—that masochistic phenomena represent a complex interplay of unconscious drives, specific defenses, and adaptive implementations which cannot be adequately described under the rubric of any one of the three structural concepts: ego, superego, or id. Following Brenman's application of Waelder's (1936) principle of multiple function, Charles Brenner (1959) further elaborated this position by stating that a single set of masochistic behaviors or fantasies in an individual patient might represent a wide range of unconscious motivations and meanings, thus uniting the often seemingly contradictory and divergent interpretations of masochism that abound in the psychoanalytic literature. He also noted that masochism invariably involves both sadistic and masochistic aims, and that it may serve to defend against the earliest fears of object loss and abandonment as well as at a later stage against castration anxiety as a defensive regression from the oedipal complex.

In this chapter, we will address one aspect of masochistic experience: namely, that it always involves two persons, the subject who suffers for and at the hands of the desired other and thus is forever restituting and re-creating the other. In addition, we will discuss the contributions of the Hungarian psychoanalyst, Imre Hermann (1936), to an understanding of this relationship, a discussion that will touch on early developmental processes, the disavowal of loss, and the problem of will in masochistic phenomena.

Hermann, a student and colleague of Ferenczi's, was the first psychoanalyst to place sadomasochistic phenomena within the context of the earliest mother–child relationship. The groundwork for such a precedent had been laid by Ferenczi (1929) in his landmark paper "The Unwelcome Child and His Death Instinct," but it was Hermann (1936) who fully developed a radical theory of the earliest mother–infant bond at a time when such concepts as primary narcissism and orality dominated the classical psychoanalytic view of the first year of life. Based on clinical observations of the erotogeneity of the human hand, the grasping movements of young infants, and the clinging and grooming behavior of primates (especially the attachment of the infant ape to the mother's body during its first months of life), Hermann postulated two primary component instincts of the libido: the urge to cling to the mother's body and the drive to go in search. The grasping reflex movements of the neonate were viewed by Hermann as being based on the fundamental instinct to cling, which seeks from the beginning to operate on another person and drives the organism toward an even more complete entity—the mother–child dual union. He believed that anxiety for the infant has its origins in the situation of abandonment or when there is danger of being separated from the mother, and that anxiety develops in the direction to cling.

The second and contrasting component instinct—the drive to go in search of new objects—facilitates, in turn, the dissolution of the mother–child dual union, the broadening of the child's world, and the taking pleasure in curiosity and discovery. Although of independent origin, it was also conceptualized as the precursor to the sexual drive. Hermann felt that the positions of sadism and masochism belonged fundamentally to this context of the dual instincts, sadism developing from the "frustration and regressive intensification of the earliest desires to cling" (p. 28), while masochism represents an attempt to separate oneself. The fantasized alienation of a part of the body (for example, hair or skin), which is then forcibly detached or mutilated, expressed for Hermann the ego's striving to experience the trauma of separation from the dual union not as traumatically imposed from outside but as self-intended, the act of a free adult.

Hermann's theory is certainly closely related to many clinical observations with regard to masochistic perversions: the importance of skin eroticism, for example, and the fact that it is often the entire surface of the body that becomes the site for pain (Anzieu, 1970), the epidermis being both the surface for attachment and clinging as well as the limiting membrane that will eventually define and delineate the self. Bonding and beating rituals join both instincts: to separate (the flaying of the skin) and to cling (to be bonded and tied). The French psychoanalyst Anzieu (1970) has emphasized the importance of the skin ego in early development and views masochism as the result of traumatic overstimulation and/or deprivation of physical contact, and the wish for attachment. The skin represents the dual union between mother and child and the process of separation, the "rupture and tearing of that common skin" (p. 31).

If we briefly turn away from the pathological manifestations of clinging and going in search in the masochistic act and examine normal development, we will rediscover Hermann's dual instincts in Margaret Mahler's (1966) description of the rapprochement phase of separation–individuation. As the toddler becomes increasingly aware of his own separateness and the unavoidable loss of his previous state of oneness with the mother, he ambivalently oscillates in his behavior between renewed attempts to approach the mother and coerce her to reinstate their former unity, and pushing away in order to advance his own individuation. It is a period of marked ambivalence (of clinging and distancing), which is in striking contrast to the earlier phase of practicing where the young toddler goes in search with exuberant feelings of mastery. As Mahler goes on to point out, if the mother becomes emotionally unavailable or rejecting during this critical period when the child must come to terms with his separateness and the slow relinquishing of his magical omnipotence, what may follow is a dramatic struggle to woo or coerce the love object, intensified clinging and grief reactions, and for some toddlers, eventually a masochistic resignation and surrendering of the child's own individuality. Esther Menaker (1953) has described a similar sequence in the development of masochism, stating that in response to traumatic deprivation and insufficient parental love, the ego sacrifices itself, its own independent development, and sense of worth, to sustain the illusion of a benign and potentially loving parent.

This tendency to cling is encountered frequently in the treatment of masochistic patients—a clinging used in the denial of separateness that can become remarkably aggressive and controlling in its coerciveness. Indeed, Berlinger (1958) has defined masochism as a pathologic form of loving, representing desperate and repetitive bids for affection and for a continuing attachment to a punitive love object through submission and suffering. The important point that Hermann makes in his discussion of masochism, however, is the dual nature of sadomasochistic phenomena corresponding to the dual and opposing instincts of clinging and going in search. Thus, for example, a suicidal act may represent simultaneously an unconscious fantasy of a longed-for merger with the lost object as a reinstatement of the dual union, and in the actual taking control of the act, an assertion of separateness that constitutes a narcissistic victory for the self, however lethal that act might be. Using a more common clinical example, the self-destructive behavior of masochistic patients that often occurs in response to a separation from the therapist or a perceived abandonment cannot within the framework of Hermann's theory be understood simply as the reemergence of the original sadistic aim against the object or as a reactive aggression meant to undo the threat of desertion. For what is also seen, in however distorted and destructive a form, are the powerful stirrings of our patient's will, which in normal development would have so adaptively subserved individuation and the unfolding autonomy of the self. In masochism, however, it becomes diverted in its aim in order to subserve clinging and the disavowal of loss—what might be called a "perversion of will" in masochistic phenomena.

In no other clinical phenomenon than anorexia nervosa is the opposing tension between Hermann's dual instincts more graphically represented. The young anorectic patient, unable to meet the adolescent task of separation and dissolve an intensely held mother–child bond, diverts this aim back to the body so that it is the soma that is repudiated and rejected. This process is highly reminiscent of what Hermann has described in masochism with regard to the alienation of part of the body that is detached and destroyed in an effort to experience the trauma of separation as self-intended and the free act of the individual's will. In severe cases, as the anorectic progressively negates her body, she achieves a symbiotic merger with the lost object (a pairing with death that is synonymous with clinging) while consciously experiencing a sense of triumph and even exhilaration in her ability to kill off that part of the self (the body) that would cling.

Louis Mogul (1980), in his excellent paper on anorexia, has pointed out the continuum between the adaptive uses of self-discipline and moderate asceticism in normal adolescents as a way of controlling the press of instinctual drives and testing the self's ability to endure pain and survive the relinquishing of parental ties, and their pathological distortion in anorectic patients where asceticism is no longer used to support individuation but becomes a lethal end in itself. One is reminded here of Freud's (1924) statement that when physical pain and "unlust" cease to be signals of danger and become ends in themselves, the pleasure principal is paralyzed and has failed in its function as a watchman not only of our mental life but perhaps of life itself.

The critical failure of separation in many masochistic individuals who must restitute the lost object over and over again in a project that is forever doomed and, in the form of a repetition compulsion is enacted in a timeless space, is very close to Masud Khan's (1981) statement that in "all masochistic fantasy or practice there is always a kernal of psychic pain that has been lived and lost" and which is replaced by a proliferation of screen fantasies (p. 420). Defining masochism as a defense that "the ego uses for holding together the self from a psychic pain that threatens to annihilate it," he goes on in greater detail to describe it as "an affect that the ego creates with characters, real or imaginary . . . to create and sustain an atmosphere of pain that stays under its control and can be libidinalized" (p. 415). This inability to endure an unbearable loss or rupture despite the masochist's immersion in suffering (a situation not unlike the fetishist who denies the mother's lack of a penis, the possibility of castration, and the irrevocable loss of their narcissistic oneness, by filling up the ''empty space'' with the fetishistic object), has been richly articulated by Anna Antonovsky (1978) in her investigation of another realm of psychic functioning, namely, the genesis and transformational nature of thought.

Recalling Freud's 1911 paper, ''Formulations on the two principals of mental functioning,'' which described the emergence of thought out of the failure of hallucinatory wish-fulfillment, Antonovsky emphasized that from the beginning of psychoanalysis, thinking was viewed as being intimately connected to the experience of absence and loss. Although it is the absence of the need-gratifying object in relation to drive and wish that becomes the motivating force for the creation of thought, she states that some frustration of drive (some delay of gratification) is necessary in order to create a space for thinking to come into being. For Antonovsky thinking represents an ultimate position of activity in the individual's effort to make his experience his own and ''we embark upon [it] in an attempt to free ourselves from being stuck in the very thereness of the given'' so that freedom for further development can take place (p. 397). This transformational activity, however, means that there must be a yielding up ''of an undiscriminating attachment to every particular of the given in its original form'' (p. 397). Thus, Antonovsky concludes that it is the capacity to bear pain that is a prerequisite for thought. It appears that it is this relinquishing that is so hard for the masochist to endure. It is at this point that we have come full circle to Hermann's theory of the dual instincts, for it is not perhaps too much of a speculative leap to draw a parallel between the opposing tendencies of clinging and going in search with the axes of metonomy and metaphor in structural linguistics; the whole realm of symbolization, encompassed within the axis of metaphor, allows the child to move away from the original object and to bear the inevitable dissolution of the mother–child dual unity. The following case example will illustrate in the context of masochism the problem of clinging to what Antonovsky has described as ''the thereness of the given.''

Case Example

Anne, a woman of 25 from the Midwest, was admitted three years ago to an open therapeutic hospital after many months of struggling with a psychotic decompensation, characterized by a depressive and almost complete collapse in her functioning. This collapse occurred after Anne once again found herself failing in her efforts to create any kind of future or independent life for herself as an adult—unable to consolidate an identity that would finally be "good enough" to win and sustain her father's affection. Her increasing panic and sense of identity diffusion eventually reached psychotic proportions after the patient (with little sexual experience) was rejected by a co-worker with whom she had been briefly romantically involved. During the months preceding her hospitalization, she repeatedly threatened to throw herself off a bridge and had homicidal fantasies of wanting to kill the "innocents" of her family, her beloved grandfather and her cousin's infant children, all of whom appeared to represent one aspect of her self representation that had become irrevocably lost and spoiled for her.

Anne suffered from multiple early losses: her mother depressively withdrew from her during the first years of her life; and her father, to whom she had a powerful preoedipal attachment that later developed into an intense and eroticized oedipal relationship, left the family when Anne was seven in the wake of a stormy and violent divorce. This loss was recapitulated at puberty when the father in a remarkably abrupt and dramatic way withdrew from his children in order to devote himself entirely to his second wife. The shattering of Anne's idealization of her father, his repetitive abandonments of her, and her inability to endure that loss had a profound impact on both her emotional and cognitive development. Anne's personality developed along the lines of what Winnicott has described as the false self organization where whatever has been nascently vital or real about the self remains inaccessible and walled off. She became a highly compliant and conforming child, cognitively constricted in her inability to "see" or tolerate ambivalence, and she vehemently attached herself as much to places as to people, often experiencing enormous inner rage whenever anything in her environment was changed, whether it be the taste of the water or a new brand of bread. Anne also evolved a highly masochistic relationship with her father in which she repudiated any dangerous impulses or independent strivings (especially around aggression, sexuality, and creativity, which made her all too much like her Bohemian and abandoned mother), and experienced all goodness, competence, and omnipotence as residing in him.

Anne's tenacious holding onto the past was represented quite literally during the first eight months of her hospitalization when she refused to change her clothes or even unpack her suitcase; but as in her life, she eventually made a kind of pseudoadaptation to her stay at the hospital, and became the perfectly good and compliant patient. As she later pointed out to me, she never made the nurses' report, never exposed any of my imperfections or flaws by joining the other patients in their flamboyant sprees of acting out. Her only complaint was her constant depressive suffering, which she saw as being my responsibility to make better since she was obviously doing everything that a good patient was supposed to do, literally to the point of caricature. Anne's fantasy was that we did indeed share a common skin. Any introduction of separateness, whether it be through interpretation, or simply by failing to return her insistent and coercive smile, or in spite of herself, by Anne's own expression of longing with regard to having a more independent life for herself, would be immediately followed by a fierce retreat back into a depressed and entrenched immobility. Just as Anne insisted on remaining completely dependent on her father (as she put it, she would rather starve and relinquish all pleasure than to give up one cent of his meager allowance to her), she refused to let go of the past until reparation for the original abandonments could be achieved and revenge properly meted out—a revenge that obviously was going to be carried out through the triumphant defeat of her own life. It was as though all of Anne's aggression was bound up in a rocklike immoveability, and that for her any exercise of will (which seemed to touch on what was most vital and alive in her) could only be expressed in an actively thwarting immobility totally in the service of clinging to that which in reality could never be regained.

Anne was eventually able to articulate the quintessential nature of her masochism at a time when she was actively playing with the idea of becoming anorectic after having successfully overcome her obesity. With a kind of sinister and malignant coldness, she stated that she wanted to die of love-sickness for me and her father—that she wanted to starve and waste away so that she couldn't even be seen. This fantasy brought together Anne's wishes for merger with the lost object by getting rid of herself, "so that she can't even be seen," for a reunion in death with the loved oedipal father, and for an ultimate revenge for all parental failings and disillusionments, since the fantasy also entailed having someone put her wasted body either on my doorstep or that of her father. She would thus bind us forever in a sadomasochistic union in which she would be internalized and held by me, the directing of the aggressive aim against the self allowing Anne to maintain her own self representation as an innocent, betrayed, and accusing child unsullied by aggression, whose only crime was to have loved too much—a parody of love and self-sacrifice so often seen in the masochistic patient.

These themes are wonderfully illustrated in a short story of which Anne was particularly fond and which she found herself rereading during a period of transient disorganization that had once again been precipitated by the loss of a young man who went off to have a sexual affair with another woman. The story is "A Rose for Emily" by William Faulkner. Quite briefly, it is a Gothic tale about a Southern woman who is extremely attached to her father, a powerful judge, and who remains aloof and apart from the town after his death. She seems unassailable and unreachable until a lusty Yankee contractor comes to pave the sidewalks; to the town's horror a courtship begins, and is then followed by the suitor's sudden disappearance. Emily never leaves the house again, and after her death the townspeople go into her bedchamber and find her dead lover, her wedding gifts to him lying beside his corpse. Emily had poisoned him in response to his planned desertion and had then proceeded to sleep beside his body for the next twenty years.

What is interesting about Anne's attachment to this story is the way in which it embodies her own clinging to her original objects and her refusal to yield up any of the given of the original situation so that some transformational and sublimating process could take place. The story also tells us something about the dynamic issues underlying the necrophilic fantasy, for it is only in death—either in the killing of oneself or the illusive, forever retreating, and unobtainable other—that separateness can finally be negated and the lost object forever made one's own. Antonovsky, in her paper, "The Thinking Cure," has stated that a major task in psychoanalytic treatment is the "enabling of enduring" (p. 399) to widen those areas of frustration and loss which the patient has not been able to suffer. Indeed, for Anne, it was her almost complete inability to tolerate or endure such a loss that led to a masochistic clinging in the service of this disavowal and that contributed to her vulnerability to psychosis. In the treatment, the central working interpretation involved her refusal to let go of her original objects, which undermined any genuine efforts "to go in search" (Hermann, 1936) and thereby curtailed the articulation of a separate identity. While the treatment was long and slow to unfold with several regressions marked by either the return of masochistic behavior or psychotic disorganization, Anne was eventually able to return to her hometown, and did manage to achieve some degree of independence from her parents, discovering for herself a modicum of self-esteem and inner certainty in her capacity to create a life of her own.

References

Antonovsky, A. (1978), The thinking cure. *Contemp. Psychoanal.*, 14:388–404.

Anzieu, D. (1970), Skin ego. In: *Psychoanalysis in France*, eds. S. Lebovici & D. Widlöcher. New York: International Universities Press, 1980.

Berlinger, B. (1958), The role of object relations in moral masochism. *Psychoanal. Quart.*, 27:38–56.

Brenman, M. (1952), On teasing and being teased: And the problem of "moral masochism." *The Psychoanalytic Study of the Child*, 7:264–285. New York: International Universities Press.

Brenner, C. (1959), The masochistic character: Genesis and treatment. *J. Amer. Psychoanal. Assn.*, 7:197–226.

Faulkner, W. (1950), A rose for Emily. In: *Collected Short Stories of William Faulkner*. New York: Random House.

Ferenczi, S. (1929), The unwelcome child and his death instinct. In: *Final Contributions to the Problems and Methods of Psycho-Analysis*. London: Hogarth Press, 1955.

Freud, S. (1911), Formulations on the two principles of mental functioning. *Standard Edition*, 12:213–226. London: Hogarth Press, 1958.

—— (1924), The economic problem of masochism. *Standard Edition,* 19:159–170. London: Hogarth Press, 1961.

Hermann, I. (1936), Clinging and going-in-search. *Psychoanal. Quart.*, 45:5–36.

Khan, M. (1981), From masochism to psychic pain. *Contemp. Psychoanal.,* 17:413–422.

Mahler, M. (1966), Notes on the development of basic moods: The depressive affect. In: *The Collected Papers of Margaret S. Mahler*, Vol. 2. New York: Jason Aronson, 1979.

Menaker, E. (1953), Masochism—A defensive reaction of the ego. *Psychoanal. Quart.,* 22:205–220.

Mogul, L. (1980), Asceticism in adolescence and anorexia nervosa. *The Psychoanalytic Study of the Child*, 35:155–175. New Haven, CT: Yale University Press.

Waelder, R. (1936), The principle of multiple function: Observations on over-determination. *Psychoanal. Quart.*, 5:45–62.

2

The Return of Masochistic Behavior in the Absence of the Analyst

Jill D. Montgomery, Ph.D.

The confusion in the literature on masochism with its complicated and contradictory formulations has to do in part with the theoretical evolution of the concept, and in part with the nature of the behavior being studied. Humans are capable of a complex variety of self-defeating, self-destructive behaviors. In our work with masochistic patients, we have become aware that these behaviors have an equally complex variety of functions and meanings (Brenman, 1952). Attempts at clarification have been made by suggesting unifying underlying principles and structures common to all masochistic phenomena. Inadvertently, a false homogeneity has been implied. In the application of theory to practice we are faced therefore, with not only having to choose from competing theoretical explanations, but also at times find ourselves forcing divergent phenomena into existing, ill-fitting unitary formulations. Rather than facilitating the treatment and developing theory, this often serves more to bind our own anxiety, an anxiety so often aroused when working with patients who engage in malignant attempts at self-destruction. In response to this problem, I began to examine my clinical experiences and those of my colleagues who had worked with masochistic patients in long-term intensive psychoanalytic treatments. I was interested in trying to see if there are groups whose pain-producing behaviors have a homogeneity that is more than superficially descriptive or arbitrarily inferred. I wondered if there are groups who represent and structure their worlds similarly, based on similar histories; who are, in other words, similar dynamically and genetically. I wondered also if this similarity is manifested clinically in the development of the transference, in the response to particular interventions and occurrences, and in the progressive self-modifications as revealed in dreams.

Two groups of patients stand out in my observations. The first is a group of masochistic women who had an overtly sadistic father and a masochistic mother with whom they are identified. They present themselves as caught in endless replications of sadomasochistic ties to males. In their treatment, they tend to project alternating sadomasochistic self object representations onto the analyst and/or reduce the analyst to the role of an impotent judge or witness in the endless battle with their abusive male lovers. Enacting the object relationships of childhood provides them with the hope of correcting these old relationships (Berliner, 1947). Cherishing this hope, they continue in their futile attempts to rewrite history while maintaining a strident status quo.

The second group, the one to be discussed here, consists of women who live within a symbiotically structured *Umwelt* (Lichtenstein, 1961) of sadomasochistic surrender and fulfillment. This is not necessarily apparent in their self-presentation, which can vary considerably, as can their level of organization and adaptive functioning. The women in this group have all had narcissistically disordered mothers who treated their daughters, and in particular the daughters' bodies, in a surprisingly overt, yet unacknowledged, sadistic manner. As Masud Khan (1979) noticed in his work on perversions, "These patients have no notion of the mother's bizarre cruelty, mother is rather idealized as a magic person who is all-knowing and omnipotent. What is absent, however, is any internal representation of the mother as a source of psychic comfort and consolation" (p. 41). Breaches in the mother's role as a protective shield, and the consequent impingements on the infant child's emergent integration, are complicated since the mother herself is the source of pain, which only later becomes eroticized. Likewise, the degree of individuation from the mother may be unacknowledged and confuse the analyst since these patients have, through mutiple dissociation, intrapsychically retained an archaic dependency, a sadomasochistic bond to the mother and environment while simultaneously having a precipitate independence (Winnicott, 1958). Their uneven development, the resultant personality distortions and strengths, lead the analyst at times to underestimate the struggle with which these patients maintain a cohesive sense of self and the reality of their anxiety over the threat of dissolution and disintegration. This anxiety is often mistakenly interpreted as hysteroid, an exaggeration and manipulation in an attempt to control the analyst. What is most important to realize is that as a consequence of the actual pain that was part of their development these patients exist within a self-constituting dyadic context that is sadomasochistic; pain is their other half. Their masochism is more than the acceptance of the sadism of a loved other; it is the fabric of the self in whatever theoretical language you might use to describe that. It follows that these patients do not have the capacity to be alone since this capacity depends on the existence of a good object in the psychic reality of the individual. As Winnicott (1958) suggests, "The relationship of the individual to his or her internal objects, along with confidence in regard to an internal relationship, provides of itself a sufficiency of living, so that temporarily he or she is able to rest contented even in the absence of external objects and stimuli" (pp. 31–32). The constant activity of these patients becomes understandable as a failure in their capacity to "be" (Khan, 1979).

Clinically, if the behavior is accurately understood, the analyst does not receive alternating projected sadomasochistic self object representations, as is the case with the previously mentioned group. Rather, the analyst functions as a wedge in the internal mother–daughter self system, which is, in a sense, an internal environment, a more primitive "space" than the idea of "introjective mother" (Winnicott, 1958). The attempt is to modify this internal environment. Most typically, the analyst is experienced as a "third," the sought for alternative who protects the nascent self and supports its existence outside of the sadomasochistic bond. During the course of treatment, the sadistic component of the self becomes more clearly experienced as "not I," but as mother, an imperfect internalization and an affectively lived history. Memories of mother's cruelty are for the first time recalled with surprising timidity, and nightmarish dreamlike affect states are replicated in the hours. The patients appear at these times to be in self-generated dreams of torture and anxiety from which the analyst repeatedly awakens them. Separation between mother and daughter is concomitant with transmuting internalizations of the analyst as awakener, comforter, mediator, modulator, and explicator of internal states.

The impact of planned separations during the treatment of this group of patients brings with it the threat of a loneliness so intensely empty and disorganizing that the only felt option is to return to masochistic acts. These acts, which we might experience with anger and anxiety, are not primarily symbolic or displaced assaults on either the analyst, the treatment, or the consubstantial body of the mother, nor are they primarily manipulations. In working with these patients we must be continually vigilant in separating our emotional responses from a consideration of the patients' intent. This is elementary, a point of good technique, but nonetheless important to restate, especially in light of the current trend in the literature on so-called borderline pathology, which almost solely addresses masochistic acts as aggressive and manipulative. The anger, anxiety, or guilt generated within the analyst is not necessarily part of the patient's dynamics or transference paradigm. Interpretations of the aggressive or guilty component of these behaviors badly misses the point. The pain, the cutting, the burning, even the suicide, are attempts at repairing the cohesiveness of the self in the face of overwhelming anxiety associated with dissolution. Their experience is of melting away; the pain creates a boundary, an edge, a pressure, a line, a meeting, and a companion. Another aspect of this that cannot be pursued here is that these patients, bound within the seemingly inescapable opposition of master–slave, repetitively enact these oppositions as paradoxes on the surface of the body. Their ability to synthesize the oppositions inherent in identity formation has progressed only to the level of paradox. Pain is paradoxically mother and not-mother since it simultaneously signifies the reunion with the mother while maintaining through externalization and tactile sensation the unitary boundedness and not-mother reality status of the daughter.

Although this behavior is well known, it tends to be described in the literature for the most part from the deficit side. The stress is on what the patient is lacking (e.g., an internalized holding object), rather than on the reparative aspect of the behavior. Also, and again another point that will not be developed here, these masochistic dynamics cross diagnostic categories. It is the degree of enactment that differs. Thus, in the absence of her analyst, one of our patients cuts her arm with a razor blade and stitches herself up with needle and thread, while another dreams "of being slit open by a fierce bad doctor and sewn up by a second"; another patient forms a new masochistic sexual relationship and is burned by cigarettes by her male lover. A fourth patient, during the absence of her analyst, lies in bed with obsessional suicidal thoughts and vivid tactile fantasies of car crashes, imagining her seering pain and bloody death. Yet another patient succumbs to a heavy depressive immobility, becoming enlivened only when she can conjure up a vivid fantasy of a cancer within her body eating painfully away at her.

Following are three brief clinical examples illustrating this group of patients:

Case Example 1

The first patient is a wealthy, intelligent, attractive woman in her mid-twenties, who, after seven years of unsuccessful outpatient treatment, was hospitalized in an open hospital. I had been working with her in the hospital for two and a half years. Since the age of seventeen, with her attempted separation from her family, she had led a chaotic, masochistically involved life of perverse, promiscuous, masochistic sexual relationships involving pseudo-slavery, bondage, torture, and beatings. Prolonged alcohol and cocaine binges would alternate with episodes of food abuse, where she would gorge until painfully bloated but not allow herself the relief of vomiting. She would fake severe pain, request emergency medical intervention, and receive unnecessary, painful medical procedures and even surgery. Recovering from alcoholic binges, she would discover that she had been involved in life-threatening situations, accidents, beatings, and overdoses. Although this woman had been in repeated therapies since the age of seventeen, she had never had a treatment survive a therapist's vacation. During the therapist's planned absence, she would disappear into dissociated self-destructive behaviors that had become progressively more life threatening. Over the course of our work together, within the open hospital setting, her treatment survived my absences, although, especially in the beginning, she severely stressed the containing environment. Her pain-seeking activity in my absences from the hospital changed over time from (1) violent enactments of masochistic sexual relationships where others were induced to participate in inflicting pain to her body; to (2) situations where alcoholic binges induced states of passivity that would leave her in danger from car accidents, falls, vomiting, and loss of consciousness; to (3) self-inflicted pain, such as starvation, gorging, exercise to exhaustion, physical injury; to (4) the beginning of more articulated, yet incapacitating and unnameable mood states simultaneous with the emergence of progressively more elaborated sadomasochistic dreams, fantasies, and symbolic acts; and finally to (5) the experience of psychic pain and an awareness of loneliness within the uninterrupted context of her daily life where she kept functioning.

Her psychosocial development fits the pattern outlined for this group. Her mother had an overly intimate relationship with her daughter's body, which the mother held sadistically in thralldom while simultaneously encouraging a precocious development. As a child, my patient was subjected to pain and overstimulation of various types at the hands of her mother. For example, when she was four years old, her brother was ill and needed injections. Bizarrely, the mother practiced giving injections on the four-year-old daughter. Further, on several occasions, my patient fell and needed stitches. Her mother would not allow the physician to give her an anesthetic, telling her sweetly that the pain ''would be good for her.'' What is important is that this torture was never named as such by any of the participants or family members, who presented a social exterior of well-mannered, attractive conventionality. These memories were all later substantiated in a family meeting where the mother, when questioned about these behaviors by her daughter, replied blandly ''maybe that wasn't such a good idea.'' This type of behavior continued throughout my patient's childhood and into her adolescence, where the mother insisted on the daughter's development of a ''sexy image,'' vigilantly enforced the daughter's weight, eating, and exercise regimen, and began sharing diet pills with her.

In my work with this patient, dreams were quite important in her developing ability to symbolize and extricate herself from masochistic needs. At a point in her treatment, when faced with the stress of separation, the patient would either act out or dream. Dreams preceding a planned separation became an important way, not only for bringing to awareness the internal pain and loneliness, but also for acknowledging her dissociated plan to seek a relationship based on pain in the face of this loneliness. A dream thus interpreted appeared to successfully prevent the acting out. Fifteen months into her treatment, in the 240th hour, in a session before my absence in December, she reported two dreams:

> She was swinging from a ceiling like a piñata. A male patient was swinging a pointed stick at her belly. He slit her open and her guts fell out.

In another dream reported in that session

> A male doctor is removing a tattoo on her leg. She is screaming.

At that point in her treatment, she could look at me and say about her dream, knowingly and with humor, "I guess if you're a victim, you're never alone." In that hour, she was also able to confess her surprise at finding herself walking dressed in a sexy and provocative manner in a dangersous part of town and could recollect her dangerous sexual adventures during past separations.

Nineteen months into her treatment, in the 304th hour, before another planned absence, she brought in the following dream:

> She dreamed that the analyst was going away on vacation and leaving her in a locked hospital with deformed freaks and dwarfs and with a mean doctor. She was terrified, locked in, and as she was being strapped down on a bed to be tortured, experimented on, and stuck with hypodermic needles by the bad doctor, she awakened in terror with the sense that maybe the dream was real.

She came to her hour with the question, "Is it a dream?" Her enmeshment in this imaginary dreamlike world delineated vividly the reality of the terror she experienced in being left with only her bad objects. "Like being left with a witch for a baby-sitter." She, with difficulty, could move to a symbolic understanding of the experience, and for the first time could find words for the terror and death anxiety she felt when alone in her room. In the work with this patient, what was most striking was that as her internal environment changed, her prevacation dreams changed. The progression was from dreams of nightmare surrender to her inner torturing world, to dreams where she appeared as a comforting person to victims who had severe traumata to their skin, such as burns, to dreams about pregnancy with the feeling of having something of importance within her and of her, and finally to dreams in which her mother was symbolically killed, which gave the patient a feeling of relief, grief, and a sense that she would be all right during my absence.

Case Example 2

Another woman struggling to maintain herself during my absence had a long history of repeated psychiatric hospitalizations with anorexia, multiple suicide attempts, self-mutilation with cutting and burning, prolonged periods of psychotic disorganization, and periods of mutism. This patient's mother had tried to murder her when she was a child and had behaved in a sadistically psychotic manner to her victim daughter with little intervention from family members. During my absence, this patient poured a pot of hot coffee on her foot and kept the wound open by cutting through the forming blisters with scissors. She explained, "I want to want to kill myself, but I can't," and "I have to do something." Her realization, many months later, was that *she* was not the one who wanted her death.

Case Example 3

A third hospitalized patient was one whom I had seen whenever her regular analyst was on vacation. In the first year I saw her, while her analyst was away, she cut herself severely on the leg. This woman's mother overwhelmed her with concentration camp stories of horror and torture. The patient had a long psychiatric history of self-mutilation, anorexia, bulimia, and obsessive suicidal rumination and gestures. During her analyst's absence, she felt as if she were "floating away." It was only after the cutting that she was calm and reconnected. This same woman, during her analyst's absence the second year of hospitalization, dreamed, while I was seeing her, the following:

> She was on vacation in a strange country. Her brother appeared and stabbed her twice in the leg, hitting major arteries. In the dream, people did not believe the story and thought that her wounds were self-inflicted. She dreamed she got ready for bed, although she was frightened that her brother was around, crazy and would harm her. She dreamed that she came, hesitantly, to my office where I gave her a hug, told her

everything would be okay, and that she should go back to bed. She returned to her room
where she found her brother who told her that it was okay, he didn't feel crazy anymore
and would not hurt her.

About the dream, she commented that, although seeing me did not
make the loneliness she felt in the absence of her analyst go away, she was
not as frightened, felt connected, and this year did not need to cut herself.
She added, "They thought the wounds were self-inflicted. I guess they
never really felt like they were."

These patients live out their masochistic behavior within a dreamlike
representational world built from a history of pain and surrender. In the
absence of the analyst the pain seeking preserves a cohesive sense of self.
In the course of treatment the analyst threatens previous adaptations while
allowing new development. The preceding cases portray a moment in the
analytic process. The patients, unable to feel complete outside of the sadomasochistic bond, still struggle with their internal sadistic objects in the
analyst's absence. It is not rage that is being expressed in their masochistic acts, but a reunion with archaic torturers who have been held at bay
by the presence of the analyst.

References

Berliner, B. (1947), On some psychodynamics of masochism. *Psychoanal. Quart.*, 16:459–
471.

Brenman, M. (1952), On teasing and being teased: And the problem of "moral masochism."
The Psychoanalytic Study of the Child, 7:264–285. New York: International Universities
Press.

Khan, M. (1979), *Alienation in Perversions*. New York: International Universities Press.

Lichtenstein, H. (1961), Identity and sexuality: A study of their interrelationship in man. *J.
Amer. Psychoanal. Assn.*, 9:179–260.

Winnicott, D. W. (1958), The capacity to be alone. In: *The Maturational Processes and the
Facilitating Environment*. New York: International Universities Press, 1965.

3

Sadomasochistic Relatedness to the Body in Anorexia Nervosa*

James L. Sacksteder, M.D.

As Winnicott (1945) notes, a great deal we tend to take for granted has a beginning and a condition out of which it develops, including, for example, the experience of the localization of one's self in one's own body. Most people, most of the time, do not give this a second thought and for the best of all possible reasons: it is never at issue. That is, their experience of their self, or their personality, and of their body has an essential unity and identity. Mental activity and bodily activity are simply different expressions of their psychosomatic nature. For such individuals, one can say the psyche indwells in the soma and the two are only rather artificially separated from one another. But, though you are born in a body and live in it and with it and through it all your life, that you are not your body, or not *just* your body is clear, because you can die and your body can survive. Karen Ann Quinlan and Claus Von Bulow's wife are two well-known examples of this tragic possibility. This is the extreme of dissociation between the life of the psyche and the life of the soma and is, fortunately, relatively rarely encountered.

More frequently encountered, however, are individuals somewhere between the two ends of the continuum. For these individuals, the personality

*An expanded version of this article appears in *The Facilitating Environment: Clinical Applications of Winnicott's Theory*, edited by M. Gerard Fromm and Bruce L. Smith, published by International Universities Press, 1989.

is not identified with and felt to be localized in their body. They and their body are quite separate and distinct and live out a life in very uncertain and uncomfortable relationship to one another. For some, the psyche experiences the soma as a complex machine that it floats in or is lodged in. For them, the psyche has to drive or operate the soma with conscious care and skill. Thus, the relationship to their body resembles what, for others, was the relationship with their car, especially when they were first learning how to drive it. For others, the relationship between the psyche and the soma is even more estranged. Here, the psyche views the soma as an actual, or potential, hostilely attacking persecutor, a source of embarrassment, shame, anxiety, humiliation, pain, or ruin. For these individuals, the soma is constantly threatening to overwhelm the psyche, so the psyche in turn attempts to achieve absolute, ruthless control over the soma, and thus a sadomasochistic relationship develops with the psyche persecuting the soma while simultaneously feeling persecuted by it.

I would like to consider briefly some factors that contribute to estrangement and alienation between the psyche and the soma and that can lead to the development of a persecutory sadomasochistic relationship between them as this is exemplified in anorexia nervosa. Anorexics experience their self and their body as quite distinct entities, rather than as a psychosomatic unity, and rather than being identified with their body, liking it, enjoying it, caring for it, nurturing and developing it, they hate it and cruelly, unrelentingly attack it. Some feel they can starve the soma to death and yet have the psyche survive, and they are surprised and then enraged when others call that belief delusional and interfere with their efforts to actualize that extreme of psyche–soma dissociation. The factors involved in this development that I especially wish to stress in this discussion are those favoring a dissociation between the psyche and the soma, those favoring a false self development within the psyche, which is the premorbid personality of an anorexic, and those favoring the development of a sadomasochistic relationship with people, between intrapsychic agencies, and between the psyche and the soma, which is the reality that obtains once the identity and life as an anorexic is established.

As I agree with Guntrip (1969) that theory only lives when it is seen as describing the actual reactions of real people, so the theoretical discussion will be interwoven with the description of the actual reactions of a real person.

Case Example

When I met Patty she was nearly thirty and had been anorexic for ten years. She lived at home and, though she was almost completely estranged from her parents, she saw no one outside the family; that is, she was virtually friendless. She was a college graduate and had many skills, but was unemployed both because she was often too weak to work but also because she could not get along with fellow employees or employers. She spent most of her time alone or, more accurately, with her body. She obsessed about its weight constantly and compulsively and relentlessly pursued ever greater thinness. She starved or, if she ate, vomited and/or purged herself with laxatives and diuretics. She exercised constantly, punishingly, and would, at times, actually beat her body with a hairbrush especially about her thighs. She was five foot, four inches tall, and she weighed 75 pounds. She, or more accurately, her body, looked like the body of a concentration camp victim or a terminal cancer patient. Naturally, she was not born this way; that is, with the identity of an anorexic and a life exclusively devoted to the pursuit of thinness.

She was born in the third year of her parents' marriage, approximately one year after the birth of their first-born child, also a daughter. Her conception completely disrupted her parents' lives. They had just moved from their hometown in the East to Europe to make a new life for themselves, her father embarking on a new career. All that was given up six months later when her mother discovered she was pregnant. She was afraid to go through the pregnancy and delivery in Europe so the new career and new life were forsaken and they returned home, now having to move in with the mother's parents, as the father was out of work. One assumes this evoked some feelings toward the unborn child.

As the firstborn was a girl, her parents had hoped for a boy. This desire increased when her mother's brother, Patrick, died in an accident two months before her birth. This brother was the golden boy of the family and his death led to a period of prolonged, intense mourning for the entire family. Patty's mother decided to name her unborn child after her dead brother and when, to her disappointment, a girl was born, she resignedly feminized the name a bit by spelling it with a ''y.'' After delivery, Patty's mother promptly collapsed, psychologically and physically. She had prolonged postpartum bleeding and was also quite depressed. She was confined to bed for three months and left the care of her infant daughter to a succession of hired nurses. There was a succession of nurses because none of them could long stand trying to care for Patty in this household. One problem was Patty; the other was her family. The problem with Patty was that she was a colicky baby, difficult to feed; she often vomited and had frequent diarrhea. She cried constantly day and night for months and no one could comfort her consistently or for long. This led first to concern and anxiety and renewed efforts to comfort her, but when they failed, also presumably, to feelings of helplessness, hopelessness, impotence, frustration, and rage. These feelings were directed primarily by Patty's family, especially her mother and maternal grandmother, toward Patty's caretakers, primarily in the form of very severe criticisms of their care of Patty. In the face of such criticism, the nurses repeatedly quit, but presumably the same feelings leading to the criticisms of the caretakers were also felt, if not expressed, toward Patty herself. Thus, Patty got off to a rocky start.

Ferenczi (1929) noted that children who come into the world as unwelcomed guests of their family are in trouble. They can observe—and by that he seems to mean they can experience affectively—conscious and unconscious signs of aversion for them, and when they do their desire to live can be broken. If it is, they die easily and willingly or, if they escape this fate, they are disposed to somatic and psychosomatic illness for the rest of their lives, and they develop a streak of pessimism and of aversion to life with the result that relatively slight occasions (i.e., setbacks, disappointments, frustrations), become sufficient motivation for a desire to die. But, as Ferenczi noted, their so-called self-destructive trends are, in fact, a desire to carry out the parents' often primarily unconscious wishes, to be free of the burden of the child's existence. How prophetic these observations are for Patty's subsequent life will become clear.

But to get more specifically to the determinants of the relationship of the psyche to the soma, let me turn to the work of D.W. Winnicott. According to Winnicott (1949, 1952, 1972), the indwelling of the psyche in the body is a gradually established developmental achievement that depends primarily on the quality of the earliest mother–infant relationship. A mother with her baby is constantly introducing and reintroducing the baby's body and psyche to each other. In this process, she conveys her own attitude toward her baby, its psyche, and its body and body functioning primarily by the way she holds and handles her baby, by how she cares for it. If the baby's existence in general or its body and its functioning in particular makes the mother feel anxious, depressed, ashamed, guilty, humiliated, frightened, excited, helpless, or incompetent, then the usually easy task of introducing the baby's body and psyche to each other becomes difficult, and, with enough disruption of the technique of infant care, the infant loses the sense of living in the body, loses an easygoing and ongoing relationship of its psyche to its soma. Thus, for Winnicott, lack of relatedness of the psyche to the soma begins with the failure in the technique of infant care in the earliest months of the child's life. There is much in Patty's life history to indicate a failure of this type in her life.

First of all, the biological mother was not available to her. She was depressed and sick and one suspects disappointed at having given birth to a girl. In any event, she felt totally incapable—at the start at least—of investing herself in her infant's care. In addition, given the constant turnover in the nurses who were primarily responsible for Patty's care, Patty never had a chance to get in tune with her caretakers and, through them, with her own body and its functioning. This is reflected in her ongoing irritability, her eating difficulties, her bowel difficulties, and her inconsolability.

I think, in agreement with Winnicott, that it is entirely possible the origins of a split between her psyche and soma originated during these earliest, very troubled months. That is not to say, of course, that her fate was determined then. Subsequent development would serve either to heal the split or to reinforce it and, if it were reinforced, to also determine the characteristics of the relationship that would come to obtain between the dissociated psyche and soma. Therefore, let us look then at some vignettes from her later life to see how it progressed.

When Patty was three, a brother was born. She was jealous and vied with the new baby for her mother's attention, often acting up to get her mother's attention, especially around feeding times. One day, as her mother was feeding her brother, she played horsey with her older sister. Her mother scolded the girls and told them to stop or she would punish them. Nonetheless, they continued the game and Patty then reached up and pulled the cord of her brother's bottle-warmer, as if it were a rein. Immediately, scalding hot water tumbled down on her. She sustained third-degree burns primarily to her inner thighs. She was in intensive care, in critical condition, for quite a while. She cannot remember her pain but it must have been very intense. She can remember feeling all alone, feeling abandoned, rejected, and neglected. She left the hospital months later after extensive skin grafting was completed.

I think this trauma further contributed to her potential to split her psyche from her soma and, in addition, was a major factor in contributing to her coming to hate her body and to develop a sadomasochistic relationship to it. From her point of view, her body at this point viciously turned on her and attacked her and caused her pain of extraordinary intensity. She was utterly helpless to do anything about it, to escape it. She had no alternative but to submit to it and try to find some way to detach herself from it from within. And not only was she helpless to free herself of her pain, so were her parents and all her caretakers. Thus, the trauma must have been doubly disillusioning. It dispelled her illusion of her own omnipotent pleasurable control over her body and its functions just after she had presumably gained such feelings by virtue of having learned how to feed herself, having learned how to walk, and run and play, and after having gained control over her bladder and bowels. It also dispelled her illusion of her parents' omnipotence; that is, that there was nothing out of their control, most especially, her own well being. Even worse, given the circumstances under which the accident occurred, she could imagine it was punishment for disobeying her mother and that her mother did not relieve her pain because she felt she deserved it. Given that fantasy, it is not hard to imagine Patty's assertiveness and mischievousness might subsequently be inhibited, especially if her mother's behavior in other ways reinforced this view of things, as well as reinforced her inhibition of her autonomy, and unfortunately, in many ways, this was the case.

Patty's mother was an imposing figure, physically and interpersonally. She was the dominant, dominating figure in the marital relationship and in her relationship with each of her children. She was a very narcissistically self-absorbed woman with very strong views about how each member of the family should live his or her life. She was intrusive, domineering and infantilizing. She was easily irritated and given to holding grudges. She vacillated widely and unpredictably between extremes of criticism and exuberant praise. She was pleased by complete submission to her wishes and reacted either with an outburst of temper or by withdrawal and recourse to somatization if this was not forthcoming. Thus, she was an expert at coercing others into submissive compliance to her by making them feel guilty about their affect on her, both psychologically and physically. She was the type of mother and provided the type of mothering in short that favored the development of a false self on a compliance basis with decidedly masochistic features in her children.

Given these characteristics, it should not be surprising to learn that following her accident Patty's primary strategy for becoming her mother's favorite child and to enjoy her constant attention, approval and love was to become totally compliant to her mother's wishes. She did everything her mother asked of her. Her mother chose her clothes, food, companions and activities for her. Both Patty and her mother could recall that Patty never yelled, screamed, rebelled or even simply asserted herself if what she wanted was different from what her mother wanted for her. Her mother said that Patty was "a perfect child," by which she meant perfectly compliant. Patty avoided her mother's wrath at all costs and when unsuccessful, which was rare, was devastated. Early on, she remembers being fearful for her life in very nonspecific ways, just something awful would befall her. Later on, in adolescence, she was tempted at times to take her life as a reaction to her mother's displeasure with her. By this point, she had internalized her mother's standards and was, if anything, much harsher in her self-disapproval and self-punishment when she failed to live up to these standards than her mother was.

Patty did appear to be very successful in becoming her mother's favorite child. Her mother wrote: "Patty became all I ever wanted to be"; that is, she was the vehicle whereby her mother could at last have the life she had always desired for herself by having her daughter live out her dream life for her. That, of course, meant though that Patty's life was not her own to live—it was her mother's—and, unfortunately, both were in agreement with that.

This brings me to Hilde Bruch's work (1973), to the literature on masochism, to Winnicott's (1960) theory of false self development, and to further explication of factors influencing the relationship between the psyche and the soma and intrapsychic personality development, and in particular, to a consideration of the effect of this type of mother–daughter relationship on these developments.

In agreement with Winnicott, Bruch traces the factors determining the relationship between the psyche and the soma to earliest infancy. The heart of child development, she notes, involves reciprocal transactional processes between an infant and his mother. From birth on, there are basically two forms of behavior in this dyad. In one, the behavior is initiated by the infant due to impulses arising from within. Here, the mother is receptive and reactive. The baby leads, the mother follows. In the second form, behavior by the infant is in response to stimulation from the outside; that is, from the mother. Here the mother leads and the baby follows. This distinction applies to the biological as well as to the social and emotional fields. Key here is the mother's response to the baby's signals. The baby is constantly giving cues and signals indicating his needs and discomforts. How these cues are responded to, fulfilled or neglected, becomes a crucial factor for the baby's progressive clarification of his needs and of the means to get them met effectively.

Dr. Bruch has stated that prior to her work with individuals with eating disorders she had rather naively assumed that the organism knows its bodily sensations and could recognize its drives and needs and count on intrinsic homeostatic regulation to ensure that unsatisfied needs led to corrective behavior. But, as she learned, all this must be learned. That is, all body and emotional and social experiences and states, including hunger, thirst, sexual arousal and pain, and the experience of affects like loneliness, sadness, anxiety, pleasure, guilt, and shame all are progressively differentiated from one another and defined from an initially undifferentiated and rather chaotic state by virtue of innumerable learning experiences occurring primarily, at least at the start, in the mother–infant relationship. If things go well—that is with good enough mothering—the child gradually learns to differentiate between various bodily needs and between bodily and emotional and social needs, and with increasing maturity becomes accurate in identifying and presenting needs and able to act in ways appropriate for their satisfaction.

However, if the innate needs of the child and the environmental responses to them are poorly attuned to each other, then a perplexing confusion in the child's perceptual and conceptual awareness will ultimately result, and the child will grow up perplexed when trying to differentiate between disturbances in his biological field and in the emotional and interpersonal fields. Such a child can ultimately come to feel helpless about identifying, controlling, and securing gratification of biological urges and emotional needs. This is especially likely when the mother fails to see the child as a distinct individual with needs and impulses clearly differentiated from her own and as defined by the child and discovered and responded to appropriately by the mother. When this fails, the mother superimposes on the child her own concept of the child's needs and thereby provides primarily distorting and impinging experiences, first in nonverbal, pre-symbolic communication, for example, in a feeding situation or a bathing situation, and then in verbal communication with direct mislabeling of the child's feeling states, such as that he must be hungry or cold or tired or happy or anxious or sad or bad, regardless of the child's own experience. This process is subsequently extended to include mislabeling the child's role and behavior in the family, at school, in the neighborhood, and in broader society and leads ultimately to the child mistrusting the legitimacy of his own feelings and experiences.

Now a child with such a mother is virtually obliged to accept these distorted conceptions about, for example, his body and body functions, his emotional and social states, in order to maintain equilibrium with the mother on whom he is entirely dependent. However, there is a price to pay, because in doing so the child is prevented from developing a clearly differentiated sense of self and a sense of competence. Ultimately, these children can come to experience themselves as not being in control of their behaviors, needs, and impulses and as not owning their bodies and not living their own lives. This process is compounded, of course, when encouragement or reinforcement of self-expression is deficient or absent and thus reliance on their own inner resources, ideas, or autonomous decisions remains undeveloped. Instead, one gets overcompliance as a way of life or, to use Winnicott's phrase, "one sees the development of a false self on a compliance basis." The benefit of such a decision on the part of the child is that there is no trouble, no obvious trouble, between the mother and the child. The cost is that there is also no real contact. The mother is completely unaware of and unresponsive to what the child spontaneously and independently wants and needs and, over time, unfortunately, the child also can become as unaware of and unresponsive to his own needs as the mother is. It is also important to note that many of the above characteristics of the distorted mother–child relationship also simultaneously favor the development of a masochistic character, as has been detailed in the psychoanalytic literature on masochistic character development. I am referring here most especially to papers by Berlinger (1958), Menaker (1953), Bromberg (1955), Eisenbud (1967), Eidelberg (1948), Pankin (1980), Bloch (1966), Brenner (1959), Brenman (1952), Stolorow (1975), and Valenstein (1973), and although there are important differences between clinicians of different theoretical persuasion with regard to how they conceptualize masochism, nonetheless, there is general agreement about the central role played by the internalization of aspects of bad objects and bad object relationships in the genesis of a masochistic character, and I think much of what I have already detailed of what Patty was like as a person, what her mother was like as a person, what their relationship with one another was like, clearly favored Patty's developing a false self on a compliance basis with a decidedly masochistic character to it.

I believe, in addition, Patty's experience of her body as a persecutory object, as a result of the traumatic burn, was an important additional contributing factor in the formation of her masochistic character. This traumatic experience was an important organizing experience for her, occurring as it did in the context of an ongoing relationship to a parent experienced as a bad object and toward whom a masochistic relationship was developing. I think it served to reinforce powerfully masochistic inclinations in general and, more specifically, any pathology of indwelling of the psyche in the soma that already obtained, and promoted the development of a sadomasochistic relatedness between the psyche and the soma, with ultimately the body coming to be experienced as a persecutory and persecuted object when Patty subsequently developed the identity and life of an anorexic. The combined bad object relationships, that is, between Patty and her mother and between Patty and her painful body, came subsequently to be enacted repeatedly, not only in Patty's relationships with significant others, but also between her intrapsychic agencies and in her relationship with her body. To substantiate that claim, I would like to return to her development and consider her next major developmental milestone, which was puberty and negotiating the perils of adolescence.

Puberty was upsetting to Patty and to her mother. Her mother hated her own body and, by implication, any mature woman's body. She especially hated her breasts which, she felt, were too large and eventually she had a reduction mammoplasty to reduce them. She preferred her daughter's reedlike, pre-pubescent body and was anxious and implicitly disapproving of Patty's budding physical maturation—a feeling and attitude, Patty promptly made her own. Patty also noted that her mother was quite uncomfortable when asked about menstruation or about anything related to being sexual, and, unfortunately but predictably, Patty became equally uncomfortable about her sexuality, its biological, emotional, and social ramifications. She was ashamed of it, embarrassed by her periods, felt helpless and out of control of their onset, duration, and intensity. Sexual stirrings confused her and left her anxious and guilty and again with a feeling of being out of control of herself, her feelings, her body and, potentially, her behavior. Thus, the entire experience of coming to sexual maturity contributed to further alienation between Patty and her body and its functions.

From her point of view, developments in the social field at this point were not going much better. As high school drew to a close, it became clearer to her that her mother expected her to go to college and to eventually marry. Thus, it became increasingly clear to her that one of the tasks ahead was to develop a capacity for intimacy with peers, an intimacy that would include mutual gratification of sexual in addition to dependency needs, and she felt woefully ill-equipped to master these developmental tasks. Because, with regard to interpersonal relationships, up to this point, pretty much all of her energy had gone into her relationship with her mother; relationships with siblings and peers had been much less important to her. She was thought by her mother and others to be popular, primarily because she made no enemies, but on closer inspection it was also clear she made no friends. She was never part of a crowd and no peer relationship had become individualized, personalized, and important to her. She had dated occasionally, primarily because her mother wanted her to. She dated boys her mother approved of and boys who were not aggressive sexually, thus not too threatening to her. None of these boys had become important to her in an individualized way. Hence, it was her mother, through her entire grade school and high school years, who was her primary companion; the only person she knew very much about how to relate to and, unfortunately, what she was about to learn was that what works with mother does not necessarily work with peers, either men or women.

Patty went off to college, hopeful of success, but worried about her capacity to achieve it. What she experienced when she got there was primarily a feeling of being lost. She did not know what to do with herself when alone with herself, without her mother to tell her what to do. She pledged a sorority and tried to establish a very tight exclusive relationship with her roommate—a woman who tended to dominate her. But the roommate was not willing to forego all other relationships in order to have an exclusive relationship with Patty, so Patty, feeling rebuffed and rejected, withdrew, moved into a single room and basically never tried again to get close to a woman peer. She began to date a boy and hoped that the relationship would be absolutely exclusive and that he would fill the void in her life. When it became clear that though he liked her he was unwilling to go along with her desire for an absolutely exclusive relationship, she again felt devastated and became increasingly depressed. She withdrew socially, turning down all other offers to date, and she began to develop the conviction that something was wrong with her body, especially after her boyfriend's ardour cooled during a petting session when he discovered her scars. She felt they were to blame for her failure to secure an exclusive relationship with him. She said she realized at that point that she had underestimated her feelings about her scarred legs previously. In the back of her mind, she had always thought that she would outgrow them or that they would somehow change or go away, or that no one else would notice them or care about them. Now, however, she was confronted with the reality that they had not and would not go away, and that their presence might effect her relationship with others, especially men, adversely. She remembers feeling at this point betrayed by her body and of hating it, and she was not sure she wanted to go on living if it meant having to live in and with her scarred body.

At college, with both her roommate and with the young man she dated, Patty had wanted an instantaneously intense and exclusive intimacy. She expected that both of these individuals would think and feel in ways identical to her own ways of thinking and feeling and would, like her, be willing to devote themselves entirely to always only devotedly fulfilling her desires as she, in turn, was willing to do for them. She was intensely jealous, very competitive for their attention and favor, and tried to eliminate all rivals. She became desperate and then depressed and apathetic when she was not able to secure this exclusive, all-encompassing relationship. She began to feel hopeless, helpless, and felt totally out of control of herself because she was not totally in control of these other people. It was clear that she did not distinguish between controlling people and controlling the thoughts, feelings, and impulses stirred up within her in response to people and their behavior vis-à-vis her. All her efforts were aimed at changing the other person, to get them to be as desired, rather than changing herself, so that she could tolerate differences between herself and who she desired and could tolerate and even enjoy multiple relationships simultaneously rather than insist, or try to insist, on forming one relationship excluding all others. However, when it was not possible for her to actualize such a relationship, she began to withdraw from the interpersonal field to her mind–body field. She realized that though people could leave her, her body could not, and while people would not do exactly as they were told and could not be absolutely controlled, her body, or at least its weight, could be. Thus, she turned away from pursuing gratifying relationships and embarked on the pursuit of thinness. It was at this point that her life of accommodation, of trying to be perfect as that was defined by someone else, came to an end. She now dedicated all her energy to losing weight instead of trying to be perfectly pleasing to others. She sought refuge in her relationship with her body and gained a sense of identity and control over her life, a feeling of competence, effectiveness, and self-respect by virtue of becoming one of the world's most accomplished weight reducers.

Unable to stand even seeing her former roommate or former boyfriend, she decided to transfer to a new school and there she became increasingly reclusive, she lived alone, socializing with no one. Instead, she spent all her time studying and losing weight. She succeeded at graduating from college; she also succeeded at losing weight. Over time, her weight fell from 125 pounds to 75 pounds. After graduating, she tried to work but could not cope with criticisms from employers and co-workers or simply the absence of exuberant and constant praise. So, she frequently quit jobs or was let go because of her irritability and passive aggressiveness. Ultimately, she was too weak to work and did not want to anyway because she did not want anything to interfere with her pursuit of thinness. Unable to support herself, she moved back home and there became a tyrannically controlling invalid, now reversing roles with her mother and dominating and controlling her mother by inducing guilt in her mother with her physical troubles in a way that mirrored but reversed their earlier relationship. Her relationship to her body was, if anything, even more tyrannical, punishing, and sadistic. Weight reduction became her way of trying to free herself of all her troubles. With sufficient weight loss, she no longer had periods or sexual feelings, thus she no longer missed men and did not long for the possibility of a good relationship with one. At this point, weight loss brought self-respect and a fleeting feeling of contentment, satisfaction, and accomplishment. Any weight gain, on the other hand, or simply the failure to lose ever more weight, brought pain, a feeling of helplessness and despair, a feeling of being totally out of control, her weight, her body, all its functions, her mind, her feelings, her relationships with people—everything. She felt a humiliating devastating failure. Peace could be reestablished only with renewed and again successful efforts to lose yet more weight. Her life had essentially shrunk to the two-person field of her and her body. No one else was very relevant. The relationship she established with her body transparently resembled bad aspects of any relationship she had ever had, most especially of course, the relationship between her and her mother. But, in addition to enacting aspects of bad object relationships in her relationship with her body derivative of her experiences with people, I also think she enacted aspects of the bad object relationship she had had with her body itself; her body, at one point, had actually been the source of very real pain and suffering to her for which she could not forgive it so she counterattacked it, and brought it pain to repay it for the pain it had caused her. Though her identity and life as an anorexic was in some ways satisfying to her because of the problems it solved for her and the self-esteem it provided for her, nonetheless, it was ultimately deeply unsatisfactory to her for she felt as Franz Kafka's (1979) hunger artist, felt. As the hunger artist lay dying, he murmured to his caretaker: "I always wanted you to admire my fasting . . . but you shouldn't admire it . . . because I have to fast, I can't help it . . . because I couldn't find the food I liked. If I had found it, believe me, I should have made no fuss and stuffed myself like you or anyone else" (pp. 89-90). Patty felt similarly about her own identity and life and that is what brought her into treatment in an effort to change both.

References

Berlinger, B. (1958), The role of object relations in moral masochism. *Psychoanal. Quart.*, 27:38–56.

Bloch, D. (1966), Some dynamics of suffering: Effect of the wish for infanticide in a case of schizophrenia. *Psychoanal. Rev.*, 53:531–554.

Brenman, M. (1952), On being teased; And the problem of "moral masochism." *The Psychoanalytic Study of the Child*, 7:264–285. New York: International Universities Press.

Brenner, C. (1959), The masochistic character: Genesis and treatment. *J. Amer. Psychoanal. Assn.*, 7:197–226.

Bromberg, N. (1955), Maternal influences in the development of moral masochism. *Amer. J. Orthopsychiat.*, 25:802–809.

Bruch, H. (1973), *Eating Disorders*. New York: Basic Books.

Eidelberg, L. (1948), A contribution to the study of masochism. *Studies in Psychoanalysis*. New York: Nervous and Mental Disease Monographs.

Eisenbud, R.-J. (1967), Masochism revisited. *Psychoanal. Rev.*, 54:561–582.

Ferenczi, S. (1929), The unwelcome child and his death instinct. In: *Final Contributions to the Problems and Methods of Psycho-Analysis*. London: Hogarth Press, 1955.

Guntrip, H. (1969), *Schizoid Phenomena, Object Relations and the Self*. New York: International Universities Press, Inc.

Kafka, F. (1979), A hunger artist. In: *The Basic Kafka*. New York: Pocket Books, pp. 89–90.

Menaker, E. (1953), Masochism—A defense reaction of the ego. *Psychoanal. Quart*, 22:205–220.

Pankin, A. (1980), On masochistic enthralment. *Internat. J. Psycho-Anal.*, 6:307–314.

Stolorow, R. D. (1975), The narcissistic function of masochism (and sadism). *Internat. J. Psycho-Anal.*, 56:441–448.

Valenstein, A. F. (1973), On attachment to painful feelings and the negative therapeutic reaction. *The Psychoanalytic Study of the Child*, 28:365–392. New Haven, CT: Yale University Press.

Winnicott, D. W. (1945), Primitive emotional development. In: *Through Paediatrics to Psychoanalysis*. New York: Basic Books, 1958.

——— (1949), Mind and its relation to the psyche-soma. In: *Through Paediatrics to Psychoanalysis*. New York: Basic Books, 1958.

——— (1952), Anxiety associated with insecurity. In: *Through Paediatrics to Psychoanalysis*. New York: Basic Books, 1958.

——— (1960), Ego distortion in terms of true and false self. In: *The Maturational Processes and the Facilitating Environment*. New York: International Universities Press, 1965.

——— (1972), Basis for self in body. *Internat. J. Child Psychother.*, 1:7–16.

4

Refusal to Learn — A Masochistic Solution to Childhood Trauma: A Treatment Case

Elizabeth S. Oakes, Ph.D.

Let us suppose circumstances in which the mothering person cannot tolerate either the child's clinging to her or the child's developing interest in the world outside, who desires compliance and conformity and conventional goodness, but *not* individuality, not difference, not separation; who keeps the child at arm's length, and yet cannot allow it to move beyond arm's length to experience the world beyond. Both "clinging" and "going in search" are impeded. The child becomes overwhelmed with the fear of annihilation if let go, yet cannot find comfort and nurturance in sheltering arms, is not able to give or receive pleasure in the maternal relationship, but is also inhibited in the experience of the pleasure of developing an independent self in relation to the world. There is safety and security nowhere.

Thus it seems to have been for the patient I will present here. This experience was compounded by traumatic physical illness in early childhood that led to her feeling abandoned, assaulted, and overwhelmed. Her experience of reality was of being persecuted by persons and events out of her control, and she developed within herself a world controlled by her own magic, giving it an order dissociated from the ungratifying and ungiving external world. She complied with external demands in the hope that her mother would love, comfort, and protect her, but inside herself she maintained magical control in order not to be victimized and overwhelmed, thus, carrying out the dual task of living with others without having to accept their definition of who she was. As she said, ''When I feel you don't understand me and I can't seem to make you understand me, I can either go away and be alone or I can stay here and be polite and smilingly pretend it's all okay, so I won't be alone and you will want to be with me—and go off in my head and make a fantasy which is where I really live.''

How then does the analyst present the new relationship to such a person, who has adapted to the situation of being kept at arm's length yet not allowed to move beyond arm's length with the masochistic solution of submission and compliance sacrificing the development and exercise of ego function? For her, masochistic behavior seemed determined and necessary to maintain her sense of self, a self acutely vulnerable to fragmentation and fear of annihilation, as demonstration to herself of her autonomous separateness, while demonstrating to her desperately loved mother a continued attachment through submission and suffering. In order to preserve this relationship, she gave up learning and growing up, and stayed a crippled child.

Menaker (1942) speaks directly to the difficulty of dealing with the masochistic factor in the psychoanalytic situation. The nature of the analytic situation includes elements that perpetuate the masochistic position. The analyst has the upper hand in the sense of understanding the patient, making interpretations, being responsible for the further progress of the therapy, making it unavoidable that the dominance–submission position is maintained and sustained in order to hold onto this new object in the transference, and the patient repeats the childhood wish for dependence and submission. The analytic situation repeats in form and arrangement the childhood situation of the patient with the deliberate purpose of reviving the childhood reactions as we see them expressed in the transference. The analyst, like the parent, seems the final authority to which the patient, like the child, must submit if therapeutic success is to be achieved. It is Menaker's position that if the masochistic component, as a defensive position of the ego, is to be analyzed and understood and eventually given up, the therapeutic situation must be altered and changed to allow for a real relationship to develop between the analyst, a real person, and the patient. The role of the analyst is to assist the masochistic patient to experience gratification and dependence while experiencing pleasure in his developing ego capacities and to experience the analyst's pleasure in this as well. Therefore the analytic situation should be managed in such a manner as to make it extremely difficult for the patient to create an image of the analyst that would correspond to the idealized all-powerful mother image on which the masochistic ego depends. What is expected of the analyst is what is expected in good mothering, that is, an attitude of respect for the person, an avoidance of authoritarianism, an expressed belief in the potentialities of the patient for growth as an independent person, a genuine sympathy for the patient's plight, and a conscious self-presentation as being both human and fallible. The analytic relationship must include a sufficient measure of reality and provide no fertile soil in which the masochistic ego can take root, thereby making a new type of identification with the analyst possible. Such identification with the analyst strengthens the ego, and interferes with a continuation of the old symbiotic relationship to the mother out of which the masochistic position of the ego has developed.

Case Example

When I began to work with A., she was twenty-two years old. Her formal diagnosis was of a borderline personality with narcissistic and depressive features and symptoms of bulimia. She had first been hospitalized following an overdose during the summer before her junior year in college. The overdose had been precipitated when her parents had become aware of her binging and vomiting. During a family argument, her mother refused to allow A. to go into the bathroom to induce vomiting. A. experienced a sense of panic, rushed to her room, and took the pills she had been collecting. She was immediately hospitalized and a year later was admitted to the Center. She had in fact been secretly bulimic and preoccupied with thoughts of suicide and death since she was sixteen, despite superior achievement academically in high school and excelling in competitive athletics. While she had continued to do well academically in her first two years in an excellent and highly competitive college, there was marked increase in bulimic symptoms and hypomanic achievement, and she began to cut herself superficially. She felt she did not know how to live in the world, feeling alone and alienated, yet she was viewed by teachers and peers as immensely talented and productive. In her sophomore year she had been sexually involved with a professor, having submitted to him because he found her "so special."

She had been able to continue college work while at the Center and had graduated. At the end of two years, her therapist was leaving the Center. Leaving had been a continuing issue during the treatment, with the patient's multiple attempts to leave to go to school or to move to the Center's halfway house, and now she talked about leaving to continue with her therapist privately. In this open hospital, she needed only to go, but she didn't. In part, she attributed that to a consultation with the Director of Psychotherapy who told her that he thought she had come here for something that she had not yet gotten. She decided she wasn't "finished." She had graduated from college, she said, in order to fulfill her duty to her parents and an image of herself.

She had sworn to herself that she would "show everybody I was not a failure by graduating from college brilliantly and then kill myself." At the moment she was most gratifying to her family and the world, she had planned to die. But the Center and her work with her therapist had allowed her a little space in which to imagine that it might be safe to try to be different despite her alienation from much of Center life.

But even as she had arranged to stay, she had rented a house two miles from town as a place to keep her dog and her rabbit. She had spent a lifetime keeping her escape routes in order, some way of holding a piece of herself in safety, and this new commitment would be no exception as she struggled with how to be with others, without surrendering to their definition of how she should behave and what should be valued. I had been her interim doctor on previous occasions when Dr. X. was on vacation and she had survived his absences "comforted," she said, by my presence, but I knew little about her, except from various hospital reports that described how difficult she was to deal with. There had been a couple of moments of genuine grief and anger and bitter sobbing in my office when she had reported that her therapist would not be as available to her for phone calls and extra sessions following the birth of his first child. I had found myself moved to put my arm around her and say, "It's hard when new babies come along and you have to give up some of the things you had before," and she said, "You shouldn't have to give them up before you're ready." At that time I thought: "She at least suggests it is possible to be ready."

She had asked me if I would be her doctor when she had decided not to leave the Center. She barged into my office without an appointment. She knew that such assignments were the responsibility of the Director of Psychotherapy and it was not my decision, and I reminded her of that, as well as the fact that I had a full caseload, which she also knew. I was away when her therapist actually left and I returned to learn that she had not yet been assigned a therapist. She had decided to stay, but none of the people she wanted to see could or would see her, and she was dragging her heels about consulting with others. I was expecting to have an open place in my caseload in a few weeks and so I told the Director of Psychotherapy I would see her if he approved. This manner of our beginning to work together was an important part of the development of our relationship as the patient clearly felt that she had chosen me and been effective in getting what she needed and wanted for herself, despite heavy odds.

She said she wanted to work on binging and vomiting because it absolutely dominated her life so that she was never free to act spontaneously, having to always plan for how and when she would binge and vomit if she needed to. Not only was she a slave to it, but she had begun to see it as a disgusting activity and herself as a disgusting person. In addition, in her two-

and-a-half years here, she had not really become attached to anyone. She was convinced that the nursing staff thought she should leave, that there was not much liking for her around the place, that she was hard, cold, arrogant, contemptuous, and manipulative and never gave anything back. She resisted human connections.

In preparing to work with her, I reviewed her history. The most striking feature from the history presented by the family, was the massive denial of any family difficulties. The reports described a model family of charming, talented, intelligent, well-adjusted, accomplished parents and three happy, healthy daughters. The father was a successful businessman and the mother, artistically talented, could have had a career of her own but chose to be a wife and mother instead. The family had lived abroad during much of the patient's early childhood. There was no word of conflict, disappointment, or failure until the patient fell victim to symptoms of an eating disorder in her sophomore year of college.

The patient's report is somewhat more revealing. The early years were filled with fears of going to sleep (that she would die), of going to school (that no one would remember to pick her up), not being able to see the blackboard because she was nearsighted, a fact that was not recognized until she was in the third grade. She had no friends, felt ugly, too tall, too clumsy, and that she didn't belong to this talented, beautiful family. But she did not feel free to reveal any of this to her parents.

Her mother worried constantly about the family's physical safety and health in a strange world. She scrubbed the children and force-fed them, warning of the dangers outside locked doors beyond the reaches of the family, with the strong suggestion that only she could protect them, and that such protection depended on their obedience to her view of the world, her values, and to staying at home with her.

By the time the patient was four-and-a-half, she had two younger sisters, one eighteen months younger followed by a second sister fifteen months later. The patient decided she would never grow up, but would wait until her sisters left home when she would be "the only child and recapture my place."

When she was four, she developed a severe combination of illnesses and was hospitalized with fever, tonsilitis, cystitis, and vomiting. Through years of therapy, she uncovered frightening memories of feeling abandoned in a dark place. Through family interviews, it became apparent that these memories were probably associated with her hospitalization, in a foreign city, where her parents reported she would be covered with feces and urine and vomitus when they visited her. Her mother reports she was told that if A. cried excessively after their visits, her visiting privileges would be reduced from the one-hour daily limit, and her mother tried to keep A. from crying when she visited. A. recalls feeling rejected, abandoned, and not understood, and postulates that if her crying upset her mother she would have concluded that her feelings were bad and she was being punished for expressing them. In addition, the hospital would not allow her to keep her prized teddy bear. She has also learned that a child in the same ward died during her stay — a fact which much impressed her parents though the patient, herself, cannot remember it.

What we dealt with in this treatment was the revelation and exposure of the patient's experience of internal chaos, the techniques developed over twenty years to defend against that experience, and her protection of that experience from the corrective light of reality. For the analyst, there was chaos in the roller-coaster experience of the introduction of reality and the clarity of that reality, alternating with the patient's rage and grief. It was as if, in her words, each day, each moment she must decide anew to live in the world or in herself, to choose anew—indeed, to choose at all.

In the first year of our work together there was much attention to a variety of somatic complaints. She experienced constant headaches, abdominal pain, and had two actual general hospital admissions for medical evaluation. I accompanied her. At the end of that year, she reported a growing capacity to live realistically with her body; to accept realistically the fact of mental patienthood; to acknowledge her part in being where she was. There was a constant reworking of illness, hospitals, doctoring, helplessness, dying, pain, and her rage that she could not control these facts for herself or deny them. The roots lay in the terrifying hospitalization at aged four of a very ill child, whose vulnerability to the assault on her sense of the goodness of life was intensified by the swift advent of two sisters and an anxious, frightened, emotionally "as if" mother, all in a foreign world, in a foreign tongue. Her current state seemed to be the result of trauma that she was unable, indeed unwilling if able, to resolve. If there wasn't terror at pain and the betrayal by her body, there was rage.

A clear pattern emerged over the months. I had noted to her my experience of having with her an hour of good work, of collaboration, usually finishing with a request from her for a hug, only to have her return for the next hour as though the previous hour had not happened. The usual explanation of "feared closeness" somehow seemed inadequate. The patient was very available for "closeness" in the hours, genuinely so. She was clearly attached to me and had been so from the beginning, and seemed very aware that I was attached to her, but this failure in continuity puzzled me. We could collaborate on a real and authentic reconstruction and when we met next, it was as if it never happened, not only not the facts of it, but more importantly not the feeling of it. A.'s response was usually "I don't remember what happened in the last hour; I don't know; I just went back and binged and threw up." It was hard to resist the impulse to meet this dismissal and what felt like conscious resistance with "I wonder why you don't want to remember," or as she later reported in a former therapist's words: "Naiveté doesn't become you, A." Her response to my giving in to the impulse was the mobilization of her own sharp tongue and quick wit and her exit from the office in high dudgeon. It was when I was aware that she came in after that and it was as if *that* never happened that I began to reconsider the evidence and a new hypothesis.

Was it possible that, in fact, she didn't remember, that there was no continuity, that there was no internal link; that, despite her accomplishments, her poise, her presence, and her intelligence, her experience existed only in the moment? She had dropped hints of this, if one chose, looking back, to see it as such. Attempts to analyze or trace back the origins of feelings of despair, of wanting to die, of hating the world that she brought into the office were always responded to with "I don't know" about the simplest of things, or "I don't remember," or "I can't concentrate," or "I never know what time it is," or "I have a headache, I didn't sleep, I'm so exhausted." She had brought in a scrapbook from her first two years here (in the first month we worked together, she said she had given up keeping it), filled with pink telephone slips which said, "Please call Mrs. M." or "Your appointment has been changed to 3:30." When I asked why she kept those she said, "They let me know I was here but I don't need that anymore." I accepted that that was where she had been. But some time in those first months I began to consider seriously the possibility that something else was operative. In the midst of the routine series of complaints of "not knowing," "not remembering," "that I was so tired I couldn't think straight," but couldn't or wouldn't sleep at night and therefore couldn't take a look at what happened from day to day, I said I thought we had to consider seriously the possibility that rather than it simply being a way of avoiding painful things, which everyone had told her, including me, she in fact did *not* concentrate, did *not* know, and did *not* remember. In other words, the confusion, the disorganization that she blamed on headaches, lack of sleep, and so on, were not a function of headaches or lack of sleep, but the way it *was* and, if we were going to work, we had to know that. As one way of addressing the issue, we agreed that she would try to sleep at night using chloral hydrate, if necessary, to try to eliminate sleep deprivation as one part of the picture. The result surprised us both. Though relieved and reassured that I was acknowledging the possible existence of something that she had struggled to hide, even from herself, she was frightened and upset with the discovery, as she allowed herself to "know" what was happening, that she did indeed lose large blocks of time; that there were "holes" in her mind, in her experience. When she said she felt like she wanted to die and I said, "What happened?" she really didn't know, really couldn't remember, really couldn't concentrate; or hadn't been aware or concentrated on what was said to her or what she said that stirred up such intense feelings. She also became aware that she moved from moment to moment, interchange to interchange, with no feeling that one was connected to the other. Between moments, between interchanges, she was somewhere else. When she left me, what had happened in that reality no longer existed and she was free to reweave it into her own fantasy, to turn it into her own truth and to operate accordingly, having it, in her own words, "both ways." She began to recognize that this was true in her relationships with nurses, activities staff, and other patients so that she never lived in the real world but most of the time in a world she made up and ordered by her own magic. In that distortion, uncertainty, and unclarity, she did not have to be victimized by any interaction, thoughts, or feelings.

But what was more devastating, and this was her own contribution, was that she was aware that *she did it*. Some place, some time back in history, she began to live by denying knowledge and experience through forgetting, through cutting out, through not registering. She could learn information to pass her tests, but it would not affect the magical view of herself in the world. That would be to be victimized and overwhelmed, forced to submit to others' views of herself or the world. So she wouldn't hear, she wouldn't learn, she wouldn't connect.

It was the beginning of the answer to a question and dilemma I posed early with her and which we met in a variety of forms throughout the treatment. How was it that she could be an honors science student, having studied the functioning of her own anatomy, and yet could insist genuinely that slicing herself up was not dangerous? There were a variety of other convictions about her own somatic functioning that simply could not be, but existed side by side with knowledge. How was it that what she learned taught her nothing about living? And so we could share a time together, share information together, share good feelings, share insight, and she could walk out of the office and there was no channel back.

In one hour, she said, "Do you remember last week when you said you thought I was so angry and full of hate that I wouldn't even allow myself to feed my mind with what I learned?" It had been a comment that had grown out of talking about some newly revealed conflicts over eating during and following the hospitalization when she was four. The dramatic climax as A. formulated it was that her mother insisted that A. had to have gravy because she had to learn that she couldn't have her own way about everything. She went on, "I heard you say you thought I was so angry and I decided not to hear the rest. I was sure you were going to say what everybody has always said— the nurses, my therapists, my parents—that I was angry and I used it to manipulate people, and to hurt people and I was cruel and nasty. Which I am, of course, but I knew what I thought you were going to say, so I didn't listen. Then, I left, but later I decided to listen again in my head and what I heard was not what I expected. You weren't telling me what I was doing to everyone else, including you, but what I was doing to myself. That is what happens [here] that is different. It gives me back to myself.'' I did think it was evidence that some change had occurred; something formerly shut was open; that though she, in the old way, chose not to hear, there was a part of her mind which in fact did hear and file away and later, in a new way, allowed herself to listen and learn.

In the midst of the most difficult time after the acknowledgment that her thinking was disordered, she had great difficulty talking to me. One day she said she was spending her time working with clay—that she didn't have to talk or think with clay—her hands took over and something was produced and she couldn't describe it or explain it but she felt relieved, relaxed, and at ease. The next day she brought in a tortured, monstrous, ugly piece. She put it down before me and said she felt better. It was a writhing mass of arms, legs, torsos, and heads, and one huge open mouth with a single tooth and the throat in the process of some violent contortion. She had great skill and I felt she had brought me her pain, chaos, and disorder and I thought I was to do something with it, but I didn't know what. I told her that. She was relaxed, at ease, not perturbed. She said she was working on another one and would bring that later; maybe it would help. Two days later she brought in the second piece. There was the same mass of arms and legs, but they were clearly assembled in human forms emerging from each other and from the clay mass. There was no mouth.

Several days later we were discussing my first real contact with her parents, and she was describing how it was in her family, and her own sense of being so different and a failure because her talents were not the same as those of her mother and sisters. She was the tallest, very awkward and gawky, and pretty clothes didn't fit her right, she said. I wondered about her own considerable talents and abilities. She explained they were not acceptable or recognized in her family. No one was supposed to be better or have different talents and what one did all were supposed to do equally or they didn't belong. I interrupted to say I thought I understood something about the sculptures. I said it was as if the first was her experience of her family as a lump, a mass of everything and everyone supposed to be the same. No one was separate from anyone else. Everybody was parts sticking out awkwardly and grotesquely. But in the second, individuals are beginning to emerge and they are coming to be whole and separately identified. She made no comment, changed the subject, and shortly thereafter this session ended.

The next day I asked her what had happened. She said, ''You may have been right, but I don't like you to get there before I do and to be so pleased with yourself for having done so.'' She was right. I acknowledged my error and my pleasure that she had been able to correct me.

But that sculpting of individual portraits from the family unit continued. New information, new memories, old information, and old memories flesh out the real persons, as the channel between what she knew and was able to acknowledge widened and deepened. From another hour: "I don't think my mother wanted me to grow up, any of us to grow up. I didn't want to go home last Christmas because it would be just like when we were little. We have to do the same things, be 'just the family.' She would read to us 'The Night Before Christmas'—nothing was supposed to change. It's so sad. She wants us all there and will when she's seventy and we are fifty. And she'll read to us, just the family, 'The Night Before Christmas.' The only way I could not be there was to be in a mental hospital. My mother buffers herself from the world by keeping her family all around—by having us feel her feelings for her, think her thoughts."

We talked about what allowed what she calls "the backward little person inside," to turn around occasionally and see what others see, though grudgingly to be sure. She says that it began with my touching her, the arm around her shoulder long ago as a gesture of comfort and later, in response to "I need a hug." The backward child never felt able to be, or to accept being, comforted by her mother whose displeasure had the power to annihilate her. "In my family, when they are angry with you, they deexist you. They don't call you for dinner. They don't talk to you. They don't touch you." She went on to describe her skin feeling like rubber as though it weren't part of her. She was in it, but way inside and not connected to it. Our physical contact "gave my body back to me." She reported that now she knew that sometimes she had a headache, but sometimes she didn't have a headache. She had thought she always had them. She had a better idea of what brought them on and that talking often resulted in their going away. She could tell a doctor where it hurt and when it was physical and when it was mental pain. And she could distinguish between a stomachache and menstrual cramps with some ideas about what to do for each.

She said the other intervention that made a difference was the "goodnight" phone call. This developed when she was having difficulty going to sleep because she felt so lonely and scared to be in her room as she became aware that that was when she so easily got into poking holes in herself, digging at her face, or binging and vomiting. Being alone in her room brought awareness of her badness, her unlovability. The masochistic acts allowed her to deal with the anxiety of abandonment and rejection. She called me a few times in a panic and then got into obsessing about whether or not she had been upset enough to call me at home. "What if I use you up?" I said I thought I could take care of myself about that, but maybe she wanted to say goodnight and she didn't have to be in a panic to do that. Several times a week she called to say goodnight before she went to sleep. It helped her feel connected, she said, and to put an end, I think, to *one* day, so she could release it with some sense that tomorrow would come and be connected to yesterday.

What follows comes from an hour twenty-four months into the treatment. It is both typical and atypical. It is typical in its process, but perhaps atypical in the swiftness with which it came to resolution. It provided a description of how she worked, and the richness and variety of imagery that was both a resource and a distraction. Often she got carried away, fascinated by her very real gift with words and images. She came in, and in contrast to her appearance for the previous several weeks, she looked disheveled, her hair mussed and rumpled, a hodge-podge of corduroys, sweater, socks, and her face splotchy, letting me know she has been picking at it. She entered, clutching herself as though holding herself together from flying apart, and curled up in the chair. Her expression was dark and brooding. It was a picture I had only recently seen, though I had long felt its presence: stubborn, resistant, turned away in mind, feeling, and spirit. We sat without words. Then, aloud, I wondered what she was thinking. She spat the words at me, "I don't know what to say to you!" followed by an angry, almost whining, old set of complaints of feeling like she's dying, wanting to be dead, not knowing what to say to anybody, not knowing what words to use, and so on. I made a few attempts to help her recall what had been happening in the weekend before that might have left her feeling like this, without success. She did, at one point, tell me that she had been trying to relieve the pain and unhappiness by binging and throwing up, and it did not work. It used to work but not anymore and "that's terrible," she added.

At last, I said that I had received a lab report that morning that she had been to see the internist last week about a vaginal discharge, that he had diagnosed a yeast infection and was treating her for that. I wondered why she hadn't mentioned it at the time. She shrugged her shoulders and said she knew I'd get the lab report. I said, yes, she knew I would get the lab report but, given that we had been doing some talking about matters physical and rather specifically about matters sexual and reproductive, it seemed likely that she might have mentioned it. She said it had occurred to her, but she didn't know how to bring it up with me, what words to use. I said, "Words like— I have this vaginal discharge and I'm wondering about it and I'm going to see the doctor to see what it is. I'm worried about it, I'm not worried about it, and so on." (Silence) I also noted that I had heard that she was complimented by nursing staff about her appearance recently and that seemed to coincide with this new withdrawal and a return to disregard for her appearance. She looked furious. "You're just fishing." I said I didn't think I was fishing—I thought I was reporting observations.

There was a pause, then she said, "I think you've missed the mark. At least I did something about the discharge. I spent a couple of days being uncomfortable with the itching. I had something like it when I was at college the first time. I ignored it. It went away. It wasn't the same thing. It was something that you don't do anything for, but I was sure *I* made it go away. I tried to remember how I made it go away before, but I knew it wasn't like that so I went to see the doctor and had to listen to his philosophy of life and be examined. The doctor had said I should have a pelvic anyway. And I had to get the medicine and put it on the bathroom shelf and make myself use it. You don't know how much energy it takes to remember, to force myself to think about needing to take care of it and doing it. My head wants to ignore it, forget it, say it isn't real or make up magic. But I'm doing what he said. It's better, and it's so depressing. I hate it. I knew what to do. There wasn't any need to come and tell you. I knew what you'd say." I covered my face with my hands and laughed, saying, "Of course you knew what I'd say. I would have told you to do exactly what *you* already knew to do."

She went on but no longer brooding and resistant: "Last night I discovered that one of my big plants has white fly and I heard myself say 'spray' and I was so depressed I wanted to die. The last time my plant had white fly I put it over the radiator, put it in a dark closet for ten minutes, put it in the icebox overnight. It died, but I knew it was because I had the wrong formula and I wanted to do it again in different order to see where I had been wrong. I didn't want the answer to be 'use spray.' " (A long pause) "Maybe you were close to the mark. Several of my plants have mites. They're like me. From a distance, they look all beautiful and lush green but when you get close you can smell the decay and see the brown leaves. I know that I should cut it all the way back and spray it and I don't want to. I want to try the magic with them, like I want to with me, count red and blue cars, figure what I did wrong that produced the mites, binge and throw up ten times. I went to look at sprays (she flashes a side look to see if I'm laughing at her). I've been to Senger's, Ward's, K-Mart, all the places. I looked and read the labels. I may buy some soon, but I may just let all my plants die."

I found myself saying with some intensity "let them die." She looked surprised. I was surprised at my certainty that I knew what she was talking about. I said something to the effect that clearly she was struggling with giving up the magic, her view of the world that she could control by her actions, rule by her actions, and the long-standing refusal to allow her knowledge about how things worked in reality to alter and effect how she worked. (I was remembering "you shouldn't have to give it up 'til you're ready," and her rage and terror at giving it up at all. That was the price of getting well and she hated it and feared it.) The magic had been her solution to not submitting to a world and a mother she felt was out of her control, to whom she could otherwise only submit. Yet it robbed her of the ego capacity to grow and live freely and safely. I went on to say I wasn't taking lightly her feeling for her plants and the sadness involved in their death, but they were replaceable and she was not. "Work it out on the plants, struggle with giving it up on the plants and spray." I told her I felt called upon to note, though I thought she wasn't going to like my noting it (she interrupted to smile wanly and say she thought she knew what I was going to say and she was ready to hear it), I said I thought that she could safely work it out on the plants because she had clearly demonstrated that she had chosen not to work it out on herself, with the decision to see the internist and follow his instructions. It was a decision for reality, for knowledge, for her body. "It wound up being a good hour," she said.

The patient was discharged from the hospital approximately a year later and arranged to live some distance away in her own apartment, struggling to complete courses to apply to graduate school. I continued to see her twice a week but the good-night phone calls continued. Her symptoms generally came under control, though they could be set off when her still tenuous new self was threatened. Her greatest problem was loneliness and in a particularly apt complaint she declared that it was an awful thing to have spent her life avoiding feeling lonely for her mother in an emotional and psychological sense, and developed a whole range of symptoms and levels of illness to protect against that, and then to have the illness and the symptoms stripped away and to be left achingly aware that the loneliness was there. Her capacity to state that, of course, was the best evidence that the healing was in process.

What has seemed to be helpful to this masochistic patient was the analyst's attempt, although not always carried out, to experience pleasure in the patient's independent actions and growth without the need to be in control nor necessarily to be right; to be realistic and to face the hard things without needing to be afraid of them or to pretend there were no real difficulties; to allow the patient to know the analyst as a real person and not simply an idealized transference object, and to provide some gratification in the relationship that served to permit the patient to feel gratification in herself and to begin to value those things about herself that she had previously hated.

Reference

Menaker, E. (1942), The masochistic factor in the psychoanalytic situation. *Psychoanal. Quart.*, 11:171–186.

5

Masochistic and Phobic Features in a Case of Schizophrenia

Cecilia Jones, Ph.D. and
Ann C. Greif, Ph.D.

Masochistic individuals are often unable to symbolize and therefore to integrate the problem of separateness and loss in relationships adequately. Melanie Klein (1948) and her colleagues place the child's capacity to acknowledge separateness and to tolerate the sense of grief it inevitably evokes at the very heart of their developmental theory, viewing it as the pivotal achievement of the depressive position. For Klein, this ability to mourn takes place when the infant is gradually able to move from his earliest and most primitive relationship to the object—where the desired other is split into a good and satisfying breast and a frustrating and persecutory one, and there is an almost complete severance between love and hate—to one in which he is increasingly able to recognize and incorporate the mother as a whole object (and thus can no longer keep the loving and hateful aspects of the relationship to her so widely apart). With these first steps in integration, Klein believes that the infant is faced with all the horrors and anxieties of the depressive position that she compares to a state of mourning. As Klein views it, the infant must contend with intense fears of abandonment and guilt over his aggressive attacks and fantasied destruction of his object (both internal and external), which he also loves and needs most. The capacity of the infant or young toddler to feel concern and despair over his aggression impells him to want to restore and repair the lost good object both inside and outside the self. This desire for reparation is intimately connected in Klein's theory with the development of symbolization and forms the basis for later sublimation.

Similarly, in her psychoanalytic exploration of aesthetics, Hanna Segal (1952) has articulated the relationship between the depressive position and artistic expression. She views all creativity as the "re-creation of a once-loved but now lost and ruined object" (p. 190). It is only when this loss can be acknowledged and born that symbolic and sublimatory activity (the desire to recreate and restore) can come into being. The capacity to use symbols represents one of the monumental accomplishments of the depressive position. They arise not only out of the child's need to find an ever-broadening series of substitutions for his impulses of love and hate (thus helping him to preserve and protect the object) but also out of his wish to repair and restore what has been lost. Symbols are experienced as "creations of the ego" (Segal, 1957); although they serve to represent the object, they never become fully or concretely equated with it and thus can be freely used in the world. Segal (1957) contrasts the capacity to use symbols with their genetic precursors, which she calls symbolic equations, where the symbol is literally equated with the thing symbolized. When regression occurs in response to overly severe depressive anxieties and the individual retreats to the defenses of the paranoid schizoid position (especially projective identification), symbols can once again collapse into concrete equations; the loss of differentiation between self and other is reflected in the confusion of the symbol with what is symbolized. Segal emphasizes that unlike symbolic equations that are used defensively in order "to deny the absence of an idealized object or to control a persecutory one" (p. 57), symbols develop out of the ego's capacity to tolerate ambivalence and guilt and are used not to deny loss but to transcend it.

One way in which a perversion such as masochism can be understood is as a symbolic equation in which there has been a collapse of meaning onto the site of the body—the acting out of an emotional reality in the realm of the concrete and physical. The infusion of a perverse aim into the character structure, such as in moral masochism, can be seen similarly as a regression from meaning in which suffering has taken hold, annihilating other affects, thoughts, wishes, and desires. The following case will illustrate the way in which the denial of separateness and defensive retreat from the depressive feelings of guilt and loss can be manifested in a failure of symbolization and a multiplicity of symptoms related to this failure. The patient to be presented clung to her symptomatology just as she clung to her caretakers in the desperate attempt to ward off experiences of pain, longing, and abandonment. She existed in a world where time had been brought to a standstill, boundaries obliterated, and distinctions between people minimized and scorned since all of these implied the possibility of loss and limitation. In the service of this denial, suffering became this patient's way of life, a daily litany for coercing the presence of actual others. For her it seemed she could thus forever capture and punish the abandoning mother of her childhood.

Case Example

Helen is a twenty-nine-year-old woman who has spent the past five years of her life in a psychiatric hospital. She went to a prestigious college where she was viewed as a gifted young visual artist, doing well academically despite one major psychotic episode and restricting phobic and obsessional preoccupations. Immediately upon graduation, however, Helen returned home to her parents, unable, as she put it, to make a separate stance. Over the next several months, she regressed into a highly deteriorated, psychotic state. During the five years of her hospitalization, Helen was relentless in her determination to achieve an omnipotent and absolute control over the caretakers in her environment; she refused to step off the property of the hospital without nursing accompaniment, and managed to defeat all nursing efforts to help her overcome her agoraphobia in graduated steps. Unable to tolerate almost any internal tension or anxiety, Helen would make trips back to the nursing station innumerable times during the day and would thus perpetually exhaust and drain the battered breast of the hospital represented by whomever she could find who would serve as a temporary external regulator of her anxiety. Despite her efforts to idealize her phobic partners and caretakers, those who fell into that category often felt as though they were little more than containers into which she could empty her tension states and persecutory body sensations.

Although Helen's difficulties are certainly consonant with the recent psychoanalytic literature on agoraphobia (Frances and Dunn, 1975), which emphasizes that the conflict over separateness is literally played out in spatial terms just as it is in the early toddler–mother relationship, Segal's work on the psychotic anxieties that may underlie phobic development is particularly helpful in understanding the severity and degree of paralysis involved in Helen's symptoms. Segal (1954) views the phobic object as the container for the individual's projection of his own bad and fragmented objects, thus binding them to a concrete external form that can be avoided. By eschewing any separate movement into the external world outside the protective realm of the hospital (which seemed to be equated with the insides of the mother's body), Helen attempted to ward off the catastrophic return of her own projected disintegration, experiencing any separateness (the potential loss of the symbiotic object) as synonymous with psychotic annihilation and death.

Klein (1948) has pointed out that when persecutory anxieties are particularly strong, the ego may become increasingly impoverished and fragmented in the successive use of splitting and projective identification as ways of expelling all the hated aspects of the self and its internal objects into the world; one disastrous consequence of this situation is the development of a crippling and slavelike dependence on an external object that must be kept in an omnipotently perfect and idealized state, the child forever fearing that in its absence the good object will have turned bad.

For Helen, nothing good could be adequately internalized or held inside of her since anything that got incorporated quickly became spoiled by her own rage; she had therefore to cling to and repeatedly confirm the aliveness of a good object in the outside world that would protect her from the persecutions of the bad mother, the latter typically taking the form of numerous hypochondriacal complaints. For example, Helen was terrified of her feces, which she feared would tear apart her body, and was constantly preoccupied with evacuation, which she appeared to experience as an anal birth. For many years she also avoided eating any solid food and subsisted almost exclusively on liquids since she feared that any bite-sized morsel might turn on her and choke her to death.

Helen's insistence that the only good state was to be inside—that she must keep her babies and feces inside and remain inside the body of the hospital—led her in the analytic situation to attack anything that might introduce some degree of differentiation or support a greater integration of her own love and hate. Helen had a remarkable way of rendering language meaningless: interpretations were reduced to platitudes, and connections developed in a previous hour were consumed and dissolved by her perseverations, thus allowing Helen to remain triumphant in her ahistoricity, tied to a caricature of her past. Through a kind of psychotic scotomazation, Helen protected herself from experiencing or having to mourn the devastation that had occurred in her life, and she searched for others who would tell her that she was still potentially beautiful and full of talent, untouched by the passing years and the horror she kept inside of her; Helen's life was only in ruins when it was named as such, and she attempted to ward off interpretations since they might evoke some painful aspect of her external or internal reality that she could only experience as a persecutory attack. Helen's efforts to achieve an absolute stasis in the treatment was obviously a reflection of her own tremendous fear of being controlled; and she played out in her life the prohibitions of an excessively severe and punitive superego, feeling that she was not allowed to enjoy food or experience any sexuality without risking the possibility of annihilation. For years Helen could only bathe partially clothed so that she wouldn't take pleasure in seeing her own body, and had dreams that she felt were specifically designed to be sexually arousing without her having to be active in any way; a compromise solution which did not totally work, however, since these dreams were invariably accompanied by a hyperventilation attack upon waking.

Last summer Helen decided that she would attend an art history class beginning in the fall with a paid companion accompanying her, thus initiating her first steps out of the hospital. Predictably, she became much more psychotic for several months in anticipation of this separation. Her psychosis also seemed to represent a major regression from her own emerging depressive anxieties, however, for Helen was increasingly becoming aware that her mother could no longer be completely rejected as all bad (as a literal witch) since in reality she was trying to be quite helpful and supportive of her daughter's plans. Unable to tolerate her own feelings of ambivalence and guilt, Helen retreated back into her persecutory anxieties. Very much in keeping with what Segal has said about the collapse of symbols into symbolic equations when projective identification is massively resorted to, Helen found the whole inanimate world becoming alive and turning into the bad persecutory mother; her purse literally turned into a person from whom she could only frighteningly flee; the Madonna in the stained-glass windows of the church across the street and the curtains in her room all sprang into life with her mother's presence, and her shoes became gaping black holes into which she would fall. Her driving companion, whom she would not allow to move more than a few feet from the classroom door (thus acting as though there were truly an umbilical cord between them), was felt by Helen to have turned into a sheep when she spotted her black wool stockings in the car, metaphor once again collapsing into its concrete equation.

Reminding us of Freud's (1923) statement that sublimation depends on the successful renunciation of an instinctual aim, Segal (1952) believes that such renunciation can only take place through a process of mourning: it depends on the ego's capacity to assimilate those objects that it must in reality give up, and it is these internal objects that in turn give rise to symbols. Thus, "symbol formation is the outcome of a loss; it is a creative act involving the pain and the whole work of mourning" (p. 196); and it is the inability to endure loss and the anxieties of the depressive position that leads to inhibitions in creativity.

For many years Helen had not been able to work on her art and the few sketches that she did produce were painfully flat and empty, static and actually deadening images of women's bodies being tenaciously held onto as though such figures could conjure up for Helen all her yearning for a homoerotic and symbiotic merger. She could not revise or change any of her drawings since they were for her perfect productions equated with the object that they were supposed to represent; and it was extremely difficult for Helen to take in anything from her teachers since revisions carried the threat that her own "perfect good products" would be stolen and contaminated by the other, just as she hated to acknowledge that she had ever learned anything from her mother since such an acknowledgment would have necessitated some feelings of gratitude and affection. Recently, however, in response to some painfully slow steps toward greater integration, and coming at a time when her therapist was leaving the hospital, Helen announced that she had finally completed a painting, which she experienced as a breakthrough; interestingly, this picture touched on the theme of loss and allowed the image of the mother to be both more whole and real, the source of both frustration and love.

Daniels (1985), in his brilliant phenomenological investigation of nostalgia, begins with its etymological roots in the Greek *nostos,* to return home, and *algos,* pain, and describes the illusory and ineluctable quality of this experience: that "nostalgia presents itself as a special moment in remembering, one in which there is a commingling of past become present . . . a constitution of the world characterized by a yearning for the hidden, a time that always was, is, and will be hidden . . [and that it is] a suffering of illusion, a searching for what cannot be found" (p. 379). Turning to Andrew Wyeth's painting, *Christina's World,* which captures a moment of almost unbearable longing, Daniels states: "Nostalgia is not only for the lost and hidden home towards which Christina alone crawls, that distant home on the horizon with its mirrored windows and hidden reflections, but the home for which we all pine, for community, that everyday life experience of inner subjectivity in the mundane world" (p. 380). This description of unfulfillable longing is very close to the concept of the depressive position—for it is only when loss and change can be acknowledged and suffered that their mediation through symbolization can take place and some transcendence be achieved.

For many masochistic individuals, depressive anxiety cannot be tolerated and situations of pain are endlessly reenacted and fiercely clung to in an effort to bind self to other ever more deeply in an illusory union. On the more psychotic end of the continuum, the patient presented here was not able to own her own love and aggression adequately, or acknowledge and mourn what had been lost, and thus literally clung to external objects, stuck in the very concreteness of her desire. She lived out a kind of half-life, continually fearing the catastrophe of breakdown which, as Winnicott (1974) has so elegantly stated, had already happened, but occurring outside the ego's realm of integration, had never been fully experienced, and was thus forever searched for in the future.

References

Daniels, E. (1985), Nostalgia and hidden meaning. *Amer. Imago,* 42:371–382.

Frances, A., & Dunn, P. (1975), The attachment-autonomy conflict in agoraphobia. *Internat. J. Psycho-Anal.,* 56:435–439.

Freud, S. (1923), The ego and the id. *Standard Edition,* 19:1–66. London: Hogarth Press, 1961.

Klein, M. (1948), *Contributions to Psychoanalysis, 1921–1945.* London: Hogarth Press.

Segal, H. (1952), A psycho-analytical approach to aesthetics. In: *The Work of Hanna Segal: A Kleinian Approach to Clinical Practice*, ed. R. Largo. New York: Jason Aronson, 1981, pp. 185–206.

———— (1954), A note on schizoid mechanism underlying phobic mechanism. In: *The Work of Hanna Segal: A Kleinian Approach to Clinical Practice*, ed. R. Largo. New York: Jason Aronson, 1981, pp. 137–144.

———— (1957), Notes on symbol formation. In: *The Work of Hanna Segal: A Kleinian Approach to Clinical Practice*, ed. R. Targo. New York: Jason Aronson, 1981, pp. 49–65.

Winnicott, D. W. (1974), Fear of breakdown. *Internat. Rev. Psycho-Anal.*, 1:103–107.

II

Identity and the Construction of the Self

6

The Hero as Victim: The Development of a Masochistic Life

Jill D. Montgomery, Ph.D.

A masochistic life is one of seemingly needless, prolonged, self-inflicted suffering and humiliation. Chronically depressed patients who engage in masochistic enactments can be terribly troubling for the analyst. These patients feel that they suffer from life; that they are untreatable, and yet in desperation demand our help, while simultaneously clinging to pain. They typically have had many experiences of treatment. Nothing in their eyes has been successful, although previous analysts might assess the treatments in positive ways. Something might become clear, but in the patient's experience nothing changes. The affective tone remains the same, as does the desperation. They continue to suffer, and they continue to participate in, and enlist others to participate in, enactments of suffering. These patients see themselves as failures living within the limited confines of an arbitrary world. Their selfhood—the discreteness, the agency, the goodness, the continuity, the aliveness, the connectedness, the integrity—has been maintained and created out of complicated masochistic accommodations and attachments (Fairbairn, 1941; Guntrip, 1969; Kohut, 1971; Stolorow, 1975; Khan, 1979). These patients have not, in a sense, developed "lived lives," lives that experientially appear to develop or unfold from within, moving more or less smoothly from

Acknowledgments: The author gratefully acknowledges the support of the Austen Riggs Foundation, Dr. Margaret Brenman-Gibson for her guidance, and Dr. Daniel P. Schwartz, whose many clinical insights are represented throughout the chapter.

developmental stage to developmental stage, prompted by developmental need, supported unobtrusively from without. Rather, they have painfully constructed, often self-consciously, a self, a body, and a life, and live as heroic victims within their constricted self-narratives.

As patients they are difficult to understand and to treat, and often become examples of "negative therapeutic reactions." Their suffering is intense, and suicide is a very real risk. Symptom has become self; and the end product is so multidetermined, serving so many functions on so many different levels (Brenman, 1952), that it is difficult to know which thread to follow.

In our work with these patients it is necessary to remember that development follows a complicated pathway. The ongoing sense of self is an active organizing process throughout development, interpreting, accommodating, assimilating, and structuring experience into characteristic shapes and patterns. Children grow within a context that includes an interaction of fantasy and reality with developing representations of their bodies, their selves, and their human and nonhuman environment. Each element of this context is multifaceted and subject to meanings that change with shifts in psychosocial task, psychosexual mode, and historical setting. For masochistic individuals what appears to have been constant from the earliest age is the presence of sadomasochistic experiences of pain and surrender, and repeated assaults (impingements and deprivations) that contributed to the precariousness of their narcissistic balance, body self-relationship, and self-unity. Central for some also was the organizing presence of an ambivalently held, powerful, yet suffering figure of authority, who served as a differentiating and integrating figure. Self-cohesion was maintained through more and more elaborated and later sexualized masochistic solutions and identifications. These masochistic solutions were returned to time and time again when these patients were threatened with loss or disappointment.

What is presented then to the analyst in treatment as a history is more a dreamlike narrative in which every element, the manifest content, leads back and away from itself in a chain of associations whose functions and meanings change with developmental level of interpretation. For the analyst each developmental modification is important and none should be focused on at the exclusion of another. The necessity of the masochistic solutions and the inevitability of the depressive outcome are understandable only when one comes to appreciate the complicated layering of repeated developmental failure and deficit. This accounts for the entrenched quality of the suffering, its resistance to easy interpretation and therapeutic zeal. A commitment to the notion of freedom can easily cause us to underestimate the necessary function served by captivity.

The following clinical study is from the intensive psychoanalytic treatment of a hospitalized male patient who had led a chronically dysphoric schizoidal life, in an unfulfilled masochistic pursuit of pain. From an isolated childhood devoid of emotional contact, with sudden abandonments, unmet developmental needs, disappointments, and severe narcissistic injury, he had built a narrative of mythic dimensions, which he inhabited as the "hero in captivity," suffering the perpetual humiliation of a hero in chains.

The Present

> *Promise was that I*
> *Should Israel from Philistian yoke deliver,*
> *Ask for this Great Deliverer now, and find him*
> *Eyeless in Gaza at the Mill with slaves,*
> *Himself in bands under Philistian yoke;*
> *—John Milton,* Samson Agonistes

The psychoanalytic narrative begins at the end with the patient telling his story in its final form and moves forward in time creating a new story while patient and analyst trace backward through the many drafts of the text.

Case Example

My patient, a tall, attractive athletic man, told me the story of who he was. There was a strangeness in its telling since his internal images and self-experience were so at odds with my experience of him in my office. With a passionate intensity he complained of a lack of passion; and told me that he had no feeling, existing only in his head. His body, he said, was dead. Most consciously he felt horribly wounded, "the elephant man." He could not look in mirrors, nor could he look at me. He dreamed of his body crawling with maggots. He writhed in my presence, and although humiliated, forced himself to further confessions of what he considered to be his "perverse sexual history." He said that he feared any sexual intimacy with men or women, and believed he resisted sexual intercourse because he could not have his penis disappear from sight. If he was a homosexual he would kill himself and demanded to know if I thought he was a homosexual. He had dressed in his mother's underwear and looked for male lovers, obsessed with a search for sexual sensation, which was maddeningly elusive. He worked hard at masturbating, which he did at regular intervals throughout the day. The fantasies of bondage and humiliation disgusted him, and he lived in dread that he was damaging his penis. If he had a gun he was afraid that he would shoot himself.

He was cautious and closed off, hypersensitive to perceived rejection. For the most part, he was despairing about himself and his chances for improvement. I was struck by the vestiges of his spontaneity and warmth, which had a delicacy that contrasted strangely with his armored physical presence. What was most clear was that I was becoming enlisted as a torturer. Five times a week he returned to my office, promptly, head down, as if sentenced, my captive, and left at the end of the hour, beaten. Speaking with difficulty, he told me that the humiliation of my glance "bound him in a net of self-loathing." It appeared as if he would explode, he was being "strangled by it." He turned red, the veins on his muscular forearms bulging; he gripped the arms of the chair, eyes closed. I had become his major problem, the source of his mortification and ridicule. He told me of his distinguished military career. He was a man who seriously studied war, a leader who had personally retrieved the dead bodies of his men from the field of combat crawling through artillery fire and had maintained the respect of his men by defeating them in hand-to-hand combat in the presence of the assembled company—a hero. He told me he was now imprisoned with "mental defectives," reduced "by a little, Jewish woman" when what he needed was "Sigmund Freud, John Wayne, and the Pope." "You," he wailed with contempt mixed with an inconsolable sorrow, "are too small even for me to sit in your lap."

It goes without saying that the qualities he ascribed to his hospitalization and treatment, a hospitalization that had become for him an irrevocable incarceration, existed for the most part as an illusion. It was a necessary enactment of which he was unaware. He was of course free to leave; it was an open, voluntary hospital. The appearance was more of an estate made up of colonial mansions than a prison camp. There were no locked doors, or orders holding him, no jailers, no uniformed staff. He was even free to change analysts. All the patients in our hospital had this option. No one was expected to be able to work with everyone. Irreconcilable problems did occur in treatment. In the reality of the hospital life there were options. A masochistic scenario was not in that sense inevitable. How he got to this point, how it came about, what it meant that he had placed himself here with his own agency unacknowledged, were to him unintelligible questions. He remained totally absent from his story, hidden in a richly evocative narrative of war stories, sports stories, fraternity stories, sex stories, stories of heroics, humili- ation, danger, pain, frustration, isolation, and suffering. The most obvious, determining, psychologically meaningful events were disregarded by him as meaningless. The effect of two grisly tours of duty in Vietnam, his leg wound, the death of his father (a Jewish surgeon and high-ranking navy official), his father's cruelty and assaults, his mother's icy indifference, athletic injuries, repeated moves, disfiguring acne, severe infantile eczema, and his father's absence, incarceration, and torture as a prisoner of war during World War II, were all of no significance. In relating his history it was as if we were watching a movie of his life, a visual presentation of images and events. The disavowal of significance existed simultaneously with profound suffering. He was held by his narrative, and like the movie hero lived in the two-dimensional melodrama bound unaware by the necessity of plot and character.

Early in the treatment he brought in the following dream.

> He was in enemy country and it was very dangerous. He was a soldier. It was an Asian country. He was captured and imprisoned. He tried to organize his men to escape, as was his duty, but somehow could not. Finally he realized that the Israeli commandoes had come to release him, led by Golda Meir, who was waiting at the gates of the camp negotiating his release. He was being led out of the camp by a small female Oriental guard. He must sign his name. He hesitated, he could not sign. He heard the voices of the guards behind him mumbling something. With agitation he was forced back into the camp where he endured two tortures. First, he had to fight a big man with cane sticks. He submitted to the big man who beat him painfully about the body with a cane stick. Next, he was contained within a chainlike constricting net that confined his movements. With any change of position the net constricted even more.

In some way that was not understandable at the time but vividly portrayed in his densely constructed dream, he "is not," outside the torture of his captivity. He cannot sign his name, he cannot "be," existing only as a "self"—unnamed—within the masochistic captivity of his life, the various functions of which were not yet understandable.

There was a foreboding of therapeutic failure in his return to the prison camp, and the failure of even this most powerful Jewish woman to effect his release. In the dream this large powerful man was unmasked. He was a child, existing within a child's fantasy of playing soldier, since like a child he could not even sign his name, and therefore we must understand that like a child he inhabited the timeless intersubjective sphere of childhood's father, mother, body.

The Father

> *. . . but that I am forbid,*
> *to tell the secrets of my prison-house,*
> *I could a tale unfold whose lightest word*
> *would harrow up thy soul, freeze thy young blcod,*
> *make thy two eyes, like stars, start from their*
> *spheres, thy nodded and combined locks to part*
> *and each particular hair to stand on end*
> *like quills upon the fretful porpentine.*
> —*William Shakespeare*, Hamlet

Thirteen years ago the patient's father died. My patient's narrative in one form could be heard simply as a story of a boy and his father. The events following his father's death, the patient's rapid and profound deterioration, his disclaimed suicidal behavior, and eventual hospitalization, could be understood as a melancholia organized around this death, complicated by the actual trauma of his own war experiences. The processes of identification by which the boy became his lost father were obvious, if only to the analyst. It should be added that the patient disclaimed any parallels between his life and his father's and most consciously rejected and denigrated his father, denying any feelings around his father's death or the possible impact of the war on his current problems.

In the treatment it was seen that the dream delineated the patient's unconscious fantasy of the psychiatric hospital as prison camp. The analyst, rather mockingly portrayed, appears in the dual role of guard and rescuer. The patient appears as his own father suffering the torments of imprisonment, entangled in the Lilliputian nets of captivity, enacting his father's four-year captivity and torture by the Japanese. This was a story he heard often as a child. At times in the transference the patient experienced himself as his father and me as the guard. The articulation of this fantasy made certain things clearer: his sense of imprisonment, the inevitability of his decision to hospitalize himself (and in a foreign part of the country at that), his intense sense of humiliation, the beatings he received by my words, the netlike constriction of my glance, and so on. But the function of the identification remained unclear. For certainly it was necessary to know more about an unconscious fantasy than just the existence of equivalencies, the "this equals that," which was of little value unless the function and history were understood as well.

If the patient's narrative was heard as a melancholia, then the patient's identification with his father and concomitant suffering would be understood as functioning to repair a loss and deal with the intolerable affects associated with the ambivalently held lost object. These would be the maneuvers of mourning with the classical dynamics of a differentiated self grappling with complicated experiences of rage, guilt, and punishment. The vengeance of the self-attack would be understood as retaliation. However, interpretations based on this understanding and developmental level of organization, presenting these themes, left the patient feeling panicky and hopeless. He had heard that all before. We had to come to hear the dream and understand the function and meaning of the unconscious fantasy in a different way. This involved four steps, which I list here as a way of articulating some important principles, rather than to suggest that they were necessarily sequential or discrete. (1) I had to acknowledge the precariousness and vulnerability of the person who was grappling to organize the loss of his father. (2) I had to hear the heroic embedded in the shame of victimization and stories of prison camp torture, and understand that the victim father was a hero in the eyes of the boy. (3) I had to seek the early roots of this identification and fantasy. (4) I then could appreciate the necessity of the prison camp enactment as the patient's attempt at maintaining integration in the face of the overwhelming anxiety associated with disintegration.

My patient dreamed he was his father, inhabiting his father's world, a prison underworld for departed fathers. This fantasy location had existed for my patient since early childhood when he experienced the loss of his father. He was two years old, living in a foreign place with his mother, older sister, and father. Because of the danger he returned with his mother and sister to the maternal grandmother's farm, leaving his father to fight the war. His father was soon captured and absent from the boy's second to fifth birthday. During those missing years, his mother retired to her room. He remembers the closed door and the sound of her crying. Sometimes she'd take him into her bed, but most often not, letting him, however, sleep on the floor outside her door.

She came from a Christian military family that appreciated the tragedy and honor of war. Her father had killed the last renegade Sioux chief—so the story went—pinning him to a tree with his bayonet. He was a frighteningly cruel man, a bull. Her brother was killed in combat. Father's family appreciated the victimization of being Jewish. An immigrant, the father as a child was chased and stoned by the other boys, ignored by his father, but put himself unaided by friends or family—so the story went—through medical school.

The boy, structuring his experiences into characteristic shapes and patterns, grew within this family narrative of male sadomasochistic heroics and female abandonment. He described this period as a time of isolation in a farm household of mourning women. The powerful parental imagos were elaborated in the absence of the parents—the mother tantalizingly desirable, the father tantalizingly grand. There was an equilibrium of sorts, a grim predictability to his isolation. He was the only male.

His father's actual return, when the boy was five years old, was experienced as a cataclysmic disruption and loss in two ways: (1) as the death of the imaginary heroic father—the father who returned from the prison camp was a beaten, cruel, rejecting man; (2) the now five-year-old son's own budding phallic sense of self, his narcissistically elaborated role within "his" household was threatened by the intrusion of this strange returning man. "You are not my father. You are a 'Jap' spy." Reality, fantasy, and developmental necessity supported this claim. He denounced his father, and with a five-year-old's belief in fairness, unmasked him, defending his household from this imposter, trying to preserve his internal equilibrium and sense of certainty. It was, however, the child who was unmasked as the pretender. His father, the patient recounts, regained his authority "arbitrarily" by spanking his son, a humiliating injustice. This was the violent end of a tenuously unfolding phallic fantasy of power and grandeur.

The child needed the power and individuating presence of the idealized missing father. Now he was bereft. Mother emerged from seclusion, to a disloyal reunion with the imposter bad father. No room was made for the son, although the older sister and father developed a closeness of sorts at bedtimes, when he would tell the tales of his torture. The son, feigning sleep in the next bed, would listen to the stories—"The Infamous Death March," "The Two Sunken Prison Ships," "The Sharks," "The Dying Men," "The Ship Smelling of Piss," "Drinking the Blood of the Dead Man."

But the son managed to keep the missing father alive with a masochistic solution that went as follows. The boy bolstered his precarious phallic organization by establishing a masochistic relationship to the returned sadistic father. This preserved and protected the now-dead idealized parent through a primitive identification that allowed him to take on and live out the heroic role of victim in relation to his new, second, bad father. He now became the hero in captivity within the prison camp of his own home. The father continued to treat him in pathologically cruel ways. For example, when the boy was nine years old the father took him to watch as he performed an autopsy on a baby, teasing him for his fear and nausea when he ran from the room. When he was twelve years old he was recircumcised by his physician/father. Reality, fantasy, and developmental need again supported the elaborated image of the bad father as a dangerously cruel man—a castrator—and the son as the victim hero.

The patient's history from this point on appears to have been one of a well-compensated, sadomasochistic character: socially withdrawn, plagued with severe acne, he engaged in successful narcissistic attempts to heal himself through distinguished action in athletics, accomplishments that the father pointedly ignored. His anchor nonetheless was the sadomasochistic attachment to his father, and his continual search for self-affirming acute sensations. This maintained his internal stability until the actual death of the father precipitated a decompensation of the masochistic equilibrium.

The actual death of his father was a major disruption. This death was experienced as the second death of the father. At this point the patient, in response to a crumbling psychic reality, regressively reactivated his early mythic identification with the heroic father (Stolorow, 1975). He felt himself to be "falling apart" and in defense began to live out the old identification. He did this by actively seeking to return to combat for yet another tour of duty to achieve a hero's life in death or to be captured as a prisoner of war. This ended when he triggered a land mine. Remarkably, after one year of hospitalization he emerged with a crippled leg, that left him only slightly physically impaired.

He had lost his father, his military career, and his athlete's body. His mythic sense of self was violated. His organizing heroic code of "Country, Honor, Duty" seemed meaningless and absurd. He felt panic-stricken. In his desperation he set out on a self-healing quest for what he unconsciously felt needed to be replaced—the all-powerful father of his childhood and a sense of his own regained grandeur and integrity (Kohut, 1971).

The following period was a desperate and disorganized time. He sought something of grandeur to hold on to and with a passionate intensity studied and discarded new careers—scholar, artist, scientist—attaching himself to a series of cruel, prestigious older males. He continued to suffer. In his search he began to read Freud and elaborated a fantasy of being Freud's patient, the "Wolfman." Freud was dead, but he found a living substitute, a possibility for actual attachment, in the impressive figure of Erik Erikson. He read a book by Erikson that in its biographical note placed Erikson on the staff of our hospital—thus he came to us for treatment.

He was not treated by the famous man, or any famous man. He was treated by me. Once again he had to resolve this unmet developmental need for the idealized male, and once again he did this masochistically. He regressively reactivated his early identification with the heroic father, while relentlessly attempting to enlist me and others in a re-creation of his father's incarceration, torture, and humiliation. Within the context of the hospital as prison camp, he sought to suffer an organizing pain—an archaic reunion with internal objects.

Restoring his equilibrium masochistically he was reunited with both fathers: (1) he had internally activated the idealized father with whom he was identified; (2) through the re-creation of the sadomasochistic relationship in the transference, I became the sadistic father of his childhood.

The patient brought me his dream of the prison camp unclaimed. In the dream he could not sign it as his finished creation, a work of art completed to be signed, understood, and put aside. He brought it to me, rather, unsigned, not to be understood, but to be lived, an "un-sign" not to point to anything beyond itself. I was not to wake him from his dream of misery, but like the guard in the dream, I was to return to the camp and inhabit it with him, to live sadomasochistically unnamed within the dream we were to enact.

But he could not sign since in signing he would name himself. Using his own first name not his father's he would be again unmasked as the pretender, as the son, not the father. With that he would become real as opposed to imaginary. The dream landscape of the prison camp would vanish and the dreamer as son, not father, would awaken alone and bereft—as he always was, without a father. A release from these early integrating and organizing representations and identifications would be tantamount to obtaining a release from the sadomasochism of purgatory into the feared primitive agony and self-dissolution of hell.

The Mother

> *Beya mounted upon Gabricus and enclosed*
> *him in her womb in such a manner that*
> *nothing more was visible of him. She*
> *embraced him with so much love that*
> *she absorbed him completely into her own*
> *nature.*
>
> —Rosarium Philosophorum

Bound by the narrative, he was true to his genre, which was not tragedy but romance.

The understanding of his story had to continue to progress by way of a shift in the thematic configurations with a reorganization of material around the mother. This mother was a condensation of early childhood's images and experiences. She was the tantalizingly absent, grieving mother, the nighttime mother, the longed-for and feared mother who was also part sister and grandmother—all of whom were ultimately cold, severe, and abandoning.

My patient told the following story about his birth: His mother was pregnant on the ship taking them to the new military base. He was expected to be delivered on the ship during the journey, but mother wanted first to settle in her new home. Although ready to be born he had to wait two weeks until she was ready to deliver him. He blamed what he felt to be his humiliating lack of will on this event.

As in the dream of the prison camp, women are the gatekeepers; they release and contain. This was the representation of the longed-for yet feared, dangerously all-powerful pregenital mother. She was the mother of separation, autonomy, and will, and also the mother of dependence, shame, and doubt. In the child's mind she was the one who sent men away to prison camps, who released and brought them home, who took her son into her bed, who shut him out, or swallowed him altogether (Daniel Schwartz, personal communication). The womb, the room, the camp all returned as leitmotivs, an unconscious thematization and imagistic configuration that the patient experienced subjectively as a humiliatingly arrested movement, obstructed will, and male personal agency. In the story of the mother, outsides became insides, as women in the role of prime mover offered no truly safe passage out but only passage into another chamber. There was only arrested personal agency, the inevitable return, pain, and humiliation. The desperation with which this patient must cling to the paternal representation through the sadomasochistic accommodations outlined above can be understood only in relation to the intensity of his conflictual struggle to maintain his differentiation from this mother. This is an important reunderstanding of the reenactment represented by the prison camp dream, whose archaically determined images portray not only the identification with the lost father but also suggest the motive force, the danger behind that attachment.

Fairbairn (1941), in describing the psychological process of growth and development, organized the data at the level of relations with this early mother-of-separation. In this process normal development is characterized as a progressive differentiation of the object accompanied by a progressive decrease in identification. This is conflictual, marked by the developmental urge to advance, and the regressive reluctance to abandon the attitude of infantile dependence, the successful resolution of which is dependent on the child's experience of his parents as sufficiently dependable, loving, and available for love to gradually allow him to renounce infantile dependence without misgiving. Fairbairn goes on to say about this conflict that

[The] behavior of the individual is characterized both by desperate endeavors on his part to separate himself from the object and desperate endeavors to achieve reunion with the object—desperate attempts "to escape from prison" and desperate attempts to "return home". . . [there is] a constant oscillation between [each attitude] owing to the anxiety attending each. The anxiety attending separation manifests itself as a fear of isolation; and the anxiety attending identification manifests itself as a fear of being shut in, imprisoned, or engulfed . . . [1941, p. 43].

If the prison camp dream is organized at a level where the mother-of-separation is the central focus, one is immediately struck by the retrograde movement of the hero. This acts as a pointer suggesting earlier developmental incapacities directing our gaze away from the manifestly differentiated objects of the surface action.

The dream begins with the dreamer in his most differentiated, seemingly autonomous, phallic aggressive position. "He was in an enemy country and it was very dangerous. He was a soldier. It was an Asian country." The dream then moves forward in its narrative as it falls successively backward developmentally from the verticality of the silhouetted soldier through five failures of action.

1. He is a soldier in an enemy country and is captured.
2. He is to organize his men to escape but somehow cannot.
3. He has to sign his name to be released but cannot.
4. He is to fight a big man with cane sticks and is beaten.
5. He is contained within a constricting net so that every time he moves it contracts.

The dream ends with the hero in his most contained, inactive, infantlike posture, curled within the strangulating chain, the prison womb of his birth story. He becomes littler and littler, inhabiting less and less space in the devolution of the dream, choosing always passivity and containment with its pain and humiliation rather than activity and freedom. The movement is away from separation in the direction of a masochistic containment that functions, as the dream leads us to believe, as a denial of separation. In the end the hero is in pain but tightly and securely held.

The patient's most conscious experience of this individuation dilemma was his painful awareness of his isolation and obstructed will, and what he experienced as his humiliating female identification. The awareness of isolation presented itself in our work as a schizoid dilemma. How two people could inhabit the same space without the negation of one in the identity of the other was the continual question posed in his treatment. My existence was his negation, his existence was my negation. The woman swallows up the man or the man must annihilate the woman. This became readily translated into sexual terms and actions. We came to understand that he believed his impotence (physical, aggressive, verbal, and sexual) functioned to save us both. How could he put his penis into a woman and not disappear? How could he express an individuated manhood other than by murder or rape? If he could only murder me he was certain he would be cured; to this end he lay awake at night obsessed with the desire to kill me, then was paralyzed in his hour the following day. The interpenetrating experience of identification, dependence, and empathy meant being "fucked." It was better certainly to be a suicide. In the treatment the attachment became intolerable, heightening both the dependent longing, humiliation, and danger, and the defensive rage, scorn, and withdrawal.

The sexual material so present in our hours was an infantile love affair, with an overlay of later developmental meanings and attitudes. To love was to urinate on, defecate on; to be loved was to be loved for one's mess, "one's shit, piss, and come." He believed that his mother, a scrupulously aloof woman, looked on his body with disgust—boys were bad and dirty, a burden. That a mother might admire and find gratification in her boy's body, its contents, and her caretaking functions was unthinkable. Love was understood as the transfer of bodily contents, insides becoming outsides to be valued and admired.

In terms of his female identification, his early dependence on the mother was experienced as an infantile identification. Was he his mother? He longed for her body. He dressed in her underwear, trying on her body. He looked for a male lover, a love fantasy of being urinated on, defecated on. The attempt was to get it right this time. The aim was to rewrite past love relations. The conscious humiliation that was the outcome of these actions came from the critical voice of a later developmental period commenting on this regression in the patient's level of organization. The humiliation was not the goal of the behavior. In replicating rather than correcting the past experience the memory of the maternal glance, the look of disgust in the mother's eye, was evoked rather than erased. What was unacknowledged in these actions was the sorrow of the unadmired self.

He brought me his "mess," and was repeatedly surprised that I understood, although I did not verbalize it, that he wished to be admired and for me to be gratified by my caretaking function. He brought me his burdensome voluminous insurance forms. He perceived the look of annoyance in my eye. When I informed him that he was correct, that I did hate reports but that I did them because it was important to me that he was cared for and further that I was proud to tell people about the work we were doing together in his treatment, atypically he began to cry. The sadness had to do with past care not given.

He alternated between wanting to be my baby with the attending affects of vulnerability and terror, and rescuing himself from the terror of fusion by then experiencing me as his father, critical, insisting that he be a man. Unable to then sustain the individuated position of a man alone with a woman, he resurrected the sadomasochistic tortures described earlier. In the story of the mother nothing was simple. His behavior was a complex weaving of necessary conditions for relatedness, wishes for corrective experiences, enactments, accommodations, and masochistically expressed wishes and fears.

When the patient brought me the prison camp dream, he seemed to point to the disappointment in the treatment, and the unmet developmental need for an idealized male figure. How could he be rescued by a little, Jewish female? But within the dream he gave it a try, reworking me into a powerful, warlike, rescuing Jewish woman, Golda Meir. He tried to correct the fault that reality once again had presented to him. But in doing this he inadvertently revealed a more primary danger, an earlier deficit— the wish expressed in "you're too small for me even to sit in your lap." This wish became a dangerous possibility. With the woman becoming bigger and more powerful she was unmasked for what she was, the fearful, all-powerful pregenital mother.

Let us consider once again his inability to sign his name, but this time in the story of the mother, we can see that, like Faust, when signing a contract, he hesitates (Murray Schwartz, personal communication). Faust must first sign a contract in blood with the devil, which would release him from earthly limitations, but must forfeit his soul forever to Satan. Faust, like the patient, is at first unable to sign. His hand will not move, he realizes the enormity of the contract, its promised freedom as well as the ultimate loss of self. Faust understands with whom he must sign but signs nonetheless. The patient, unlike Faust, does not sign. He knows the danger of the merger that it implies and the hell of dissolution. The patient unconsciously perceives the danger of the wish to reinstate the original mother/child unit. In the dream he returns rather to be beaten by the big man. This is not as the surface suggests an abdication of the oedipal wish, but rather the necessary condition for self-continuance, integrity, and manhood.

The dream however will not let him go so easily. The wish/fear has been glimpsed and ruthlessly makes itself known as he shrinks, becoming smaller and smaller as the unacknowledged wish/fear returns in his last torture. He is swallowed in this final torture, which becomes the containing womblike net where he must wait to be delivered. The end of his story becomes a repetition of the beginning, his birth narrative.

The Body

Jonah is swallowed by a monster.
But the Belly of the Leviathan becomes a womb:

An egg is formed around the imprisoned man:
An intense heat prevails, so violent that
the hero loses all his hair:
When the monster casts him out, he surfaces
on the primordial sea as bald as a newly-born.
            —*Maurice Aniane*, Notes sur l'alchimie''

The prison camp dream that I have presented repetitively in its unfolding interpretations was held in my mind and not returned to in the treatment. It was only retrospectively that I was able to find the tracings backward of the same path by which the treatment progressed, the inverse path of the development of his masochistic life. The dream was first understood as a comment on the unconscious fantasy of the hospital as prison camp, the repetition of which, in the present, was seen as the mobilization of an unfolding representational world (Stolorow, 1978). The re-creation within the transference of the sadomasochistic tie to the father was then understood as a masochistic solution maintaining self-organization in the face of the loss of the idealized father. The dream was then understood in relation to the mother who was seen to be the danger behind the masochistic attachment to the father. The dream now can be presented in one last reading, as the story of the body, the patient's attempt to build a body and develop the ability to inhabit it. In this last understanding of his narrative we came to appreciate how early somatic assaults and severe failures in his holding environment all interfered with the attainment of psychosomatic indwelling (Winnicott, 1945), a state of awareness in which the child experiences himself as a unit located within his body and bounded by his skin. We came to see that this patient (as outlined above) created inevitably and of necessity persecutory relations to the father, in relation to the mother, fulfilling a variety of psychological functions and developmental aims. The persecutory paradigm functioned also on the level of the body, where pain and bondage came to define boundaries for a self, constituted from the very beginning within a primitive, maternally toned context of pain. We came to understand that it was through the acute sensation of actual and fantasied pain and repetitive masturbatory rituals that the patient sought to affirm his existence. The patient's history was then seen to be a series of persecutory relations building up a self, beginning with the body, in which each subsequent developmental mold was informed by the shape of the previous casting. It was the tenuous sense of a self within a body, a self constituted out of a defining context of pain and isolation that was the danger behind the dependence–individuation dilemma of his relations with the mother.

His imperfect body–self relation was formed in the painful and absent touch of his earliest history. Immediately following his birth, mother and baby both developed a severe "tropical rash" that lasted for months. He "screamed and screamed until red and breathless." No one could hold, touch, or comfort him.

For one month he sat silently writhing in my presence. My experience was that every word and movement I made seemed to cause him great pain as he recoiled visibly from their impact. My attempts to soothe him seemed to add to his distress. Then one day he brought me a newspaper clipping, a photograph of a disgustingly monstrous, screaming infant, tightly held, facing outward in front of an equally monstrous, grossly obese, frowning woman. He looked at me directly, a startlingly rare occurrence in itself, demanding to know if that was how I saw him. I answered, surprised by the sudden boldness of his actions and words, that it was obvious that that was how he thought I saw him. He became silent. After a pause, I informed him that I was not certain how useful this information would be for him but that I didn't think he should underestimate the impact of that horrible painful rash that left him screaming and unholdable for the first months of his life. His experience was that he was unsoothable, untouchable, not really there, that every touch caused pain. He began to sob quietly.

The patient's inconsolable one-month period of silence and distress was a reliving of an early psychic reality, not verbally encoded, imagistically and kinesthetically lived out, a psychic reality of which the patient needed to become aware (Winnicott, 1949). At the level of the body the story is of the lack of relation of psyche and soma, the sense of depersonalization, and the feeling that the center of gravity of consciousness exists only tenuously in the kernel rather than in the environmental shell. The environmental shell that creates edges, a sense of thereness, does so through a painful contact. Further, his consciousness of a self became located in "mind" dissociated from "body," a mind that made up in thought for environmental failures.

At the level of the body, Winnicott describes this embedded relationship of soma, psyche, and environment:

> Before object relationships the state of affairs is this: that the unit is not the individual, the unit is an environment-individual set-up. The center of gravity of being does not start off in the individual. It is in the total set-up. By good-enough child care, technique, holding and general management the shell becomes gradually taken over and the kernel (which has looked all the time like a human baby to us) can begin to be an individual. . . . How deceptive this can be is shown by the fact that often we think we see an infant when we learn through analysis at a later date that what we ought

to have seen was an environment developing falsely into a human being hiding within itself a potential individual [Winnicott, 1952, p. 99].

We came to glimpse within the lived reality of the treatment the psychic reality, built out of a prolonged early infantile experience of pain and absence. His "edges were made of fire." The treatment was "a skin graft that might or might not take." There was a poignant dissociation of mind and body, a sense of loss and longing for a body lost and never inhabited.

He told me he was dead; without a body. He pounded his legs. He told me that he could not feel. They lacked feeling. He insisted that I validate and understand his subjective experience of physical deadness, that I did not insist he was feeling when he was not, that I believed it as real. It was his goal, "nothing else would do, no compromise." He must feel. By that we came to understand he meant "inhabit his body." And that by my understanding I would hold inside of me his body in its deadness, his unspoken fantasy of rebirth and resurrection, the body reunited to the soul within the healing maternal environment he had never experienced in his life.

Sexual sensation enacted in his compulsive masturbatory actions and sought for in life became his most conscious attempt at reclaiming his body. The repetitive masturbatory actions became understood as the affirmation of the enfeebled self (Stolorow, 1975), and the reclamation of his body and its rebirth within the longed-for nurturing context of infancy. The masturbation ritual in its first and most revealing form, began in early adolescence.

He tied a cord tightly around his waist and lay in a bathtub. He made his mind a blank. The warm water of the bath would slowly rise and he would have a spontaneous orgasm. He felt fully alive and there.

While the bondage and tying protected him from dissolution by affirming the boundaries, the water held him, providing the longed for context (Stolorow, 1975), and the possibility of transformation, renewal, and rebirth. His fear, guilt, and confusion in the aftermath of his actions necessitated the addition of progressively more complicated requirements of bondage and holding, accommodating to developmental changes, incorporating actual experience and individuals.

The prison camp dream on the level of the body is a sad and honest story of a hero's protest against the insistence that life be lived even if lived falsely. It is not, as in the story of the mother, an abdication of will or action but rather a powerful assertion of will, a "no" in the face of life's arbitrarily delivered assaults, deprivations, and compromises, which produce a facsimile of a self. The dream began with him standing apparently free as the soldier, a heroic individual, but a hollow mannequin, a false self, the integrative achievement and outcome of the complicated accommodations necessitated by his life. In the dream he refused the distorted freedom and stopped the forward action. By returning and moving inward, he sought to inhabit himself, to rewrite his history. He moved developmentally backward toward his beginning. Crouching within the net he awaited an adaptively attuned new beginning that would be a mutually enacted deliverance.

Conclusion

The development of one man's masochistic life has been presented here, stressing the complicated developmental layering that accounted for the tenacity of his depression and masochism. Early in his treatment this extremely intelligent man presented a densely constructed dream that integrated three major levels of organization, while simultaneously commenting on the treatment and his goals. Each level was organized here around one of childhood's developmentally central representations, father, mother, and body, and understood in light of a particular theory or theorist who seemed to best describe the issues.

A life is a complex creation. The multiplicity of its relations and outcomes is best studied by repeated experiments in restructuring the material—believing with humility that nothing is given but the phenomena, of which our understanding is but an approximation—and by maintaining our attitude of spontaneity and aliveness that allows for the appreciation of the heroic within the seemingly pathologically entrenched.

References

Brenman, M. (1952), On teasing and being teased: And the problem of "moral masochism." *The Psychoanalytic Study of the Child*, 7:264–285. New York: International Universities Press.

Fairbairn, W. R. D. (1941), A revised psychopathology of the psychoses and psychoneuroses. In: *An Object-Relations Theory of the Personality*. New York: Basic Books, 1954.

Guntrip, H. (1969), *Schizoid Phenomena Object-Relations and the Self*. New York: International Universities Press.

Khan, M. (1979), *Alienation in Perversions*. New York: International Universities Press.

Kohut, H. (1971), *The Analysis of the Self*. New York: International Universities Press.

Stolorow, R. (1975), The narcissistic function of masochism (and sadism). *Internat. J. Psycho-Anal.*, 56:441–448.

——— (1978), The concept of psychic structure: Its metapsychological and clinical psychoanalytic meanings. *Internat. Rev. Psychoanal.*, 5:313–320.

Winnicott, D. W. (1945), Primitive emotional development. In: *Through Paediatrics to Psychoanalysis*. New York: Basic Books, pp. 145–156, 1975.

——— (1949), Mind and its relation to the psyche-soma. In: *Through Paediatrics to Psychoanalysis*. New York: Basic Books, pp. 243–254, 1975.

——— (1952), Anxiety associated with insecurity. In: *Through Paediatrics to Psychoanalysis*. New York: Basic Books, pp. 97–100, 1975.

7

Failed Efforts at Identification: The Masochistic Patient's Response to the Analyst's Pregnancy

Ann C. Greif, Ph.D.

There has now long been an appreciation of the adaptive and defensive aspects of masochism (Menaker, 1942; Brenman, 1952; Berlinger, 1958; Eisenbud, 1967), even though this perspective on masochism still has at times to contend with being seen as competitive with or contradictory to models of instinct theory. But the patients' fear of giving themselves over to a resourceless dependence on the analyst and their consequent inclination to dissociate and split off their masochistic wishes is often not given the emphasis it deserves. Rather than being unambivalently eager and ready to inflict their masochistic stance for the purpose of manipulation, coercion, self-protection and need-gratification, patients with histories of self-defeating, pain-inducing, and self-destructive behaviors dread the reenactment of the sadomasochistic bond (Balint, 1932). They fear once again being enslaved within the context of a nongratifying attachment that leads nowhere and satisfies few if any needs, except perhaps the most basic one of all, which is simply to be related to another human being no matter how painful this relatedness may be. There is, of course, resistance to the evolution and emergence of the transference. However, what I think needs to be appreciated is that some patients rightly mistrust their own capacity to turn their suffering into the aim and goal of the analytic process rather than what treatment hopes to eradicate. Menaker (1942) made a similar observation when she suggested that the analyst institute parameters to prevent the flowering of a transference neurosis with masochistic patients. It would seem Freud (1923) came across the same type of clinical dilemma with severely masochistic patients, when he coined the term ''negative therapeutic reaction'' to describe the technical difficulties encountered. Gorney (1979) redefined the concept of negative therapeutic reaction as negative therapeutic interaction, stressing the patient's and the analyst's fear of the patient's regression to a resourceless dependence on a depressed maternal introject.

This fear of regression is especially powerful when the analyst appears to be vulnerable, physically or psychically. Then the patient has good reason to fear a repetition of early trauma having to do with loss, abandonment, and deprivation. The dynamic is even more powerful when there is a resonance between the real life events of the analyst and what has been troubling and problematic for the patient. This is some of what seems to take place regularly for more severely disordered patients when their therapist becomes pregnant. They are confronted dramatically with the feared and hoped for equating of the analyst with the powerful preoedipal mother whose presence still overshadows their emotional lives. For masochistic women, in particular, with their denigration of themselves and other women and their concurrent intensely ambivalent tie to an idealized, all-powerful mother, the therapist's pregnancy stirs tremendous feelings of rage and envy, fears of abandonment, wishes to merge and to flee, and finally hopes for identification and individuation as a way out from under the narcissistic injury and dependency. For masochistically disordered men, the route of identification is no less complicated and problematic, often stirring up powerful resistance as it potentiates fears related to homosexuality and passivity that were already present.

Ruth Lax (1969) wrote a clinical paper describing how the event of the analyst's pregnancy is responded to in a manner characteristic of the patient's neurosis. With regard to her descriptions of the therapeutic process, Lax reported a major reliance on identification as a defense with her three female patients, all of whom she describes as being of borderline psychopathology and with strong masochistic trends, as well as with one of her male patients whom she described in similar terms diagnostically. She explains the use of identification as an effort to defend against narcissistic mortification. She writes, ''this mechanism of defense affords for narcissistic gratification and compensation'' (p. 370). To extend Lax's formulation, I would add that this type of patient experiences the therapist's pregnancy as an abandonment and narcissistic injury partly because it threatens the fantasized union and possession over the mother's body, which now comes to be graphically represented by the analyst's body.

I do not share Lax's discouragement over the intrusion into the treatment of such a reality event, although I agree with her that it places special burdens on the analyst in terms of managing countertransference problems at a time when the analyst is likely to be highly vulnerable and in a state of psychic flux and reorganization herself. Rather, I think, the analyst, at least in her own mind, should place the stress on the opportunity that the pregnancy presents to the patient and analyst for examining the entanglement of reality with the transference. Technically the analyst needs to proceed patiently and thoughtfully, accepting the patient's criticisms and accusations and avoiding interpretations that subtly blame the patient for having a reaction to the pregnancy.

Feeling excluded and pushed aside, these patients are hypervigilant for any further slights. The analyst should not shy away from those occasions when the patient may legitimately be included. For example, if changes in appointment times have to be made, and if the patient shows interest, it is desirable to let him or her know for what reasons things have been changed around. Several of my patients were concerned that I would deliver prematurely over a weekend or between sessions prior to our agreed upon stopping date. While these fears were analyzed in terms of the patient's dread of separation, unconscious hostility, and infantile fantasies about childbirth, it was important to share what I actually did know about my medical condition before the analytic work could proceed.

Like most of us, masochists hate things to change. As they have had inevitably to confront loss and abandonments in their lives, they have responded, as Freud (1923) said we all do, by attempting to use the precipitates of their past relationships to build up identifications and to construct psychic structures, including the degraded and idealized images of self and others that constitute the ego ideal and superego. Brenner (1959) has drawn attention to the ubiquity of masochistic phenomena in the resolution of the oedipal complex, given that the superego is formed out of the child's surrender to parental dominance and authority and will ever after exact punishment and inhibit self-expression. In a sense, we all make use of identification in the formation of these structures to protect the self and others from sadistic impulses, to heal the narcissistic mortifications associated with feeling unloved and mistreated, and to remain connected with those persons whom we have passionately loved and hated. Masochism becomes part and parcel of being human. Yet, there are differences of a qualitative as well as quantitative sort between different types of masochistic phenomenon.

As one might expect, one difference between what Brenner has referred to and what can be observed with more seriously disturbed masochistic patients is the absence of reliably internalized and well-differentiated self and other representations. Instead, these patients exist in a symbiotically

structured *Umwelt* (Lichtenstein, 1961) of sadomasochistic surrender and
fulfillment, which has prevented the integration of a coherent identity. The
actual cruelty and desperation that have filled their early years, and the
concomitant rage and disillusionment that has been repressed and dissociated are central to the thwarted process of identity formation and to the sense
of alienation and unreality that permeates masochists' lives. These patients
do not feel themselves to be truly separate or to possess a unique identity.
They are still tied to the image of the mother as it was made known to them
within the family of their childhood. The father when present as a consciously known other is felt to be painfully absent and/or guiltily excluded.
Identification with the parents as a means to redress childhood wrongs and
to recoup narcissistic supplies has been interfered with. Sometimes it may
have been the rigidity of the early attachment, a critical attitude toward
efforts at independence, and sometimes it has been blatant parental hostility
or envy that left the patient feeling unloved and like an outcast, but whatever
the reasons for the failed identification with the parents these patients live
out an existence which does not change, in which the past still dictates the
present.

Masochistic patients are unable to individuate to such a degree that
they can create an identity based on the precipitates of their past relationships. Of course, the failed identity integration and the failed individuation
go hand in hand. Optimally, the experience of separateness, as not
traumatically imposed but as wished-for independence (Winnicott, 1971),
is followed by modest doses of disillusionment that ultimately leads to
healthy and constructive identification (Behrends and Blatt, 1985). In the
developmental scenario associated with a masochistic disorder in adulthood, there is considerable evidence to suggest that these patients had
neither the expectably good-enough experiences with separation–
individuation nor with their efforts to become Iike their parents, to see in
their parents qualities they themselves would someday hope to possess for
themselves. The ''normal'' masochism that is usually played out intrapsychically between the different agencies of the mind is instead lived
out in masochistic surrender to real others from whom the self seeks
fulfillment and the completion of an identity.

Now that the stage has been set for talking about the masochist's
difficulty in using identificatory processes to cope with loss and separation, specifically from a maternal figure, I will report two clinical vignettes. These two individuals, a man and a woman, were seen during a
period of time when I was pregnant. Both individuals had major characterolo-
gical problems, primarily of a masochistic type. While neither of these
patients were schizophrenics, there were marked periodic lapses in reality
testing within the therapy and probably brief periods of overt psychosis

outside the hours associated with feelings of loneliness and abandonment. My pregnancy marked a significant turning point in each treatment. Both patients found the news of my pregnancy traumatically disruptive; efforts at identification with me often occurred as both reparative gestures and defensive measures to deal with rage, envy, and the concomitant guilt and shame. Neither patient was able to sustain a treatment alliance and each patient decided ultimately to transfer to another analyst during my maternity leave. Perhaps this was a means for them both to reclaim their autonomy and to escape from an identification that had felt not self-created but traumatically imposed.

Case Example 1

Terri was twenty-four when she entered an open hospital. For nearly ten years she had struggled with, at times, life-threatening anorexia nervosa. She was a "cutter" and had made several serious suicide attempts. She had been through electroconvulsive therapy (ECT), LSD therapy, megavitamins, and antidepressant as well as antipsychotic medication. None of these interventions directed toward and acted out on her body had worked, and she agreed reluctantly to a trial of psychoanalytic treatment. Emaciated, dour-faced, dressed all in black, she felt imprisoned by her symptoms. Over the course of the next two years, she became increasingly vital and energetic in my presence. She had moved from feeling imprisoned by her symptoms to feeling imprisoned by her body, and finally to feeling alternately trapped and held by her attachment to me. She had come to realize that her obsessive need for control was a direct precipitate of her mother's intrusive concern with her body. (Her mother had overseen every bowel and bladder event until she was well into adolescence. In addition, this mother had encouraged and authorized the sundry physical therapies mentioned above.)

Even before I announced my pregnancy, Terri had had several dreams that indicated at least an unconscious awareness of my pregnancy. In one dream, for example, she was a child with a rare disease that made her younger and younger until finally she became an infant. In another dream, she watched an anorexic young woman being given a transfusion of blood and then felt rage and indignation when she died without warning. Terri's association to these dreams indicated her wish both to be like me and to be my baby, as well as her fears of abandonment and attendant rage. But there was nothing easy or straightforward about her identification. Soon after learning directly of my pregnancy, she found herself a job for the first time in nearly six years. By this, she seemed to be simultaneously conveying her struggle for greater independence from me as well as her loyalty to me as a career woman, which for Terri also implied a repudiation of me as a mother. Another example of the conflictual nature of her response, with its efforts at identification, was her manic flight into greater physical activity. While her activity mimicked a kind of nesting, it also resulted in her becoming thinner and thinner and looking more and more like a little boy, as my pregnancy advanced. She was consciously aware of wanting to free herself from any dependence on me, and she was terrified of a regressive return, in fantasy and actuality, to a sadomasochistic relatedness with her actual mother. She felt depersonalized and out of touch with her own body, which I interpreted as a response to her fear of losing me, and her sense that she had already lost her affectionate attachment to me and my body. During this period, Terri for the first time in her life also experimented with some homosexual attractions and activity, and while she hoped thereby to discover "who she really was" she was left feeling empty, hopeless, and abandoned by these affairs. She felt afterward even more desperate and clingy toward me. One particular event late in the pregnancy seemed a remarkably rich condensation of Terri's conflicted "masochistic" reaction to my pregnancy. For weeks Terri had been considering taking off from the hospital on the spur of the moment that is, without notifying me, and she carried a packed suitcase with her whenever she left the hospital grounds. She only realized after she had told me about the suitcase that it represented for her the suitcase I must have packed ready to take to the hospital. After this had been discussed in a Friday hour, Terri did take off impulsively, went to the nearest large city and got her hair cut, and then got herself involved sexually with her male hairdresser. As this was all taking place and then later in the middle of the night, she frantically called the nursing staff about her inability to extricate herself from the unfolding drama she was creating. She felt prematurely and precipitously involved in this heterosexual liaison, and experienced herself as bad, damaged, and dirty upon her return to the hospital. I was particularly struck by the richness of this metaphor for representing Terri's dilemma. As someone who had in the past repetitively cut the surface of her body in an effort to cut out and yet preserve her attachment to the mother, it seemed particularly apt as she struggled with these same issues with me that she would cut some part of her body, namely her hair, and also go to bed with an anonymous man, much as she felt I had brought another anonymous man into her relationship with me.

Case Example 2

John came for treatment as an outpatient when he was in his late twenties. He was a significantly depressed paranoid man with borderline liabilities who had been involved in a fiercely sadomasochistic relationship with a woman for the past eight years. At the time treatment began, he was concerned that this relationship might be ending and he would be faced with the terror of utter aloneness. John was the middle child in a family of three boys. His was a chaotic, violent family in which the parents fought continually until the time of their divorce when the patient was five. The father who was already a distant, unapproachable figure, left without keeping in touch with his sons. The mother, who was a very troubled narcissistic woman herself, moved the children from place to place, and threatened them with abandonment for any misbehavior. I had been seeing John for a year and a half when he learned about my pregnancy. He had guessed very early on that I was pregnant when I had only the suspicion of being pregnant myself. At that point I did not confirm or disconfirm his suspicion, and in any case he rather characteristically presented this fantasy as simply that, as a fantasy he hoped I would not shatter or try to take away from him by bringing in any mention of reality. When he subsequently learned his suspicions were correct, he was delighted with what he felt was his empathic connection with me. I think on a deeper level he was reassured by his correct intuition because it represented to him his ability to control me and my actions. But this positive response quickly faded and a malevolent paranoid vision set in. He felt unfairly outmaneuvered by me as if the pregnancy were an effort to control him. He treated my pregnancy as if it were an interpretation and spoke of how unempathic I was being. At times he went so far as to wonder whether I had intentionally engineered the pregnancy to provoke some feelingful reaction from him and to spur on the work. At times he reflected on his wish to be "reborn" by me. Unlike my female patient, he focused most of his attention on wanting to be my child, and could only briefly acknowledge his identification with me, as evidenced by his escalating hypochondriasis, renewed fears about homosexuality, and recent twenty pound weight gain. He began to threaten to leave his girl friend and became irritable, erratic, and sometimes downright cruel with her, alternating the roles of sadist and masochist. While the connection between this behavior and his wish to turn passive into active and to leave me rather than have me leaving him was discussed frequently, he continued to live out his rage with all women, and thereby to repudiate within himself his own femininity and its relationship to his still powerful identification with his mother.

For John my pregnancy felt like an assault. I became the crazy, emotionally abusive, and intrusive mother who was seductive one minute and rejecting and cold the next. John was preoccupied with who the man was who had fathered the child. Needless to say, John held a very sadomasochistic view of heterosexual relationships, in general; he mocked and ridiculed me for becoming pregnant and subservient to this man in my life, whomever he was.

John felt tortured by such thoughts and by the guilt and rage that lay behind them. Despite John's very real efforts to maintain a sense of being with me, he and I could never recapture a clear sense of mutuality. It was as if all previous meaning constructed between us was fractured and words could not penetrate the problem. In a sense John was absolutely right; my pregnancy was for him an empathic failure that resulted in the dissolution of an idealizing transference and his loss of me as a reliable self object. Efforts at identification did not mend the rupture, and John ultimately changed analysts as my patient Terri had done.

It would seem that a life transition for the analyst of this magnitude, in which the patient in a sense is forced to participate, places severe strain on the treatment situation, the patient's defenses, and the analyst's capacity to endure. Identificatory processes for these two patients were unsuccessful in the sense that they were not able to contain their impulsiveness nor were they able to find a way to continue in the treatment. The effort to use identification often took on a very masochistic cast—for example, in Terri's promiscuity or John's weight gain—and seems to point to one possible avenue for the psychogenesis of masochistic symptoms; namely, the failed use of identification, in the face of separation that is felt to be traumatically imposed by a maternal figure, leads to masochistic surrender as the best available avenue to remain connected with, yet separate from, the mother.

Discussion

I have tried to show with these clinical vignettes how identification is used in an effort to cope with a disruption in the treatment and the impingement of a real event in the life of the analyst, and how this process epitomizes the function of masochism, which is to somehow manage to stay connected with and at the same time separate from a dangerous maternal introject. These patients sought to use identification to bridge the gap they felt was created by their analyst's becoming pregnant, but yet they found this process difficult to sustain due to their intense anger and feelings of betrayal, disappointment, and abandonment. The pregnancy of the analyst as it indicated a separateness from them was traumatic, and left them feeling incomplete and helpless, floundering to find a way to manage their aggression and other painful affects now that the analyst was no longer felt to be a reliable "container," either because she was seen as too fragile or she was felt to be already filled up with thoughts and feelings about the child she carried. These individuals reverted to their previous masochistic solutions as their best effort to maintain their separateness from the analyst, while finding some security in the revival of the original attachment to their own mother.

References

Balint, M. (1932), Character analysis and new beginning. In: *Primary Love and Psychoanalytic Technique.* New York: Liveright Publishing, 1965, pp. 151–164.

Behrends, R. S., & Blatt, S. J. (1985), Internalization and psychological development throughout the life cycle. *The Psychoanalytic Study of the Child,* 40:11–39. New Haven, CT: Yale University Press.

Berlinger, B. (1958), The role of object relations in moral masochism. *Psychoanal. Quart.,* 27:38–56.

Brenman, M. (1952), On teasing and being teased: And the problem of "moral masochism." *The Psychoanalytic Study of the Child,* 7:264–285. New York: International Universities Press.

Brenner, C. (1959), The masochistic character: Genesis and treatment. *Amer. Psychoanal. Assn.,* 7:197–226.

Eisenbud, R. (1967), Masochism revisited. *Psychoanal. Rev.,* 54:561–582.

Freud, S. (1923), The ego and the id. *Standard Edition,* 19:1–66. London: Hogarth Press, 1961.

———— (1924), The economic problem of masochism. *Standard Edition,* 19:159–170. London: Hogarth Press, 1961.

Gorney, J. (1979), The negative therapeutic interaction. *Contemp. Psychoanal.,* 15:288–337.

Lax, R. (1969), Some considerations about transference and countertransference manifestations evoked by the analyst's pregnancy. *Internat. J. Psychoanal.,* 50:363–372.

Lichtenstein, H. (1961), Identity and sexuality: A study of their interrelationship in man. *J. Amer. Psychoanal. Assn.,* 9:179–260.

Menaker, E. (1942), The masochistic factor in the psychoanalytic situation. *Psychoanal. Quart.,* 11:171–186.

Winnicott, D. W. (1971), *Playing and Reality.* New York: Basic Books.

8

Thoughts on the Positive Value of a Negative Identity

James L. Sacksteder, M.D.

As Stolorow (1975), in a wonderfully lucid and becomingly modest paper on the narcissistic function of masochism (and sadism), noted, "masochism is a complex, multi-faceted problem, the manifestations of which appear in many forms and guises" (p. 441). These range from a normal element in the functioning of conscience to sexual perversion. He notes that ever since Margaret Brenman's (1952) application of Waelder's (1936) concept of the principle of multiple function to the understanding of masochistic phenomena, it has been clear that masochism, in its various manifestations, is best understood by considering it from multiple perspectives at different levels of analysis, including, for example, its functions:

"as an Id phenomenon" (p. 441), reflecting oedipal and/or preoedipal conflicts over sexual and aggressive drive development;

"as a Superego phenomenon . . . arising from guilt and from the need to be punished for forbidden impulses" (p. 441);

as an ego phenomenon, reflecting especially defensive and adaptive functions of the ego, including its functions;

"as a mode of relating to external and/or internal objects with the aim of warding off various infantile danger situations and dreaded object relations" (p. 441);

as a phenomenon, reflecting conflicts and associated arrest or regression in the process of separation–individuation; and finally

as a phenomenon reflecting incomplete self/self object differentiation derivative of severe narcissistic pathology.

Thus, careful clinical investigation is required to determine for any given individual the specific functions of his masochistic behavior at any one given time, as well as at different times over the course of his life.

My goal here is simply to add one more to the above formulations: that is, I want to suggest that masochism can also profitably be considered from the Eriksonian perspective of the concept of ego identity or, more specifically, from the point of view of Erikson's (1956) concept of a negative identity. My hypothesis is that a masochistic identity is a type of negative identity, which, however costly and pathological, nonetheless represents for some individuals their best possible effort at creating and maintaining a separate and autonomous sense of self, one that salvages for them a modicum of satisfaction, security, and self-esteem and thereby staves off tugs toward identity diffusion, psychotic regression, and/or suicide.

Before presenting clinical material, I want to say a word first about how I am using the concepts of identity, identity diffusion, and negative identity. Erikson's (1950) concept of identity fits within his wider conception of the human life cycle as reflecting an epigenetic principle that envisages a gradual unfolding of the personality through phase-specific psychosocial crises. One's identity is formed gradually by successive ego syntheses and resyntheses throughout childhood of the psychosexual and psychosocial aspects of the personality derivative of mastering or failing to master specific conflicts and tasks associated with each stage of development. As consolidated in late adolescence, one's identity represents a unique new gestalt integrating "constitutional givens, idiosyncratic libidinal needs, favored capacities, significant identifications, effective defenses, successful sublimations and consistent roles" (Erikson, 1956, p. 116). Thus, the concept of identity encompasses conscious, preconscious, and unconscious, psychosexual, psychosocial, and structural aspects of the personality. Of importance, for my argument, is Erikson's emphasis on the great relevance to the young individual's identity formation, of the ways in which he is responded to and given function and status as a person. The gradual growth and transformation of an individual's identity requires that it be recognized, encouraged, supported, and approved of by those who count most to the individual. Thus, who and what one considers oneself to be is powerfully shaped by the reflected appraisals, especially those subsequently internalized and made one's own, that one encounters all through development. To a variable but important extent one tends to become who and what those important to one expect and desire consciously and unconsciously.

Unfortunately, as Erikson explicated, some individuals come to their developmentally normal adolescent identity crisis with apparently unintegratable positive and negative identifications, and thus with apparently uninte-gratable positive and negative self and object representations. These individu-als find it impossible to coalesce an identity sufficiently acceptable and grati-fying to them and to their society and, instead, experience identity diffu-sion. These individuals, painfully unsure of their sexual, social, and vo-cational identity, become increasingly confused, ashamed, self-conscious, anxious, and guilty about this state of affairs. They withdraw into pain-ful isolation and inactivity because consistent engagement in any type of activity or relationship truly meaningful to them threatens them with in-creased disorganization. For such individuals, suicide can become a seri-ously considered option as a means to end their depression and their sense of the meaninglessness of and their failure at life, and/or as a desperate al-ternative to and escape from the threat of psychosis.

A different way to end the ongoing pain and confusion associated with an identity diffusion, however, is to establish a negative identity. A negative identity, as defined by Erikson (1956), is "an identity perversely based on all those identifications and roles which, at critical stages of de-velopment, have been presented to the individual as most undesirable or dangerous and yet, at least in some ways, also as most real" (p. 131). In other cases, or, in addition, "the negative identity is dictated by the ne-cessity of finding and defending a niche of one's own against the exces-sive ideals, either demanded by morbidly ambitious parents or seemingly already realized by actually superior ones" (p. 131). Thus, the choice of a negative identity by an individual represents "a desperate attempt at re-gaining some mastery in a situation in which the available positive iden-tity elements cancel each other out. . ." (p. 88), as occurs when all accept-able roles appear unattainable with the individual's inner means. When this is the case, "it is easier to derive a sense of identity out of a total identi-fication with that which one is *least* supposed to be. . ." (p. 132). Thus, for some, it is better to be *"nobody or somebody bad, or indeed, dead —and this totally, and by free choice — than be not-quite-somebody"* (p. 132). I believe a masochistic identity is one such negative identity for some individuals and, to make that point, I want to examine briefly some fac-tors contributing to the origin, evolution, and functions of masochism for one man I have worked with and learned from. As it is this man's iden-tity formation I am especially interested in, I will stress, in the clinical pre-sentation, the positive and negative identity elements available to him by virtue of the characteristics of the individuals who raised him, and the char-acteristics of his life experiences, and of the reflected appraisals available to him derivative of them.

Case Example: Michael

Michael was in his mid-twenties when he presented himself to me and I began to work with him. He was about five foot, eleven inches, blond, fair, with blue eyes, well proportioned, and could be quite graceful. He was potentially a very attractive man. However, my first thought on meeting him was that he looked like a derelict from skid row. His body was unwashed, as were his torn and rumpled nondescript clothes. He smelled bad. His longish hair was in disarray, and a scraggly, unkempt beard added to his dissolute appearance. He was thin to the point of emaciation, and looked pale, pasty, and ill. He slunk into my office as if ashamed of himself and as if he expected to be shunned or scolded or ridiculed and attacked by me. He spoke haltingly, at first in vague generalities, and frequently glanced furtively at me as if to see whether I was laughing at him or was contemptuous of him or repulsed by him.

What he told me was that his life was in shambles and this despite having been born into a wealthy and powerful family, and despite his own quite considerable intelligence and talents. For reasons painfully unclear to him, he had not been able to take advantage of any of his advantages. Instead, he had progressively taken on the identity of the family failure and problem because he had repeatedly failed at every social, educational, and vocational initiative he undertook. At the point at which I had met him, he had stopped all educational efforts and, after having flunked out of three colleges in succession, and because every occupation he considered or attempted seemed meaningless, he did no work. He was very withdrawn, isolated, and lonely, and mostly eschewed the company of other human beings because any move toward closeness repeatedly ended up with Michael being rejected, either quietly, or after having been attacked, ridiculed, and humiliated. This was because, despite the best of intentions, he nonetheless repeatedly engaged in behaviors that invited, and indeed provoked, the public humiliation, contempt, scorn, attack, and rejection he repeatedly encountered. This was especially true of his efforts to secure sexual gratification. Such efforts occurred only when Michael was intoxicated and typically they horribly misfired. His few sexual experiences with women were all with prostitutes. Initially, he was either impotent or had premature ejaculation, which embarrassed and humiliated him. However, he learned that he could sustain an erection and obtain some pleasure by imagining he was the woman prostitute, and with the actual prostitute above him he would then fantasize having breasts and a vagina and have the experience of being penetrated. Michael also had occasional sexual experiences with men. He would go to bars and arrange to get picked up by powerful, menacing men whom he would provoke into being contemptuous of him, and into humiliating him and sexually abusing him. However, actual sexual behavior with other human beings was relatively rare. His primary form of sexual gratification was masturbation and, while masturbating, Michael often would fantasize himself in the role of a woman, sadistically enslaved and dominated by an overwhelmingly powerful man.

As I mentioned, most of Michael's sexual behavior occurred when he was intoxicated. When he was sober, he was markedly anti-instinctual and appalled by the nature and intensity of his sexual and his erotized dependent, narcissistic, and aggressive urges. He controlled them by allying himself with a severe, primitively punitive superego. Thus, he was contemptuous of himself for his needfulness and punished himself or arranged to be punished by others when guilty about it, as well as when there was any upsurge in his ongoing guilt, shame, and humiliation about his ongoing failure to make anything of himself, as happened frequently when initiatives undertaken, regardless of how slight, nonetheless failed.

When I first met Michael he was totally estranged from his family, not having been in communication with them for over a year. Prior to that, and for years, their relationship had been characterized, from his point of view, primarily by hurt, frustration, anger, pain, disappointment, humiliation, and an increasing sense of helplessness, hopelessness, and despair about being able to do anything about this state of affairs. In addition, though, it was clear to Michael that one function his life and identity as a total failure served was to express powerfully his rage at his parents for the ways in which he perceived them to have failed him. It was thus an attempt to wreak revenge on them, regardless of the cost to himself.

Naturally, things had not always been this way, and I would like to trace now some of the factors that appear to have contributed significantly to determining the increasingly masochistic course of this man's life.

The Family

As I mentioned previously, Michael was born into a wealthy and influential family. The family fortune had been made spectacularly by the paternal grandfather. Until early middle age, this man had had to struggle hard just to make ends meet as he was a poor, Appalachian dirt farmer. One of his jobs was to haul logs to a nearby paper mill. The paper mill suffered various types of reverses and ultimately went bankrupt, at which point Michael's grandfather somehow managed to buy it. Subsequently, he pretty much singlehandedly built it into one of the largest paper manufacturing companies in the world. Michael never knew his grandfather, other than as a legend. Said Michael: "He was like Superman. His brothers were all dirt farmers collecting Social Security, and he was driving around in Cadillacs." He was the model of success in the business world held up to

Michael, to ideally emulate and equal, and it goes without saying, he was a tough act to follow.

Michael's father's solution to the problem of how to follow in his father's footsteps was to go into another field, after he first worked briefly and unhappily in the family-owned business. Taking advantage of his inherited wealth, he went into public service and performed ably in this capacity, ultimately achieving much recognition at a national level for his contributions. Thus, he also achieved a type of success with which it would be hard to compete. Nonetheless, growing up, it was his paternal grandfather and father that Michael was encouraged to emulate and, in fact, best. They were the models that were used to shape his ambitions and ideals, and he felt that were he to achieve a success less spectacular than theirs, then he would be a total failure and would be considered such, not simply by himself but also by his family and society.

Michael described his father as a shy, socially unskilled, hardworking, emotionally withdrawn, lonely man, more interested in ideas and causes than people. Michael felt his father had no friends, only acquaintances and associates. He engaged only in carefully ritualized and formal socializing and much preferred more solitary activities, such as reading and watching television. He lived his life by rigid codes of conduct that did not allow for much spontaneity or passion or simply fun. Instead, they seemed to demand constant, humorless self-sacrifice and total commitment, even slavish devotion, to serving others.

In contrast to his father's family, Michael's mother's family was thoroughly conventional and totally undistinguished. Their achievements were not idealized and held up as models but some aspects of their way of life was. Michael's maternal grandfather, a merchant, lived his whole life in a mid-level position in a business owned by his family. He was a puritanical, domineering, opinionated man, who especially abhorred drinking and any form of unrestrained instinctual expression. His children were raised to be abstinent and to be compliant. It was understood they were to maintain a socially correct and reserved appearance at all times. Michael feels his mother deeply loved her father and he feels her attachment to him and loyalty to the way of life dictated by him was one reason she rarely dated and was nicknamed "icy" in college.

Michael's parents met in college and were married shortly after his father's graduation. His mother never finished college, and this was one source of her ongoing insecurity and feeling of inferiority. As a couple, Michael's parents relatively quickly settled into a reasonably comfortable, socially correct relationship, but one that seemed totally devoid of any passion. Very quickly, Michael's father became a virtually absent husband and even when physically present, was usually emotionally unavailable. He made it clear he preferred to read or watch television rather than to talk with his wife, and this despite her protests and repeated pleas that he pay more attention to her. This simply led to increased withdrawal on his part, and that style of relating later served as an important model for Michael.

Michael's mother was an attractive, stylish, reserved, but nonetheless imposing, woman. Because his father was mostly absent as Michael grew up, it was his mother who was the dominant and dominating force in the lives of the children. It was hard for Michael to think of her as a person, separate and distinct from himself, and thus to describe her, but, from his descriptions of her, she came across as insecure as a woman with her peers, as a wife with her husband, and as a mother with her children. Michael said she was very status conscious and, like her father, abhorred drinking, spontaneous instinctual expression, and was very preoccupied with appearances and anxious for the family to be seen as a harmonious unit, living lives above reproach. Michael felt she settled for the life of a glorified servant, assigned the tasks of keeping the house clean and performing as a social hostess, completely subjugating her life in service to her husband and his career, and this despite his apparent lack of interest in and affection for her.

Childhood

Michael was the youngest of three children, as was his mother in her family. He was named for his maternal grandfather and appeared to have been special to his mother all his life. She described him as a happy, contented, undemanding, quiet, easily cared for, and controlled baby. Thus, he seemed, possibly on a constitutional basis, to have been somewhat passive from the start. This feature, however, even if present from the beginning, was subsequently greatly reinforced. He was raised early on by a series of nurses and adjusted to their comings and goings, perhaps too easily, with too little protest over their loss, reflecting too little individualized and personalized attachment to their person, as opposed to their role and function. His mother, in a pattern she was to maintain over the course of his entire life, tended to vacillate between being nearly totally uninvolved with him in a personal way, delegating his care at such times to others, and, alternately, with being, from his point of view, overwhelmingly overprotective and intrusively overinvolved with him, or at least her idea of him. Michael said that even when intensely involved with him, "she didn't actually see me; she never saw me as I am. I was her toy or her plaything or her possession or a part of her. I've never been able to get out from under her, to not be a part of her, as my brother and sister have been able to, and she likes that. She likes having me around, needing her, even though she always denies that and says she wants me independent of her.''

Early on, Michael learned that it was important to be good, to keep up appearances, to cause no trouble, and thus to suppress his assertiveness, spontaneity, and differentness, if these led to conflicts with his parents. It was important to be compliant to his parents' expectations if he wished to maintain a good relationship with them, and thus, over time, Michael became very good at being the way whomever he was with wanted him to be. This led, I believe, to his consolidating, at least for a while, what Winnicott (1960) calls a false self organization built up on a compliance basis which in order to maintain it, required repression, suppression, dissociation, and splitting as a way of life.

In his early years, almost all interactions were with his family and relatives, as he was raised in a family compound set off geographically and psychologically from the rest of the world. Thus idiosyncratic ways of relating peculiar to the family, especially those that, however useful within the family system were, nonetheless, not useful outside of it, went unnoted and uncorrected because of the lack of opportunities to interact with nonfamily members. Thus, Michael's acquisition of social skills was significantly interfered with right from the beginning.

This problem was compounded just as Michael began school because midway through his first-grade year, just as he was getting to know his local peers, the family moved to the New York area, following a new government appointment for his father. Subsequent moves, all necessitated by his father's career, repeatedly disrupted Michael's schooling and the network of social relationships he was building. These moves were major contributors to Michael's increasing sense of passivity about his life as he was repeatedly uprooted due to parental necessities in a manner totally beyond his control, and maximally disruptive to him in terms of his ongoing relationships and activities, and without any acknowledgement or empathy by his parents of the traumatic effects on him of these moves.

Another factor contributing to his sense of passivity, his feeling of a lack of control over his life and experiences, however, was an ongoing problem he had with enuresis. This was, in addition, an ongoing powerful source of embarrassment, shame, and humiliation for him. Years later, the difficulty was identified as being due to a congenital urethral flap, but this was not known at the time. All Michael knew, growing up, was that he wet the bed, and continued to do so despite every effort he undertook to correct the difficulty. His parents' attitude toward the problem was to largely ignore it and the seriousness of its effects on Michael. They advised Michael to keep it a secret, reinforcing its shameful aspect, and he said it was his enuresis that prompted him to get into keeping secrets as a way of life. This problem also helped tilt his development toward an identity associated with doubt and shame, as opposed to autonomy. Michael's parents scolded his brother and sister when they teased Michael about wetting the bed; nonetheless, the bed-wetting obviously left him at their mercy any time they wanted to hurt him by teasing him and ridiculing him about it. His brother, especially, hurt him deeply, when angry with him one time, by telling some of Michael's friends that Michael wet his bed, thereby exposing Michael to further ridicule and humiliation about this difficulty.

As Michael was growing up, he had virtually no contact with his father. His upbringing was left to his mother and, over time, their relationship became increasingly problematic. From Michael's point of view, the nature of the relationship was primarily determined by his mother and her needs, thus reinforcing Michael's passivity and his need to be passively receptive and responsive. Michael's mother's relationship with the patient was very variable. At times, she was so busy with the social obligations that went along with her husband's position that she had very little time, energy, or apparent interest available for her son. At such times, Michael felt as if he did not exist or, because she took no notice of him, his activities, or relationships, he felt that they were not important and, by inference, that he was unimportant, uninteresting, and insignificant. And, because her attitude toward him was reinforced by his father's apparent attitude toward him, Michael ended up feeling that no one cared about him, that he did not count, that he did not deserve attention, respect, or love. At other times, though, and in contrast to his experience with his father who, he felt, never had much interest in him, his mother would involve herself very intensely with him. This could be in ways experienced as deeply pleasurable, but, more frequently, it was experienced by Michael as overwhelming, with the result that he felt invaded, taken over, and controlled by her. It was as if his life, interests, and activities were taken over and became hers, and he somehow got lost in the process.

When involved with him, Michael's mother would share with him her grandiose ambitions for him, but the nature of the ways in which she hoped he would succeed seemed more in the service of her needs, desires, and interests than his, and involved her wish for him to attain what seemed like impossibly high standards and goals. At such points, Michael's mother was intensely admiring and inflating of Michael, and extravagant in her praise of any of his actual achievements that buttressed her belief in what he ultimately would be able to achieve for her. However, because this mirroring was marred by the aspects of merger involved with it, as well as by his increased awareness that what was admired was more her idea of him than his actuality, the entire experience became increasingly disturbing for him.

During these years, Michael often tried to turn to his father, both for help with his difficult relationship with his mother and, in addition, simply to establish a good, ongoing relationship with him. Until adolescence, Michael idealized and even idolized his father. He was proud of his achievements. He admired, respected, and loved him, and desperately tried to get his attention, affection, and admiration. Said Michael: "My father was a God to me but I could never get through to him. He just wasn't interested in me. If I tried to talk with him, he never seemed to take me seriously or he'd tell me 'Be quiet'- because he was reading or watching TV. I guess I wasn't interesting or important enough to him. I wanted to please him but nothing I did ever seemed to." The one exception to this, for a while, was a shared enjoyment of tennis and golf. These served temporarily as very pleasurable shared activities and interests, but most of Michael's efforts to develop a good relationship with his father failed. An additional factor complicating this effort was Michael's feeling that his mother interfered with his efforts to get close to his father. He felt his mother was possessive of him and rivalrous with her husband for his time and attention. She would sit Michael next to her and "with the women" at dinner parties and interfered with Michael's efforts to sit next to his father and join "with the men" in their discussions. His relationship with his father was further complicated when, during his latency, his mother sought him out for companionship when her husband was unavailable to her. This often left Michael feeling anxious, guilty, and disloyal to his father, and fearful of his father's disapproval and wrath, because of his taking his father's place with his mother. The combination of his mother's possessiveness, engulfment, and exploitation of him and his father's withdrawnness from him largely left Michael without a serviceable relationship with his father to facilitate the identifications with him that would have helped Michael to separate and individuate from his mother and emerge from their complicated, dependent, narcissistic, sexualized, and symbiotic relationship with one another, and grow into a comfortably secure male identity.

Michael's relationships with his siblings might have helped him with these tasks. Unfortunately, however, he never established a good relationship with either of them. He viewed them in ways identical to the ways he viewed his parents; that is, he saw his older sister as like his mother and thus as either uninvolved with him or overinvolved and overprotective of him in ways that left him feeling humiliatingly infantilized. In addition, he felt at other times that she was straightforwardly contemptuous and rejecting of him. The same was true of his brother. Michael tended to idealize his brother, as he did his father, and wanted very much to join with him in his activities. However, his brother did not include him, did not seem to like him, and either ignored or ridiculed him. What was missing, obviously, was any sense of acceptance by his brother or his sister as a peer and as an individual they were interested in, liked, wanted to be with, and admired. Instead, he felt they either ignored, exploited, or rejected him and, unfortunately, these same qualities of relatedness were subsequently to be transferred from his sibling relationships to his peer relationships. What was missing in all the family relationships was a consistent, accepting, interested involvement in his life and him as he was actually experiencing it and himself.

Early Adolescence

As Michael entered puberty, the family moved yet again and things went from bad to worse. Just prior to the move, Michael had made some friends in his neighborhood and at school and, for the first time ever, was really absorbed in and enjoying extrafamilial peer relationships and activities. Thus, he was understandably devastated when his parents announced that they were moving and went ahead with the move despite his protestations. Michael said: "I've hated my parents ever since that move. I had a few friends before that move but, because of that move, I lost all my old friends and I never found new ones. After the move, I never fit in. I was lonely. I stopped playing." Alienated from his parents, he stopped sharing with them much of what he did outside the house. When at home, though, he remained superficially compliant and, because he caused no trouble there, his increasing difficulties outside the home went unnoticed. At school, it was as if his now "bad mother" and "bad father" were reincarnated in the form of a bad, mean, older woman teacher and a "sadistic ex-Marine coach." Michael hated them both for what he perceived as their picking on him, singling him out for public ridicule and humiliation. This development seems a very fateful one because, subsequent to it, Michael lost access to two potentially neutralized arenas of activities and relationships that might have led the way to positive recognition and social success. Instead, schooling and the activity of learning became spoiled for him because of the contamination of his bad relationship with his mother with a bad relationship with a mean woman teacher. And, similarly, sports, for which Michael had some considerable aptitude and which had previously been one pleasurable activity he shared with his father, were now spoiled for him by the contamination of his bad relationship with his father with the bad coach.

As Erikson (1956) reminds us, it is during the elementary school age preceding puberty and adolescence that the child "is taught the prerequisites for participation in the particular technology of his culture and is given the opportunity and life task of developing a sense of workmanship and work participation" (p. 83). The child has the task and opportunity "to reidentify with parents as workers and tradition bearers rather than as sexual and familial beings, thus nurturing at least one concrete and more 'neutral' possibility of becoming like them" (p. 83). When development misfires during this era, more neutralized identifications with the parents are interfered with, leading to ongoing conflicted enmeshment with them. Similarly, a sense of workmanship and work participation can fail to sufficiently consolidate, paving the way toward very serious problems later, as was the case for Michael.

Michael's difficulties with the teacher and the coach contributed to his being teased and shunned by classmates and teammates, so he withdrew from this peer group and turned to younger boys for companionship and, for a while, enjoyed their company. Unfortunately, he was teased about these associations so he became self-conscious and ashamed of them, and discontinued them. He then fell in with some older delinquent boys who primarily exploited him but who, nonetheless, provided him with some companionship. These boys, somewhat like his mother, vacillated between total uninvolvement with him and intense involvement with him; an intense involvement, however, determined by their needs and their desire to exploit Michael. For a while Michael engaged in some quite serious delinquent behavior. This included shoplifting, petty thefts, and breaking and entering. This behavior gradually diminished, but not engagement in the other behavior his companions introduced him to, that is, substance abuse. In their company, and then, increasingly when he was alone, Michael began to drink and smoke pot, and, unfortunately, he liked the experience of being intoxicated, "unfortunately" because being intoxicated subsequently was to threaten to become a way of life and possibly death for him. It was during this period, of course, that, for the first time, Michael consciously and deliberately engaged in behaviors he knew would appall his parents. However, at this point, he kept his rebellion a secret from them and remained compliant when in their company.

None of the relationships with the delinquent boys ever became truly personalized, individualized, and meaningful to him. He says he never trusted any of them enough to open up to them. Nor did he open up to anyone else, as he was increasingly ill at ease with all of his peers. He became increasingly shy, self-conscious, anxious, and exquisitely sensitive to rebuff, and constantly preoccupied with whether or not he was making a good impression. Unfortunately, very often he was not because he was simply so socially unskilled and most of his overtures toward peers were so maladroit and tactless that they most often evoked, and even provoked, rejection and ridicule, or at the very least, withdrawal. And, unfortunately, rather than learning from experience and becoming more socially skilled, Michael became increasingly inhibited, and he increasingly avoided undertaking any kind of social initiative. These accumulating failures to be a success in school, at sports, and with peers contributed further toward tilting his development from trust to increasing mistrust; from any sense of increasing autonomy to an increasing sense of doubt and shame; from confident initiative to guilt; and away from an increasing sense of industry toward an increasing sense of inferiority.

Adolescence and College

His parents, busy with their own lives, almost unbelievably insisted they had no idea of the seriousness of the delinquent behavior, or the substance abuse, or his ongoing difficulties with his peer group and with teachers and coaches. What eventually brought Michael's difficulties to their attention was that he became obviously depressed at home. He became withdrawn, reclusive, and isolated there. That prompted his parents to make two interventions into his life. First, they had Michael reevaluated for his enuresis. It was at that point that the congenital flap was discovered and, at $14^1/2$, Michael had an operation on his penis that finally corrected his difficulties with enuresis. Then, Michael's parents informed him that they were going to send him away to a private boys' school. They hoped that would improve his spirits. These two interventions were both traumatic as Michael first felt assaulted and then rejected and abandoned, and this also powerfully increased his passivity, as well as his ambivalence toward his parents, their way of life, and their aspirations for him.

Michael said that though he didn't particularly want to go to the private school, his parents were adamant about it, so he passively went along with the plan and he stayed at the school until he graduated from high school, even though he hated it. He was very lonely and isolated. At this point, he waited for others to first take social initiatives vis-à-vis him. If no one reached out to him, he in turn never reached out to anyone. Unfortunately no one seems to have reached out to him and to have connected with him during the entire course of his high school years. He reported that over time he talked to virtually no one, except to give very prefunctory responses in the dining hall, in class, and in hallways. He said he was mostly "numb" during these years, just going through the motions, and though he must have been a transparently lonely, sad, obviously isolated, obviously interpersonally insecure, and socially unskilled youth, nonetheless Michael says this apparently went totally unnoted. He could recall no interventions prompted by this state of affairs either by the faculty at the school or by his parents. So, apparently unnoticed, he withdrew from people and increasingly engaged in behaviors he could pursue alone. These included, most prominently (and mirroring his father's behavior) the activities of reading and watching television. He made absolutely no efforts to date (again, like his father, he indicated little outward interest in women). His sexual behavior was limited to masturbation and his fantasies increasingly took on a sadomasochistic cast, with Michael identifying alternately with the man and the woman in the fantasies but, over time, increasingly with the woman. Actually, beyond his sexual relationships, virtually all his relationships with people at this point were primarily fantasy relationships; that is, he largely lived in his imagination and rarely thought to try to realize, to actualize any of his fantasies. The importance of this, as Erikson (1956), A. Freud (1958), Blos (1967), Laufer (1976), and others have noted, is that whether or not adolescence leads to progressive development or to regression is determined in a major way by the opportunities provided to an adolescent by his peer group, and for Michael they were virtually nonexistent. Thus, again, he was largely cut off from the types of relationships and activities that would have helped him out of his enmeshment with his parents and that would have helped him to master the developmental tasks of adolescence successfully.

After graduating from high school, Michael attempted college three times at three different schools, and this was his last effort to achieve success, as his family defined it. Michael had become increasingly conscious of being very torn, vacillating between wanting to please his parents by conforming to their wishes and realizing their ambitions for him, and the impulse to do the exact opposite; that is, to displease them, to rebel, and create a life for himself that realized their worst fears about him — one that would be the opposite of anything they would desire for him. Eventually, it was the latter course of action that prevailed. Thus, though Michael went to each college with the best of intentions, hoping to find himself at last and to achieve the spectacular academic and social success that would have pleased his parents and himself, it never worked out. He simply could not achieve the types of positive successes that would have consolidated a positive identity. Instead, academically, after repeatedly making promising starts, he then had difficulty with his attention and concentration and with disciplining himself to study. He also obsessed so much about what course of studies to major in and about the type of life to create for himself that the net result was increasing paralysis. He would get progressively behind in his schoolwork, which left him anxious and depressed. He would then drink to calm himself down and cheer himself up, but that interfered with studying and resulted in his getting even further behind. Ultimately, he would flunk out, reinforcing his image of himself as a failure. Similarly, socially, after first having been invited to join various fraternities and then being blackballed by them because of his behavior, he became completely withdrawn and isolated and lived alone, anonymously, in rooming houses, trying very hard to be utterly self-sufficient, needing no one for anything. When the loneliness became intolerable and began to stimulate thoughts of suicide, he would drink to decrease his anxiety, shyness, self-consciousness, and inhibitions, and go out and engage in the types of sexual behaviors with men and women discussed earlier in this chapter. These encounters allowed a dissociated gratification of various types of dependency, narcissistic, aggressive, and sexual desires, dystonic and forbidden when sober, but impulsively and compulsively sought out and gratified when intoxicated.

During this same period, Michael was involved in an escalating series of automobile accidents that were barely disguised suicide attempts. He destroyed several cars and narrowly missed losing his life. His accidents always occurred when he was driving intoxicated. In each instance, he was "protected" from the consequences of his behavior by his family. They had the charges of drunk driving removed, and they replaced each car in succession. And, as previously, Michael's long period of enuresis in childhood, his juvenile period of delinquency, and the adolescent pattern of increased social withdrawal and substance abuse, so now, too, the repeated failures at college, his increasing alcohol abuse, and the very serious threats to his life posed by his drunk driving, the seriousness of this behavior was largely denied by the family. Almost unbelievably, they never talked with him about what he was doing, or attempted to help him integrate it, understand what it meant, and help him with his increasing troubles. Instead, they more often acted as if nothing was happening, which, in turn, again led Michael to feel as if nothing he did mattered to them, including endangering his life. If no one he cared about cared about him, what was the sense of continuing to live, or struggling to make something of his life?

In addition to the fatalism and despair involved with this way of life, though, Michael also became increasingly and consciously enraged with his parents and, as the estrangement between him and his family grew, he no longer dissociated his rage at them while in their company. At times he threatened their lives.

Conclusion

Michael had come to realize that his failures could be turned into a type of success because they were a way powerfully to attack, worry, and reject his parents. So, increasingly, he devoted himself to succeeding at failing, and to developing a life that was the exact opposite of all that his parents ever hoped for him. Thus, he was not a success, he was a failure; he was not sober and industrious, he was drunk and dissolute; he was not a source of pride, he became a source of shame, embarrassment, and guilt; he was not making good use of his intelligence, talents, and wealth, instead, he was wasting them; he did not marry well, he did not even date, instead, he lived in total isolation or engaged in sexual behavior with anonymous men and women that would have shocked and appalled his family. In terms of his negative identity, he was well on his way to becoming a chronic alcoholic, a sexual and moral masochist, and probably, eventually, a successful suicide. From his point of view, part of the "success" involved in being a failure was to bring to his parents' attention their inability to impact on him in any manner that would halt and reverse his progressive deterioration. They came eventually to feel as helplessly passive, as frustrated, impotent, hopeless, and helpless in the relationship to him as, I think, he had previously felt in his relationship to them. Now, they, like he, alternated between anxiety, rage, and despair.

Michael's development led eventually to his hospitalization and to our meeting in psychotherapy. The aim in the preceding presentation was not just to delineate the gradual growth and transformation of Michael's identity, but more importantly to stress what in our first meeting was certainly least apparent, and that was the positive value of Michael's negative identity.

For painful as this state of affairs was for all concerned, it nonetheless represented, Michael's best attempt at separating, individuating, and differentiating from his family of origin and making his way in the world. His masochistic identity allowed him to gratify and solve needs and conflicts relating to his dependency, his sexuality and aggression, and his narcissism. In addition it served as his best possible solution to the needs and conflicts relating to his incomplete separation–individuation and self/selfobject differentiation. Though Michael led a tortured and torturing life, his adaptation was, nonetheless, successful in the sense that it served to keep him alive and nonpsychotic. The integration and maintenance of an identity and the satisfaction of diverse needs and demands are motivational principles in human development. In the psychoanalytic work that followed our first meeting it was necessary for me to acknowledge simultaneously the very real failure of Michael's life, while understanding and appreciating it as an integrative achievement.

References

Blos, P. (1967), The second individuation process of adolescence. *The Psychoanalytic Study of the Child,* 22:162–186. New York: International Universities Press.

Brenman, M. (1952), On teasing and being teased: And the problem of "moral masochism." *The Psychoanalytic Study of the Child,* 7:264–285. New York: International Universities Press.

Erikson, E. H. (1950), *Childhood and Society.* New York: W. W. Norton.

——— (1956), The problem of ego identity. *J. Amer. Psychoanal. Assn.,* 4:56–121.

Freud, A. (1958), Adolescence. *The Psychoanalytic Study of the Child,* 13:255–278. New York: International Universities Press.

Laufer, M. (1976), The central masturbation fantasy, the final sexual organization, and adolescence. *The Psychoanalytic Study of the Child,* 31:297–316. New Haven, CT: Yale University Press.

Stolorow, R. D. (1975), The narcissistic function of masochism (and sadism). *Internat. J. Psycho-Anal.,* 56:441–448.

Waelder, R. (1936), The principle of multiple function: Observations on over-determination. *Psychoanal. Quart.,* 5:45–62.

Winnicott, D. W. (1960), Ego distortion in terms of true and false self. In: *The Maturational Processes and the Facilitating Environment.* New York: International Universities Press, 1965.

III

Absence, the Father, and Recognition

9

The Analysis of Masochistic Features in a Young Man

Frank Marotta, Ph.D.

Paul, a young man, came for hospital treatment after he had been beaten severely by two men in a prostitution district. What prompted him to come for intensive treatment was not simply the seriousness of this latest incident but also his recognition that he had provoked each of the half dozen beatings he had received in the prior two years.

Along with this recognition came a greater willingness to admit his dread of losing control over all his bodily functions, and that he had been fighting for some time the compulsion to cut off his penis, to kill babies, and in a variety of ways to harm himself and others. He deeply feared that he would some day fail in his struggle to resist these very powerful and relentless urges. Paul was a college graduate, highly articulate, and of superior intelligence. He read widely and had a long-standing interest in the theater. I believe that a retrospective analysis of this case contributes to our understanding of masochistic phenomena.

The setting and framework of this treatment might be considered to be ideal. The patient was in a long-term, unlocked hospital. We met in psychotherapy four times weekly for two years and four months and then on an outpatient basis for five months more. In addition to all of the more usual aspects of holding that are provided by a hospital setting, the unlocked facility placed the responsibility for maintaining suitability to remain in the open setting squarely in the patient's hands. This is an essential condition necessary for an intensive inpatient psychoanalytic treatment. The open setting is a feature particularly relevant in a case of masochism in light of the obvious fact that a locked setting may have specific and complicated meaning for a masochistic patient. Moreover, the treatment setting was ideal in that every treatment in this hospital was reported to the entire staff on a regular basis, thus affording more public scrutiny and discussion.

Despite the rather ideal setting of his treatment and my commitment to adhere, to the best of my ability, to good psychoanalytic treatment, this patient made only marginal progress. Indeed, he stated at termination that while he had made some important internal changes, he had been unable to understand or in any substantial way to change the central core of his masochistic complex. I agreed with him and bid him well in his move to a large city and his pursuit of further treatment.

I knew at that time that something of substantial importance had remained unfocused and unrecognized throughout the course of Paul's treatment. Recently, I came upon Gilles Deleuze's (1971) lengthy study of masochism. Through the work of Deleuze I came to realize that Paul had been struggling to say something through his actions and words that I could not receive at the time. Paul had been trying to articulate a complex question about an absence, a question that might have gone something like, "How can the father be realized to exist?"

Where traditional psychoanalytic ideas about masochism assume that the masochist's torturer is a representation of the father, Deleuze maintains that it is actually the image of the father within the masochist that is beaten, humiliated, and ridiculed. It is not a child but a father who is being beaten. Deleuze argues that there are no real object ties for the masochist and no identification. This stands contrary to the usual understanding of masochism where masochistic behavior is seen as the regressive identification with the passive victim mother in the service of sustaining an object tie to a father perceived as dangerous. Deleuze states that the masochist constructs a world devoid of real objects. The "perversion" is not a passive sexualized connection with the sadistic father but the destruction of the image of the father. This destruction is in the service of the masochist's pursuit of a frozen, antiseptic state which places the masochist as hero in a perfectly ordered existence.

The masochist accomplishes his goals by two powerful and simultaneous acts of disavowal directed at the parents. First, the real mother is abolished through distorting idealization. This is an important point and, although it cannot be developed fully here, I would like briefly, even if cryptically, to mention it. Where conventional psychoanalytic conceptions detect the presence of the father behind the ever-present torturer, Deleuze finds the presence of a maternal ideal. Deleuze describes this figure as the complicated, heightened aggregation of three separate, mythic maternal aspects: the oral (good), the oedipal (punitive), and the uterine (seductive) into an all-powerful central ideal. Through exaggeration and drama, this ideal defines a symbolic order. Its means are punishment, seduction, and reward. Its promise is perfect existence. The second disavowal follows then as the father and any otherness to the dyad are abolished. In this order the magnified mother now lacks nothing, while the father literally is nothing.

The inevitable failure of the masochist has to do with the general fact that nothing can be abolished without fear of its return. Indeed, what has been banished poses the continual threat of return, furiously unmediated by symbolic contextualization, as hallucination — on the body, in the realm of the real. The masochist must relentlessly guard against the prospect of the banished father's aggressive return, a prospect that continually disrupts his pursuit of being a singular hero within a perfectly ordered dyad. Inescapably this image does return and in its return the image of the father is drawn on the masochist's own body. This is the desperate nightmare in which the dreaded reasserts itself from within.

In this chapter I will present chronologically, and in some detail, my hours with Paul in order to convey the texture of this type of clinical work, and also to present Paul's struggle to engage in the psychoanalytic situation and the difficulty with which he remained attached, alive, and nonpsychotic while simultaneously attempting to purge his world of real objects. The reader may then draw his or her own conclusions. Paul was certainly a profoundly troubled young man, and our work could not be said fully to have accomplished its goal. In our day-to-day contact with each other, however, something of importance developed that is difficult to specify in an abstract way.

It will be obvious to the reader that I proceeded with conventional ideas about masochism, about Paul's attachment to his mother, about his attachment to me, and about his manhood. In the text of the treatment the reader might look for both, that which has given rise to traditional psychoanalytic ideas about masochism and that which supports the ideas suggested by Deleuze.

Case Example

Paul was a twenty-five-year-old, unemployed, single male at the time of his admission to the hospital. He stated that he was suffering from severe anxiety and that he was "as depressed as a slug." He was plagued by obsessive thoughts of cutting off his penis, of stabbing himself or someone else, of losing control over his bodily functions, and of killing a child. He had intermittent chest pains, which seemed anxiety related. Consultation with several cardiologists revealed no positive findings. His developmental history was noteworthy for the parents' divorce when he was five, for his inability to get along with his stepfather, and for his desire to be with his father: "I would suck the slime off the floor to be with my father, even though he is an alcoholic and a sleaze.''

The first several weeks of psychotherapy meetings were marked by Paul's complaints about my age. Paul stated emphatically that he desired to be in treatment with a certain famous older man who had been on our staff. After naming a whole list of prominent elderly men he wished to affiliate with, he stated that on his own he was referenceless. ''I need someone to take me under his wing and make the world listen to me, someone who could say 'yes' to Paul.'' He mentioned that he had written a lengthy letter to a famous novelist but got no reply. ''If I ever finally cut off my penis maybe I'll stuff it into a bottle and send it to that bastard.'' Also, he believed that he would never have been admitted to this hospital if it were not for his mother, since she undoubtedly must have ''pulled some strings'' to get him in. It seemed to him that all of his important advances in life were due to his mother and that he was nothing on his own.

Despite his apparent disappointment with me he pressed on to fill each hour with many things. Sessions would often start with some sort of hostile or provocative comment such as, ''I came, I saw, I conquered''; or ''You look like you had sex last night. Am I right?''; or ''Do you smoke marijuana?'' My efforts to have him expand on his comments would go evaded. In one meeting, after a string of particularly provocative remarks to which I made no response, he told me that he was testing to see if I attended to comments he made at the very beginning of an hour. Each hour in these early weeks seemed to be a dramatic performance that would begin with a theme or topic statement. Before long, however, he would be associating from one story or description or memory to another. These would be so mired in references to characters or lines in movies and plays, lines or whole stanzas of Shakespeare, quotes from books, and so on, that it was impossible to follow any coherent line of thought. Any attempt by me to focus on one point would lead him to become even more disorganized. He would stumble for a moment, at times indicating that he did not even comprehend what I had said, and then resume his associative barrage.

In the first several weeks of treatment Paul frequently spoke of the argument he had with his stepfather just prior to his hospitalization. With intense animation he would describe repeatedly the process by which he consciously provoked the argument. When his stepfather became very angry Paul ''got him even more hot and just when I thought he might hit me I went right up to him, stuck my face into his, and shouted [obscenities] at him.'' Later Paul's stepfather told his mother to ''get that jerk out of this house or I am leaving.'' With increasing anger and speaking to me as if I were his stepfather, he shouted, ''You can get this jerk out of the house but you can't get me out of my mother's mind.'' Paul described his mother as someone who cycled back and forth between being "so good that it is frightening" and so bad that he was sure that she was quite mentally ill.

A story he told me at the beginning of the third month: A man was in a room with his psychiatrist and his puppet. The puppet had begun to take on an identity of its own and to turn against the psychiatrist, attempting to bite him, but the man threw the puppet down and smashed it to pieces. The man then strangled the psychiatrist to death. Immediately after completing the story Paul announced that he wanted to show me something and launched into a few minutes of very skillful dramatic improvisation. When he stopped he sat silently looking at me for a moment or two. It seemed he was saying that if I was misled by his acts, his false images, his imitations, he would want to kill me. Also, it seemed he was saying that in some way I mattered to him, that it was important to him that I not mistake his presentation for him. However, I did not know just what to say to him. He said, "You have a face like a poker player," and then went on to describe how hurt he still was over having been kicked out of a public swimming pool because people thought he was someone else. At the end of the meeting, halfway out the door, he said, "I need to know where you stand with me."

In the very next meeting I repeated something he said. He became disorganized, stumbling on his words as he attempted to resume his thought. I asked what happened and he described himself as becoming anxious and unable to remember what I said. He went on to say that he feared I might be more intelligent than he ever could be, and that I must be more persevering since I have a job while he could not work. He was frightened that I might humiliate him in some way. He had a feeling of admiration for me, and also felt very jealous and competitive. In the next meeting he spoke of his dog and how this pet had consistently loved him over the years. Tearfully, with building dramatic momentum, he said, "No matter what obsessions, ugly thoughts, or anything else that might be in my head my dog would always love me. He lets me hold him and, in letting me hold him, he is holding me. I've always had the image of a girl and me, naked in a room, holding each other, watching the rain fall. She knows nothing about me and I nothing about her, not even names. I need to hold someone and love them."

Meetings now started to have somewhat less of a hostile provocative beginning and were less hard to follow. Quite often Paul would refer to his obsessive thoughts. "The thought of cutting off my penis is very strong. It's hell. Everything I see I translate into a means to cut it off. What if I see scissors or a knife? I'm always afraid. If I see a light socket with no bulb in it, I think of sticking my penis in it and turning on the electricity. What if I lose control and stab someone or throw acid in their face or pull a baby out of a carriage and kill it?" After a pause, he resumed with, "I admit to stealing and cheating and lying and looking at my asshole in a mirror and wanting to sleep with my mother. What will it take to get rid of these obsessions?'' I began to say something and he interrupted, then stopped and observed that he "cuts off" what I say. After another moment he said, "I thought you were going to say that you don't like me, I just felt a strong sense of guilt." He went on to say that in his fraternity he started out as the least popular member and hated the most popular one. When things changed so that he was the most popular person in the house he would not allow himself to hate the previously most popular person anymore. He knew what it was like to be down and never knew when the tables might switch again. "So I can't hate you. Besides you listen to me. The worst hell for me is talking and not being understood, being negated."

Soon after the beginning of Paul's hospitalization I began to receive letters from his mother. She wanted me to begin him on "megadose vitamin therapy," to have "endocrine studies" done, to begin him on "endorphin treatment," and so on. As time went on Paul began to speak more directly about his relationship with his mother. He said that she would rapidly oscillate between intrusive love and neglectful hate, and that he never knew what to expect. At times she would tell him he was beautiful, competent, and precious to her. She would arrange dates with women for him; she got him into schools; she urged him to begin sports; and she was forever giving him the names of people to contact who would surely give him a good job. She consistently pressured him during his hospitalization to get a job and to make progress. "But I don't hate her or blame her for anything. She is my only supporter. She does the best she can." Despite all of her blatant provocation Paul would stop short of saying he had any anger toward her. His clear denial of anger seemed like an open invitation for me to make the mistake of "making" him see his anger toward her. This he would surely have experienced as my trying to take him away from her. Yet when I made no comment he would become intensely depressed.

In one particular interaction Paul began by saying that he was feeling depressed. I asked what he did when he felt this way. He replied that he typically got himself beaten up. I remembered that our previous meeting was filled with his attempts to get me to point out his anger toward his mother. I began to ask Paul what had happened between that meeting and this, and when did he begin to get so depressed. Angrily he resisted, saying that yesterday was gone and dead. Equally strenuously I persisted, suggesting he might learn something. He recalled his first psychiatrist saying something about closeness. Gradually letting down his angry demeanor, he began to say that he was pushing me away. "I can't love a man. It's homosexual. My mother says love a woman not a man, find a woman." In the very next meeting he told me that he was beginning to paint on canvas the image that he had been carrying in his head for quite a long time. The image was of him and his mother. Both are naked. She shoots him in the genitals and, as he slumps over, she shoots him in the head.

In the course of our meetings in the third and fourth months, we slowly were able to establish that while Paul's mother would constantly initiate threats and interruptions to the treatment, Paul's management of these depended on what was going on in the therapy hours. For example, once Paul arrived several minutes late to an hour telling me that he had forgotten the form his mother had sent him. She wanted me to fill out a form so that Paul could be evaluated at another hospital for psychopharmacological treatment. Paul again said that he forgot the form and that his mother was paying more and more each month for his hospitalization while their insurance benefits diminished. I said it sounded to me that these matters were threats to the treatment. Paul's obvious bristling turned into outright rage and menace as he said, "I'm not threatening the treatment, I'm threatening you. The name of the game is control. I'm going to control you before you control me." I wondered quite persistently what was going on and finally he reminded me of the previous meeting in which he cried throughout the whole hour as he talked about his longing for his father. "You were inside me on Friday and I have to destroy you, keep you away. When I let someone see me as much as on Friday, I am vulnerable and besides it's only fifty minutes at a time. Am I going to get into wanting you to hold my hand or wanting to sit in your lap?" He then went on to state that he could get his mother to help him in modulating the intensity of what was going on in the therapy by taking up her suggestions, which always amounted to an interruption of the treatment situation.

At this point in the treatment the first staff case conference occurred in which I presented my work with Paul so far. The following three excerpts from the conference are from three different sources. First, a paragraph from the test report:

> Paul's feminine identification appears in part to be in the service of making contact with an older man who, although potentially violent, is also viewed as a possible source of nurturance when compared with an aggressively intrusive and dangerous maternal presence. This image of the maternal figure as an exciting but frustrating and dangerous object is exemplified in his drawing of a female on the DAP who has phallically jutting, almost weaponlike, breasts but no arms to hold. In this regard Paul's preoccupation with castration concerns appears to reflect a much earlier and premature "severing" from a symbiotic relatedness. Having to remain hidden and armored in the presence of the mother, he is left with the choice of offering himself up as a victim to men—to be masochistically beaten like a woman in order to hold onto the other. Such contact is made at a tremendous cost. Paul needs to deny and contain any aggressive and competitive strivings within himself and this leads to a profound sense of immobilization.

The second source of commentary was my own synthesis of the case at this time:

> The patient longs to be held and dependently attached to another in order to somehow correct or compensate for his sense of having been pushed too quickly out of dependency. He sees becoming the narcissistic extension or sexual object of another's desire as the necessary condition for this connectedness, and he oscillates between searching for this form of attachment and rejecting it. While the attachment is sought in order to "be someone" and to alleviate feelings of emptiness, he rejects it as a situation in which he has no independent identity but is exploited. He identifies with and prefers the role of the woman, the characteristics of suffering and being beaten constitute an identification and preservation of very early relatedness with his mother, a woman who was often beaten and abused by her husband. Also this identification is in the service of a search for nurturance from an older man, nurturance his mother was unable to provide during those times when she was in conflict with her husband and depressed. On the defensive side, feminine identification functions as a way of avoiding competition with and becoming vulnerable to the tremendously aggressive and brutal characteristics he ascribes to men. Finally, this identity serves as a defense against Paul's own desires to beat and brutalize his mother in retaliation for her aggressively intrusive and sexualized orientation toward him.

The third source of commentary was the staff discussion at the first case conference. The staff discussion for the most part focused on the points made above. One comment, however, stood out at the time as both different and intriguing:

> This young man really lives the role of a phallus in this family and in a way that is perverted. The test report does mention that his desire to cling is perverted into a position whereby any contact renders him a narcissistic object of somebody else's desire. But I think that some sort of a basic or unconscious structure of perversion is what prevents him from being psychotic. It is what gets him beat up periodically. It is what organizes his rage. That makes me wonder if at times he would try to get you [the analyst] to beat him up, and really have to get beat up in order not to be psychotic. How do you deal with that when the going gets rough? I personally find it difficult to think about this patient as a simple narcissistic character, or to feel optimistic. I think it is a very lonely situation as I understand it.

By the middle of the fifth month Paul was telling me that his life was destined to be a disastrous scenario of death and destruction. This treatment would be at best my attempt to defuse the bomb prior to the disaster. He would use his mother in the disaster scene and me as an extension of this. Possibly I could listen and help him to see what he was doing so he could have some measure of awareness and choice. In the very next meeting Paul told me that his brother had just had a heart attack. While describing this to me Paul held in his hand a postcard from a famous author. Knowing that his family had a history of early heart attacks and that Paul had also demonstrated some signs of this vulnerability, I assumed he would be frightened. Paul corrected this rather quickly by telling me he was convinced I would take a "so what" attitude to his postcard as his mother had. The postcard from this author rendered him real in some way and in response to that he assumed I would want to keep him down. In the face of this I could only keep quiet and listen. Paul felt angry with his brother for having a real attack while he only had chest pains. Once again Paul was the phony, someone else was real. But all of this was "crap," he said. On the postcard the author told Paul to put his hand down his pants at least once each day to remind himself that he had a penis and that he was a man. This author understood what was real and important. After two or three sessions Paul finally heard me say I understood the postcard was important to him. With this he immediately began to tell me how selfish and bad he felt for placing greater importance on the postcard than on the news of his brother's heart attack. He loved his brother deeply. He began to cry with increasing intensity as he described his brother escorting him back home after a debilitating anxiety attack. On this return flight, air turbulence caused the plane to shake. Paul noticed his brother became somewhat anxious and yet his brother put his arm around Paul. Paul put his arm around his brother and they held each other as the plane went through the turbulence.

In the next meeting Paul was provocative again, telling me that analysts really ought to learn more about how to help patients get a job so that they can work on their own. He was in no way interested in sucking my penis or sitting on my lap or following me across the country. As this continued over the next few sessions, he told me that he could find my button, push it, and provoke me into rage, even into hitting him, without his ever laying a finger on me. He also explained that when he was feeling as agitated and as paranoid as he did at the moment, I should not move right in on him because the situation was a dangerous one. He then went on to speak of a fight he had precipitated with his brother the evening prior to his departure from his home to find work in another city. He was having a hard time with the idea of leaving his brother and his mother. He said something provocative to his brother regarding his brother's wife. A physical fight ensued in which Paul, his mother, his brother, and his brother's wife all took part. Paul observed that his brother fights to win while he, Paul, fights to lose. And in that Paul wanted them all to hold each other before he left; he won.

In the very next week, I began working with a new patient, Kathy. On Kathy's second evening after admission, she and Paul slept together. On the following evening she became involved with another patient, and Paul and this other patient managed to have a physical fight over her. Paul wanted me to beat up this other patient for him. He also wanted me to beat up his stepfather and the director of the hospital, these latter two for not stepping forward to resolve his financial problems. Since his brother was not there to protect him I was the next closest. I ought to beat up these people for him. I asked, "What then?" He responded that he would then want me to hold him, adding that while all of this seemed so dramatic it was related to not having had a relationship with his father.

Regarding the situation with Kathy, Paul described what he saw as a triangle with three features. The first was that there are two men competing for one woman; the second, that the woman's very presence disrupts the relationship of the men; the third, when the men are too close to each other the woman becomes jealous. A fourth aspect, one he did not include, was the woman and one man colluding to keep the other man out. This fourth aspect was adequately demonstrated in a meeting in which Paul and I had explicitly planned to speak with his mother by phone. Just prior to the meeting his mother called and canceled the phone discussion we had planned. Paul, not knowing this, came to his hour ragefully. I said I could see he was in no shape to have a phone conversation with his mother. He grinned. I said I was very impressed with how he and his mother could work in concert toward a mutual end, and told him that his mother had just canceled. He was not surprised. He pointed out that all of these machinations constituted his working with his mother's support against any real emotional change. I was the enemy. They would protect their relationship from me at all costs. I said he was paying a very high price to protect their togetherness and also that he did not need to be in this hospital to protect himself from emotional growth.

Soon after this he brought to his hour a collage he had just completed. This collage was made of a number of magazine cutouts of various kinds and the most prominent feature was the picture of a naked woman in a provocative position. He propped the collage up on a small table directly in my view and proceeded to talk about something else. After a short while I said, "I guess you want to see if I'll pay more attention to the woman than to you." He responded immediately by telling me that "a man's cock is what rules him," and then went on to describe how he had felt manipulated by Kathy. He thought he could trust her. When he saw her with another male patient he felt humiliated and emasculated and remembered having these feelings when a football player had been dating his mother. The football player arrived at the house shortly before Paul was to leave to meet his father. Feigning illness he managed to stay in the house with the idea that his presence would keep some control over the behavior of the football player with his mother. He said he hated women and wanted to know how Kathy's being my patient would affect my listening and valuing him. He said I could never convince him that she and I were not sexually together and laughing at him.

Several weeks later Paul entered my office once again in a very provocative manner. He was wearing sun glasses and had a camera with him. At various points he would look through the camera at me, focusing it, "threatening" to take a picture of me. My attempts to address his behavior led nowhere until I asked what function these operations served. He said it was intended to make me submissive, and then I would be on his side and in his control. If I was submissive he could then possibly trust me and talk with me. In my being submissive he would be dominant. He became anxious in saying this, pointing out that it all seemed very sexual, and it made him nervous because submissive really means female and dominant means male. He then said that he had sexual feelings toward me but beyond these physical feelings he also felt "a deep loyalty and caring" for me. He did not want to lose our relationship. In the process of saying this he emphatically banged his fist on the table. I pointed out that this banging was perhaps a continued effort to get me to feel submissive. He agreed. I responded by saying I bet he did this in himself somehow, banging down the troubling feminine, submissive thoughts and feelings. He was startled by my saying this, yet added that in his fist-banging there were really two motions: the fist going downward was the pushing down of feminine submissive desires; the pushing up of the fist was the raising of a dominant masculinity. Submissive desires were "crazy like psychosis" and when they were in his awareness he felt literally like nothing. He went on to say this was at the heart of why he would get beat up. To be punched in the face was actually the action of getting someone else to do what he could no longer control in himself — namely, to push down the submissive desires. When these feelings were prominent, he would feel not only that he was dissipating into a boundless nothingness but also an intense worthlessness. Thus, to be hit by someone else accomplished many things. The first was to push out the submissive desires. Second, because he could take the physical punishment he must be masculine. Third, if he was actually recognized and punched then he must exist, and it is at this point that he feels worthwhile once again. Sobbing, he ended the session saying that it felt important to him to be recognized and that when he does feel recognized he cries. Finally he guessed he was saying these things directly to me.

The following week was horrendous. The meeting reported above occurred on a Friday, and Paul opened the Monday meeting by stating that he was indeed leaving the hospital at the end of the month. He was more paranoid, hostile, and provocative than I had ever seen. My attempts to ask him how his feelings evolved between Friday and Monday went nowhere. In fact, he said he could not remember Friday and did not care. He started the next hour in exactly the same way. My first comment was, "Well, if it isn't Mr. Brutal again." Paul stopped short with this comment, almost began to cry, and asked me just what I meant. I told him that it was clear he was brutalizing himself and brutalizing me in an effort to provoke me into brutalizing him. While these comments diminished the intensity of his hostility, he still seemed unable to take perspective on his behavior. On Friday, the last meeting of the week, Paul walked in and immediately said, "Well, are you going to be calling me Mr. Brutal again?"

I said no, that in fact I wondered if he might show me his work at the art show. He immediately burst into tears and said that he had been sorry that he had been brutalizing me and himself in the way he had. Moreover, he knew that he was repeating the pattern that we discussed on the previous Friday but felt that this had gotten out of his control. He knew that after the Friday meeting, and then over the weekend, he had become aware of strong feelings of a different kind toward me. While he wanted to talk about this in another meeting, now he wanted to show me his contribution to the art show.

The following Monday Paul began by saying that he was still thinking of leaving. I rather casually said, "Well, I guess that's it then." He responded by saying that he felt there was too much pain and humiliation involved in getting close to me. The intensity of his desire to be close to me was frightening to him, and left him feeling disoriented and disorganized. While he was unable to answer why he chose to act out these feelings instead of talk about them with me, he did recognize very clearly that he had chosen action instead of discussion on the previous Monday morning.

A few meetings later Paul told me that his mother wanted him to have a consultation with a specialist at another hospital. He added that to him her communication meant that she did not want him to develop a relationship with anybody but her. In the course of this he made the observation that the organs of his body upon which his self-destructive thoughts focused — namely, his mouth, his eyes, his penis, and his heart — are all organs of connectedness. He also observed that his obsessive concern with losing his hair during his last year of high school began right after his brother got married. Someone made the casual observation that he seemed to be losing a few hairs. The thought Paul immediately had was "No, I'm losing my brother." Subsequently, he lost this thought but stayed focused for the next two years on the concern with losing his hair. After his long description of all the factors that worked against his expressing his feelings around his brother's marriage, he said that losing his hair really meant "don't leave me."

The next three weeks or so were very much taken up with the issue once again of financing Paul's hospitalization. His mother asserted that she was intent upon "cutting off the funds in a dramatic way to get Paul to feel he was in crisis, to snap out of his dream state, and to begin to make plans for living." Finally, Paul's mother and brother worked out a more formalized agreement whereby they would share the expense of hospitalization. Paul's brother assured the hospital that if she withheld funds he would make up the difference.

This further consolidation of the financial aspect of Paul's hospitalization marked a turning point in therapy. He moved gradually toward focusing more on feelings regarding his father and me. In one meeting he commented on "public" and "private." He wanted me to make a public acknowledgment before the whole hospital staff about the relationship we had developed in private. He said that in some way this relationship was not real if not acknowledged. Simultaneously, he said he had a sense of shame about the relationship. He could not specify what this shame was but recalled a specific episode. At around age eleven, he was with his mother on a walk. When they came to their house they found Paul's father sitting in his car at the end of the driveway. Paul's eyes met his father's, but his father started the car and quickly drove off. Paul wondered if his father saw himself in Paul's eyes and felt the pain of his own shortcomings such that he had to turn away. He said that while his father had to turn away because of shortcomings, he, Paul, felt ashamed. He felt his love was all he had to give his father and that was not good enough to keep his father with him. He felt that he had to perfect his love or to correct something in order to regain his father's presence. They could only be privately and illegally together, such as, for example, in his childhood when they spent weekends at a men's club bar, a place in which children were not allowed.

In another meeting Paul was again focusing on the relationship with his father and how his desire to cut off his penis might be involved. He said that as he was talking he was having an undercurrent of thought in which his penis was saying to him, "Don't forget me." He realized that this undercurrent became stronger whenever he got closer to anything of value to him. He described how his father had made raisins bob in water, and through his animated descriptions made the raisins come alive. He said that it was his father's presence that made something alive. He then wondered if somehow his father's absence and his own desire to cut off his penis went together in some way.

About a week later he was late for a meeting and in the remaining fifteen minutes he said quite a bit. The one thing that stood out in my mind was his reference to his girl friend touching him. He wanted this and yet he wished to destroy it. This reminded me of the fact that I had indeed put my hand on Paul's shoulder as he walked out the door several days earlier. In the very next meeting, now on time, Paul once again referred to his girl friend's touch. I commented at this point that I too had touched him. He said he remembered this and had kept it as a photograph in his mind. I said I had been thinking about the fact that I had touched him and that perhaps he was feeling frightened and confused. Paul agreed with this immediately and added, "Yes, this therapy relationship was in fact legitimate." There had never been a legitimate intimacy between him and his father. There was always something wrong or illegal with that. When I touched him he realized how much he had wanted that touch and for me not to let go. He realized even more how lonely he was.

The next day Paul was once again provocative, saying that he did not even remember the previous meeting. I remained quite insistent, referring to the previous meeting to help understand today's provocative and rageful behavior. Paul finally made the observation that he was being very "obstreperous." He said, "I'm pushing you to slap me. If you must touch me, make it a hit. If I feel close with you, I feel all the more like shit. I feel lonely and afraid, afraid that I'm going to make you shitty too. I want you to be with me. When I felt close with my father and then had to leave I wanted him to walk into my house with me. I wanted him to sleep with me. I wanted him to stand up to my mother and say, 'He's with me.' I would feel close with my father but that had to be kept secret and private. I couldn't tell my mother that. She would say, 'Did that alcoholic bastard feed you?' He would say, 'Hurry and get out of the car before that bitch finds me here.' They expected that I would understand all of that but I didn't."

In the following meeting these themes continued. Paul spoke of having felt raped by his father and yet that it was not his mother but actually his father with whom he wanted to sleep. He went on to say that his father never allowed anger. In the face of Paul's anger his father simply and quietly walked away. "He cut you off." He realized that his mother colluded with his father in this inability to be angry by taking Paul's anger upon herself. I took the opportunity here to say, "So the trouble here seems to be that you feel angry toward me and you run to your mother. Rather than telling you to go back and work it out with me she colludes. She says yes, stay with me, we'll find some other way." Paul agreed with this very much, saying that her posture is always one of encouraging him to stay with her, telling him that she is the only one who will listen to his anger.

Paul told me that in his mind there were only two ways to be with a man: one was to be his woman and the other was to bash his head in and humiliate him so that he is disarmed and not dangerous. Following this meeting Paul appeared depressed. He reported feeling just about dead. He said he had given up hope here, in me, and in therapy. I asked if "dead" was a way of being with father. "No," he responded. "I'm going to leave him. He left me, now I'm going to leave him." He reported feeling empty, unreal, aimless, and exactly the same as he did in the first few hours after receiving his last support check from his father when he was approximately twenty-three years old. "Why didn't he at least include a note with that last check. Nothing. What about me, Dad? I'm not her, I'm not the divorcé, I feel a loss of support. My depression and obsessions are now competing. The depression is now just as strong as the obsession but I can't do this alone. I feel a loss of support." I asked how I might have dropped him. He asserted quite strenuously that indeed I hadn't but that he was feeling the loss of support from his father to be present now everywhere in his daily life.

A few weeks later Paul came to his meeting very quietly and sat motionless for several minutes. He then held out a postcard he had received from his father. For the rest of the meeting he said virtually nothing but cried for the whole time. I found myself deeply moved even though I was not really clear about what was so moving. I thought about what Paul had done on previous occasions to things of emotional value and as he was about to leave I said that if he ever wanted to rip up that card to call me first.

I will only sketch the salient points of the last five months of the treatment. The move toward termination did not feel as sudden as might appear in this written account. However the reasons for the termination, beyond certain practicalities, have never become clear.

Soon after Paul received the postcard from his father he began to intensify his plans to move out of the hospital and continue his treatment with me on an outpatient basis. I outlined my concerns about this arrangement, and after much discussion I agreed to see him as an outpatient. My principal concern was whether or not Paul could sustain himself in a reasonable way while living alone to enable the treatment to continue. He did prove himself able to do so. For the next few months we discussed how Paul gave away his feeling of closeness with me, and also his recognition that he felt in himself "a central gap" within which he feels and is nothing. He wanted to fill this gap with "something real."

Soon after Paul began to speak of feeling "a central gap," a topic he could only discuss with great discomfort, his girl friend moved out of the hospital to a large city several hours away. He began to focus on whether or not to move in with her and continue his treatment in that city. I told Paul that I wondered both whether he was giving away closeness and if he was truly filling the gap he experienced with something real. I said that while I thought these were the central questions, I also would not stand in the way of his moving. He began to take trips into the city to be with his girl friend and to interview with various analysts there. He asked me to recommend analysts to him and, while I gave him three names, he never mentioned whether he met with any of them. Instead, he gradually became angry with me for my willingness to let him end his treatment with me. He envied me for not needing him and felt frightened to leave me and the protection he felt within the treatment. Simultaneously, he felt ready to take the steps necessary to test himself "standing in the clear, by myself, to find my way in life." He decided on an analyst and he also decided to live near his girl friend but not with her.

In our final few meetings he discussed his view of his strengths and weaknesses at this point. He no longer felt like a time bomb and had made substantial progress in feeling more aware of himself, more consistent in his feelings and more confident. He also knew that he had not really gotten to the core of his problem. The thought of cutting off his penis was still very much with him, although it sometimes was strong and sometimes present just as background. Also, he was troubled that he still sometimes felt profoundly depressed.

Several months after Paul moved away we happened to meet on a street near the hospital. He was with his girl friend and was visiting the area for the day. We spoke for a few moments and I could tell that he was feeling anxious and yet warmly toward me. He looked well and said he was doing well. I felt warmly toward him, and also felt the same feelings of anger and relief that I felt when he ended his treatment. I could see that Paul was experiencing complicated feelings in my presence, too.

Discussion

Deleuze's theory of masochism rests on the premise that in usual development the mother's interaction with the infant consistently implies that rules exist that constrain the infant's and the mother's desire, and that there is always a third to the dyad. The conveyance of these rules eventually creates structurally and perhaps consciously in the infant the realization that the dyad is limited. What is other to the dyad is a realm in which displacements and substitutes for the infant's desire might be found. With the development of this structure the infant begins to become a psychological subject. A symbolic world has begun to form. Central to this symbolic world is the acceptance of limitation; in other words, the structure has been established to conceive of agents or representatives of otherness to the dyad. Of course the first and the one with most impact as an agent of otherness to the dyad is the father.

In masochism, according to Deleuze, the early relation with the mother leads the masochist to abstract and transform aspects of the mother into a symbolic structure governed not by the reality of otherness but by the promise of unity. Further, this unity is not with the mother as a "real object relation" but is a unity that transcends mundane and limiting reality. This unity with a maternal ideal promises to the masochist the possibility to be a singular, unrelated hero in a realm of sentimental, antiseptic perfection, devoid of sadistic sensuality, cruelty, and aggression. Several consequences, according to Deleuze, follow from this symbolic structure:

1. The real mother is disavowed, replaced by an all-powerful and complete ideal. That ideal is not equivalent to the actual mother but to the symbolic structure itself.
2. The father and any place to conceive of the father is nonexistent in this symbolic structure — this place is antithetical to the nature of the masochist's symbolic structure.
3. The masochist's sense of coherence depends on the maintenance of the integrity of this symbolic structure.
4. What is banished from the symbolic order returns in the realm of hallucination.
5. What is being beaten, humiliated, and ridiculed is the image and likeness of the father within the masochist.

With the assistance of the above five points, I will attempt to illustrate that Paul was articulating the question "how can the father be realized to exist?" Through the totality of the transference and as a dilemma of the treatment he was saying that an internal structure to conceive and accept the authority and legitimacy of the role of the father, of otherness to the dyadic unity he pursued, could not exist.

Paul's mother and he clearly maintained a complex ambivalent relationship. Without question, she participated in his sustaining a view of her that played an integral role in his pathological organization. However, it is not true that "without her [he was] nothing," and that she was responsible for every one of his accomplishments. What is central here is that Paul experienced himself as nothing without her and that he thought of her as serving all functions powerfully and completely. His notion of her cycling between adoring him, intrusively negating him, and being the supplier of all things for him was his effort to represent to me his positive idealization, to mythic proportion, of the good, punitive, and seductive aspects of a maternal ideal. The combination of these maternal aspects set up a symbolic universe that was revealed often in the course of treatment and was more determining in the transference and in his daily life than was any "real" relationship with his mother.

Paul represented a portion of what was centrally valued in this symbolic system in his image of "a girl and me, naked . . . holding each other, watching the rain fall. She knows nothing about me and I nothing about her, not even names." He also represented the fullness of this symbolic system's punitive power in his image of his mother shooting him in the genitals and then the head. The first image is of a sentimental, sexless, nameless unity. The second image, presumably portraying punishment for some violation, involves his being shot in the genitals. The structure that governs these images provides no place for a penis.

Paul articulated a rule of this symbolic system when he referred to feelings of closeness toward me for the first time and said, "My mother says love a woman not a man, find a woman." There is no contradiction between this rule and the prohibition of the penis noted above: a woman is to be loved without the presence of genital sexuality.

The wish for relationship with a father is clearly evident in Paul. However, the father Paul wishes to find is a figure of a particular type for, again, this relationship must include no penis. Rather, Paul wishes a relationship to make him "reference-full," to give him a name, to make him real and admired, and ultimately to further his pursuit of being a hero in a perfectly ordered existence devoid of sensuality and cruel sadism. His requirements of this man: he must be older (sexless and nonenvious), submissive, unashamed (legitimate), and totally protective and holding of Paul. Paul said provocative things at the beginning of his hours to see if I attended to these: he was posing here the question of whether I would come to him, submissively, unashamedly, nonenviously, protectively, or if he must find and satisfy my cruel, heinous, and sadistic desire before I would listen to him.

These requirements of a father conform to the rules of the symbolic order that guides Paul. His conformance is further illustrated in the monstrous qualities of "the father" or man he constructs and dreads. This is the phallic man, the monster of affection who demands subjugation to cruel and sadistic sensuality, horrific torture, and subservience in any manner he wishes. This man requires complete submission in exchange for any sense of identity that affiliation with him might afford. This is the reality of the penis, and this reality is banished from the symbolic world. "A man's cock is what rules him"; "must I suck your penis, sit in your lap, follow you across the country?"; "I'm going to control you before you control me"; these are a few of the comments through which Paul represents this prohibited man.

On the occasion of my taking a female patient into treatment, Paul articulated three features of "a triangle," three dilemmas intrinsic to the rules of his symbolic structure. Two men compete for one woman, the woman's very presence disrupts the relationship of the men, when the men are too close the woman becomes jealous. I added: the woman and one man can collude to keep the other man out. At the center of these "features" Paul poses the core of his dilemma and the question for the treatment, for, in his system, there is no possibility for anything beyond the dyad. If one is in relationship with a woman there is no place for a man. How can otherness to the dyad, the place of the father, be realized to exist?

I would like to focus on the meeting that started out with Paul's "threatening" to take a picture of me. While there were several repetitions of his feeling close to me and then violently withdrawing, this example seems particularly instructive. Within this meeting he stated that he felt "a deep loyalty and caring for me." His initial presentation of wanting to intimidate me into being submissive so he could talk to me was directly related to his feeling affectionate toward me. He defined this as having sexual elements to it. Condensed within these statements and what he said subsequently about getting beat up is the following: Feeling affectionately toward me is experienced as my being inside him. If I have a penis and am inside him then the monstrous, dreaded man is inside him. To have this dangerous and foreclosed figure within him courts fatal punishment from the oedipal (punitive) aspect of mother for violating the rules of her symbolic order. To lose alignment with this mother and her symbolic order is to lose both the prospect of becoming the hero in an antiseptic realm and to lose the identity and coherence-rendering effect that adherence to this symbolic order provides.

Within this dilemma being beaten is the only recourse. What is being beaten is the image of the father. Forceful beating is the only means to match and possibly dominate this ruthless, dangerous figure, especially in the context of having to preserve a symbolic order on which one's psychic life depends.

When Paul says in this meeting that "the fist going downward was pushing down the feminine submissive desires," I take him to be referring to the experience of having his sense of himself lost to, inundated by the sadistic, sensual aspect of the foreclosed father. This inundation eradicates the symbolic order of the mother in which he experiences identity; he feels as if he is dissipating into a boundless nothingness. To be hit mobilizes bodily sensation, and this anchors him against dissipation into nothingness. "Taking the physical punishment" indicates that he must be equal to or more forceful than the cruel monster who has inundated him. To have "being recognized and punched" lead to feeling he must "exist and be worthwhile" is to say that someone saw his dilemma, cared about him, and helped him, held him again. Indeed, he spoke of feeling indebted to those who hit him.

This meeting ended, of course, in a way that set up the same problem once again. Paul felt recognized by me, held by me, and finally, invaded brutally by the image and likeness of a "male identification." He returned in the next meeting, bristling provocatively. One might ask why he returned. I would suggest that he does not return to be beaten by me in actuality, although he engages in all the operations that might lead to being beaten. Rather he returns to show me the problem: that he has no way to receive and accept identification with me or the process of treatment without becoming internally disorganized to the point of psychotic fragmentation. Also, he shows that the foreclosure of an identification is both unknown to him and out of his control. My calling him "Mr. Brutal" stopped him momentarily. He wished to know what I meant, unable to discern at that moment if I have begun to beat him or if something useful was being offered. My explanation helped but was not enough. In retrospect, and insofar as his identity was inundated and fused with the disavowed, my calling him "Mr. Brutal" began to name that which was banished from his symbolic realm and had no name. Again in retrospect, I might well have followed this action of naming with a question central to the treatment dilemma: "What is it in you that you wish for me to beat?"

The final matter I will address is the question of how to understand Paul's wish to sever his penis. Paul states clearly that the penis is "an organ of connectedness." He does not, in saying this, show himself to be organized in terms of a differentiated oedipal structure. Further, he always associates his references to cutting off the penis with wishes to cling and to be held: at one time by a naked nameless woman while watching the rain; at another time, under the wing of an elderly man who makes the world listen to Paul. At best his wish is to find personification of his maternal ideal. For Paul what has been banished from the symbolic order that governs him is otherness to the dyad. The penis, the organ of connectedness, condenses into one image this otherness and all that has been banished with it. The father, limitations in the original dyad, limitations of self, sadistic sensuality are all expunged from meaning. There is no "paternal metaphor." What is kept out of representation in the symbolic order, however, continues to exist and to reemerge on the body for physical or "real" representation. For Paul the wish to sever the penis is not the wish to culminate a "passive feminine identification" in the service of being with the valued, although cruel and dangerous, father. This construction presumes already in place a structure for triadic relating. Rather, Paul's wish is to eradicate for all time the basis in himself for likeness with the father in that the penis is equivalent to the entirety of the father. The wish is to preserve unity with a maternal ideal that recognizes no rule above or otherness to its own symbolic realm. To sever the penis, then, would be to seal the dyad, forever to rule out separateness, to place Paul as exclusively central in this maternal ideal's eye, and to establish himself as a singular hero in a perfectly ordered existence.

The viewpoint suggested by Deleuze is primarily a structural analysis: he is concerned with how the aberrant development of a symbolic order constitutes the subject masochistically. In the case of Paul the question of "how can the father be realized to exist?" is brought into clarity and is contextualized in terms of the absence of a structure within the symbolic realm that would enable displacements of desire and evolved substitutes to be desired. From the standpoint of Deleuze, masochistic organization and behavior are not a repetition of the past, although an understanding of the past certainly informs the analysis of masochism. The analysis of masochism is more properly the analysis of what the masochist envisions and pursues, and the understanding of the conditions under which the analyst becomes the maternal ideal or the dreaded disruption of the masochist's pursuit. Finally, in analyzing the masochist's inability to form identifications and the exclusivity of his relation to an abstract symbolic ideal, Deleuze's position contextualizes just how profoundly lonely and immobilized is the masochist's situation.

Reference

Deleuze, G. (1971), *Masochism, An Interpretation of Coldness and Cruelty*. New York: George Braziller.

10

The Master–Slave Relation in Psychoanalytic Impasse

James E. Gorney, Ph.D. and
John P. Muller, Ph.D.

For this consciousness . . . was afraid for its entire being; it felt the fear of death, the sovereign master. It has been in that experience melted to its inmost soul, has trembled throughout its every fibre, and all that was fixed and steadfast has quaked within it [Hegel, 1807, p. 237].

Here, at the pivotal moment of the struggle between master and slave, Hegel pinpoints the emergence of the self-consciousness of human finitude as the first step in the slave's overcoming his bondage and realizing his own desire. How is this philosophic proposition relevant to the psychoanalytic process, specifically in terms of transference and countertransference? We are proposing the master–slave dialectic as a paradigm of the counter-transference–transference struggle between analyst and patient that may eventuate in impasse.

The French psychoanalyst Jacques Lacan, adapts Hegel in order to explicate the evolution of self-consciousness and the revelation of desire during psychoanalytic treatment. This process constitutes the essence of "the talking cure" and central to it is the constitutive role of language. In exploring the technical relevance of Lacan's adoption of Hegel, we will examine a single analytic case in which impasse occurred and was then resolved. Before turning to the clinical material from the perspective of

*An earlier version of some aspects of the following clinical material has been published in *The Psychoanalytic Review* (1982), 69/2:241–248.

the relationship of master and slave, we must touch upon some of the broader dimensions of Lacan's theoretical framework.

The Symbolic Order

Lacan describes the master–slave relation that sustains psychoanalytic impasse in terms of what he calls "the imaginary order." This is sharply differentiated from "the symbolic order" of language. To understand the special characteristics of the imaginary, we must first consider Lacan's conception of the symbolic order.

"Man speaks," Lacan tells us, "but it is because the symbol has made him man" (1966, p. 65). Here "the symbol" refers to the pervasive presence of signifiers, structured according to the laws of language. The signifier is the sound image of a word, while the signified is its meaning, and the link between the two is arbitrary. Thus there is no intrinsic connection between the notion of death and the sound-image "death"—*thanatos, mors, Tod* in their respective languages serve as well. Within a given language system, these linguistic signs are distinguishable from one another not by themselves but only through a reciprocal differentiation; that is, the word has meaning only in reference to the whole language that forms a closed system. The laws of language govern the functioning of these signs along two broad axes. These are what Jakobson (1956) calls the principle of combination and the principle of selection, and they have great importance for understanding the linguistic processes manifest in dreams. The principle of combination, which governs the proper order of words in a sentence (such as this one), is identical with the figure of speech called metonymy where contiguous relations are paramount (e.g., in the use of container for thing contained: "to drink a glass"; part for whole: "thirty sails"; place name to designate where an event took place: "the Watergate scandal"). This process of associative linkage based on context and contiguity Lacan equates with the dream process of displacement as described by Freud in *The Interpretation of Dreams* (1900-1901) (an excellent clinical example of metonymic linkage is provided by Levenson [1978]). The axis or law of selection, on the other hand, governs the proper substitution of one word for another based *not* on contiguity but rather on some kind of similarity (as in the above substitution of "law" for "principle") and is identical to the figure of speech called metaphor. Metaphor, in turn, is equated with the dream process of condensation (for further elaboration, see Muller and Richardson [1978]).

The symbol is not identical with the word, but can be anything—object, dream-image, gesture—that is significant insofar as it is embedded in, and takes its meaning from, a pattern broadly structured by the underlying grammar of combination and substitution. This underlying grammar operates in a largely unconscious manner; it is other to consciousness, "an other scene" Freud calls it, and Lacan calls it simply "the Other," with a capital "O." It is a third dimension mediating exchange and making conscious discourse possible. "The Other" is "the locus in which is constituted the I who speaks with him who hears"; this locus "extends as far into the subject as the laws of speech, that is to say, well beyond the discourse that takes its orders from the ego, as we have known ever since Freud discovered its unconscious field and the laws that structure it" (1966, p. 141). The principles of contiguity and similarity structure our human lives in a pervasive manner. We see them operating when structuralists like Lévi-Strauss and Barthes apply them to cultural phenomena such as cooking or dress, when Jakobson suggestively classifies the history of literature, art, and cinema along these two axes, or when Frazer in *The Golden Bough* organizes his mass of ritual and myth according to these two same principles.

The symbolic order, then, is constitutive of our functioning as human beings in a consensually validated (though largely unconscious) network of discourse and meaning. Indeed, central to Lacan's interpretation of Freud's fundamental discovery is his assertion that "the unconscious is structured in the most radical way like a language" (1966, p. 234) and not like a pseudobiological system borrowed by traditional psychoanalysis from nineteenth century science. How one gains entry into the symbolic order, the domain of language, and the unconscious, within the psychoanalytic situation is of critical importance.

The Imaginary Order

The imaginary order is the order of images and distortion. Within this realm individuals struggle for recognition and approval according to the paradigm of master and slave. Lacan identifies the image as a structure that allows for a point-to-point fixity, a point-to-point spatial correspondence, in the way that an image reflected on a screen retains a point-to-point fixity with the object or picture being reflected (1964, p. 86). It is this intrinsic iconic and spatial reference that is constitutive of the imaginary order and is precisely what is not relevant to the structure of the symbolic order. As was noted earlier, within the constitution of language there is only an *arbitrary* relationship between the signifier and the signified and there is always a reciprocal differentiation of signs within any given language. The symbolic order is thereby free, unfettered by a rigid system of one-to-one equivalences, and, as Freud recognized in the fort-da game of the child, language provides symbols that make objects present in their absence. It also negates the immediacy of objects by providing distance from them by virtue of postulating them in discourse.

By way of contrast, the primarily visual, one-to-one illusory correspondences of the imaginary order involve captivation and seduction in a dual relation from which the Other is excluded. Lacan illustrates the functions of the imaginary order with examples of animal studies (1951, p. 14). That sexual development in certain species is dependent on the visual recognition of another member, that mating and combat rituals involve visual displays that captivate the other in a sexual or aggressive response: this is the heart of the imaginary order.

In humans, the first experience of captivation by an image occurs in what Lacan terms *the mirror phase*. Between eight and eighteen months of age the infant can recognize his reflection in a mirror and responds to it with jubilation. The reflected image of the total body offers the promise of motor coordination, mastery, unity, and stature that contrast with the turbulence and motor incoordination felt by the infant. This experience of bodily fragmentation is now camouflaged by the imaginary identification the infant makes with its reflected image. This identification is typically made with the image of the mother's body, perceived as a whole Gestalt, and this identification sets the stage for the development of the ego in a fictional direction. Why the ego? Because this idealized image structures later identifications, serves as narcissistic model for control and mastery, and functions as a defensive armor and source of resistance to the recognition of unconscious desire. Why fictional? Because as reflected image it distorts relationships (e.g., in the mirror right and left are reversed, size is distorted, and so forth), the image is external to the self, and founds the perception of the world and self in alienation.

This distorted recognition at the mirror becomes prototypic of the distortions the child receives in identifying with the reflected appraisals of those around him. So intrinsic is this early distortion that Lacan asserts a fundamental misunderstanding henceforth pervades all human understanding. This conception of the ego as the locus of misperception and imaginary identification of course differs from the formulations of contemporary ego psychology. Here, in Lacan, the ego inhabits the domain of the imaginary order.

As the ego develops, misidentification extends to social relationships. The child begins to compete, engaging in a dual, unmediated struggle for dominance in which it seeks to be recognized by the other as the object of the other's desire. The child longs to be the completion of the other: the complete and fulfilling object of the other's desire. The linguistic signifier of the other's desire, of what is lacking in the other, is the phallus—the impossible object that symbolizes the imaginary completion of the mother's desire. The human desire for recognition, particularly as expressed in sexual desire, thus becomes structured by the phallus as signifier with its subsequent derivatives. The wish to become the imaginary phallus, the completion of another's desire, rigidly structures the ego. It leads to a use of language that is objectifying, rather than subjective, and ultimately disguises the subject from himself and from his own desire. This disguise alienates him from the unconscious—the domain of the symbolic order, the domain of the Other.

This desire for recognition takes on explicit Hegelian overtones as Lacan draws on the master–slave struggle and adapts it to his own purposes. Here it illuminates the early stages of the ego's struggle, in the imaginary order, to consolidate its defensive position. It is also directly related to the transference relationship established during analysis.

The Master–Slave Dialectic

The master–slave dialectic occurs at that point in *The Phenomenology of Mind* when conscious understanding realizes it plays a key role in constituting the object of knowledge, and therefore the focus shifts now to consciousness turning to itself as self-consciousness. Thus the origin of self-consciousness must now be examined, not by analyzing the state of knowing, in which the knower is passively absorbed in contemplation of the object, but by examining desire, in which the subject becomes aware of himself as a lack, as wanting. The proper object of human desire, as distinct from animal desire for a given object, is another human desire, another lack like itself. To become fully human, human desire seeks to be recognized by another human desire as its proper object. Hegel poses the hypothetical encounter between two desiring subjects, each of whom seeks autonomous recognition from the other. In order to affirm his autonomy, and in order to fully distinguish himself from the animal's mere sentiment of being alive, the desiring subject must be willing to risk his biological life.

This gives rise to a struggle to the death for recognition. But if one self-conscious object were to kill the other, all possibility of recognition would be lost, so a compromise solution is found in which one subject surrenders to the other in a master–slave relation. The slave becomes and remains a slave by virtue of his paralyzing fear of death. By choosing not to risk his life, he thereby becomes subservient to the master who shows no fear of death.

But this relation between master and slave is an unstable solution. The master, for example, is gradually forced into the realization that he has come to a dead end. For rather than gaining equal recognition from another autonomous subject, he is only partially recognized by a slavish self-consciousness that is unable to grant recognition on equal terms. Moreover, the master's relation to objects is mediated by the slave's work and his satisfaction lies in enjoying the objects of the slave's labor. Although the slave is not initially aware of it, he can find the truth of his self-consciousness in the master's capacity to grant him recognition. Moreover, the slave in his work sustains an active relationship with given objects insofar as he directly works on them. He thus transforms objects and leaves his enduring imprint on them.

The slave's work becomes truly transformative as he comes to experience his fear of death in a new light. At this moment he has the realization that to become truly human, to transcend the merely animal concern for the preservation of life, he must be willing to face his own death for the sake of his human desire. It is by facing death that the master became master and that man is given proof of the essential difference separating him from animal reality. Through recognizing and overcoming his fear of death, and continuing to engage in transformative work, the slave begins now to approach the master on equal terms. He thereby overcomes his bondage, and (in Hegel) can move on to achieve autonomy (for further elaboration, see Kojéve [1947]).

For Lacan this struggle as it unfolds between parents, and children, or analyst and patient, is complicated by the imaginary identifications that determine it. It is a dual, ego-to-ego struggle for prestige in which captivation by the image and desire of the other leads to aggressivity and a struggle for dominance. In our view, this struggle has special relevance for understanding the nature of psychoanalytic impasse. The process of impasse can be viewed as an imaginary struggle to the death for recognition of one ego by another within the transference–countertransference. It may also be regarded as a critical interactional dilemma that contains within itself the seeds of its own resolution as illustrated in the following clinical material.

Clinical Material

History

David was in his late twenties when Dr. G. first consulted with him. During the first meeting, this tall, muscular young man kept his head bowed, gazed at the floor, and seemed to shrivel in his seat as he outlined his "desperate" and "humiliating" situation. For reasons obscure to him, David had quit his job with a prestigious law firm after feeling "put down" by some mild, but justified, criticism from a senior partner. Plunged into an inexplicable state of malaise and obsessional self-doubting, he reported with shame that his current employment consisted of working the night shift loading garbage onto a truck, and he asserted that this job was an apt reflection of his essential image of himself. With a hint of a smile, he noted that his upper middle-class parents were now forced to be evasive or to lie when friends or relatives inquired about him. David reddened when asked how his recent troubles had affected his relationship with his wife. With considerable difficulty, he reported that he had become impotent just prior to leaving the law firm. Indeed, the impetus for seeking treatment was his wife's ultimatum that she would move out if he did not make some active move toward resolving his problems. After an extended series of consultations, David unenthusiastically accepted the therapist's recommendation to begin psychoanalysis, meeting four sessions per week. He passively accepted all conditions of the analysis stating, "I guess I have no choice other than to put myself completely in your hands."

As David reviewed his history, he described both his parents as successful professionals and the family as marked by affluence, propriety, and high expectation. The mother was a cold, distant, cerebral woman who rarely smiled and notably avoided physical contact with family members. For as long as David remembered, she had taken to bed with episodic bouts of depression and withdrew into mute unresponsiveness for days at a time. While the mother was presented as a shadowy, absent figure, David's experience of his father was remarkably vivid and intense. This imposing, authoritarian man ruled with an iron fist, demanding obedience from his wife and children. David viewed him as larger than life, trembling in awe of his "icy stare," "huge muscles," "booming voice," and "strong will." He struggled lifelong to gain his father's recognition and approval, for as the first-born son David was expected to embody the family tradition of high achievement and strength of character.

His earliest years were largely in the care of full-time nursemaids as his mother divided her time between long hours at work and periods of "being too sick" to come out of her room. There was a vaguely upsetting memory of her having gone away "to the hospital" for an extended period when he was very young, but this memory was fragmentary. For as long as he could remember, David had turned to his father for nurturance and guidance. Their special and exclusive relationship set them off from the rest of the family, becoming over time fixed and ritualized. The father would typically present his son with a series of expectations, tasks, rules or moral injunctions, to be executed exactly as prescribed. Thus, when David was eight he was expected to dry the dishes, take out the garbage, feed the dog, sweep the kitchen floor, and shine his father's shoes (as well as his own) to a mirror finish, precisely between 6:30 and 7:00 each evening. At exactly the appointed hour, the sink, garbage pail, dog, floor, and shoes were inspected. A successful completion of the assigned tasks was recognized by an approving nod and the words, "You may prepare for bed now young man." A light pat on the back would follow, sending a thrill of pleasure through David's body. However, if his work deviated in any way from what was expected, he would then be met with a terrible silence and a steely gaze that seemed to cut right through him. Feeling terrified and humiliated, David would quickly correct the mistake and then run up to his room and sob uncontrollably on his bed.

With the onset of adolescence, David's relationship with his father intensified further. David had few friends and was unbearably shy with girls, yet he barely noticed his loneliness. Each day he would race home from school, complete his chores, and anxiously await the sound of his father's car turning into the driveway. Years later, David recalled how a neatly mowed lawn or a perfectly shoveled driveway would elicit a "look of love" from his father that "thrilled" him, more than compensating for the contemptuous lectures and subsequent mute withdrawal that greeted any mistake. When David turned sixteen, his idealized image of his father was shattered. At this time the father began an affair with a young woman just a few years older than David himself. Despite his professed puritanical attitudes, the father made no attempt to conceal the affair. Soon the father purchased a flashy sports car, a toupé, and a wardrobe of "hip" clothes. David reacted with mounting feelings of abandonment and betrayal.

After resisting the temptation for years, David began to masturbate. He experienced this forbidden act not primarily as an outlet for sexual gratification, but rather as a secret means of outwitting his father. Similarly, he felt a secret triumph in finding ingenious ways to skimp on his chores or schoolwork. Such feelings and behaviors were concealed until his high school graduation. Toward the end of the ceremony David was awarded a handsome scholarship for being the "most outstanding" student in the class. He was not especially surprised by this honor, yet as he approached the podium and saw his father in the audience "with love in his eyes," sitting between his wife and his mistress, David was consumed by a feeling of "unreality." To his own and others' shock he heard himself say, "I cannot accept this award because I don't deserve it and I don't need it." He sat through the rest of the ceremony "in a fog." That evening he was lectured unmercifully by his father who was in a white rage. Tearfully David stammered out how he resented his agreement to go to the prestigious college his father had selected for him. Indeed, he was not really sure he felt ready for college at all. Then for the first time in his life David saw tears come to his father's eyes. Nothing further about this was ever mentioned again between father and son. A few months later David began college at the school of his father's choice.

Throughout college and law school David buried himself in his work. The days would begin with an hour of solitary jogging and end with an hour of solitary yoga. After completing his studies, he returned to the city in which his parents resided, and joined a well-respected law firm. Initially, he functioned at work just as he had at school: efficiently and effectively, with no discernible pleasure or passion. Soon David became infatuated with a young woman. After a long courtship they married, despite his father's disapproval. David described their first year as "the happiest time of my life." After some initial problems with potency, he came to enjoy and feel confident in sex, but when his wife desired to become pregnant, the thought of fathering a child filled David with an ill-defined sense of dread. Wishing to please his wife, he agreed to discontinue contraceptive measures, but immediately became impotent. Within a few months he had gone from law firm to garbage truck. Feeling on the verge of inexorably ruining his marriage and career, David reluctantly decided to seek treatment. As he saw it, he was on an irreversible descent into skid row, turning all that mattered to him into "trash and garbage."

Treatment (Dr. G.)

As our first interview ended, David asked some questions about the requirements of analytic treatment, such as why it would be necessary for us to meet so frequently. I mentioned as part of the rationale the development of "intense feelings" that might arise in the therapeutic relationship. The next day David entered visibly agitated, sat down in the chair wide-eyed, and his face froze into an expression of pure terror. In commenting on this I asked him to share his thoughts. Flushing, David breathlessly spoke of how my phrase of the previous day, "intense relationship," had been haunting him. Unsure at first what my words implied, in the middle of the night he came to a sudden realization. "I had the fantasy that when I came today you would take off your clothes, tell me to take off mine, and we would have sex on the bed (sic) over there." I asked him to describe what he had imagined. Looking at me as if I were a fool to have asked such an obvious question, he replied, "You were screwing me over and over again—in the ass."

David swiftly entrenched himself in a frozen posture within the transference. His self-label of being "nothing but a bum" constituted his essential image of himself. With some chagrin, he noted that "bum" was also the very word his father now hurled in accusation during frequent telephone lectures and then underlined in red in his weekly hortatory letters. Identifying me with this omnipotent figure, David could do little else but catalog his feelings of shame, incompetence, and unworthiness. Over time these complaints condensed into a repetitive obsessional litany, leveling his words to a droning sameness. My jacket and tie made him feel embarrassed about his sport shirt; my seeming competence at my work made him feel a failure at his; fantasies of my big penis and sexual prowess reduced him to feeling weak and unmanly. Through the pose of deferential respect and obsequious compliance there emerged a persistent demand that I use my omnipotent power to say or do something that would enable him to feel manly and whole.

David's mounting silent reproaches and suppressed, impotent rage created a climate of persistent, unequal struggle. He was unable to work with, or derive any benefit from, my interpretations, claiming they sounded like "a psychoanalytic sermon." Indeed, whenever I would make an interpretation, no matter how delicate or casual my tone, he would experience his body shrinking on the couch while he simultaneously imagined I grew larger in size, looming over him from behind. My words could only be heard as an accusation, a threat, a command, or a moral injunction, and often they could not be heard at all. On one occasion I commented that he was persistently reacting to my words before he could reflect upon them, adding "reaction without reflection is a means of erasing words." He replied dryly, "That sounds like something you read on a tea bag."

As the transference intensified, I began to feel unrecognized in my role as analyst, for David's servile protestations of ineptitude cast me into the transferential role of a cruel despot. His failure to respond to my repeated interpretations of this dynamic were most troublesome. Eventually, I began to experience his refusal to recognize me as a benign analyst as reflecting a more fundamental refusal to recognize me as a reasonably well-intentioned, caring human being with some modicum of integrity. This led me into a countertransferential quandary, for I began to doubt not only my skill as an analyst, but my personal worth as well. When David would bemoan his sad lot and compare his fate invidiously to my "astoundingly successful life," I would begin to feel vaguely guilty about the relative ease of my life compared to his. At other times, ruminating about my real shortcomings, I became depressed as I realized how far short I really fell from his idealized image of me.

Our psychotherapeutic difficulties began to escalate into an active, belligerent impasse. David recalled a series of childhood memories of how his father had cruelly shamed him before the whole family whenever he brought home a report card, even when the grades were excellent. Following a long lecture at the dinner table, David would burst into tears, run up to his bedroom, and sob under the blankets. A few hours later, his father would come to the room, sit on the bed, put his arms around his son and grant temporary forgiveness, after extracting a solemn promise to do better. David would become sexually aroused as his father sat near him. Feeling manipulative in order to gain closeness through his guilt-provoking tears, he thought it worth any price to gain, even momentarily, his father's sympathetic recognition. He then expressed the fantasy-wish that I sit beside him on the couch—which he persisted in calling "the bed"—and put my arm around him to comfort him. He was furious at me for my not having intuitively recognized that this was what he wanted and needed. My failure to provide him with even this small token of regard was perceived as an act of deliberate cruelty, designed to keep him subservient and worthless in the demeaning role of a "sick patient."

Complaining bitterly that analysis had only served to make him "feel worse," he defiantly quit his job on the garbage truck and determined to live out his image of himself as "a bum." Using his meager savings to pay his analytic bills, he pleaded with me to reduce his fee significantly or allow him to run up a debt. When I declined, he flew into a demanding rage, claiming he would commit suicide if I actually terminated his treatment over an unpaid bill.

My refusal to budge made him feel as if I were only interested in his money and in no way "wanted" him. Repeated confrontations and interpretations that he was reacting to me as if I were his father and that he was trying to make me take sole responsibility for his analysis and, indeed, for his life, were to no avail. Finally, with an intense sense of humiliation and undeniable provocativeness, he said that his suicide threat was itself a manipulative hoax, since I had not even provided him with enough manly courage to risk killing himself. Should treatment stop, he then would shamefully apply for welfare, living out his miserable life as a psychoanalytic casualty and permanent cripple.

That evening, David had a terrifying nightmare. In the next day's session, he lay down on the couch, clenched his fists, and in an embarrassed whisper related his dream: "I cut off my pinky with a letter opener, put it in my pocket, and carried it around. My wife and I were going to go to the movies together, but she was late. So I decided to put it in the freezer, which was empty except for two ice cubes which had melted together. Suddenly I saw the blood gushing out of me and I went into a panic. I wanted to call you or an emergency room to get it sewn back on. I picked up the phone, but I couldn't speak—only a scream came out. When I woke up I had the feeling that something was worse with me than I really knew."

Alerted that here was an important message to be heard, I asked him what the word "pinky" brought to mind. He recalled that as a small child he had used his mother's word *tinkle* to refer to urination and then, in his own creation, had coined the phrase "tinkle with my pinkle." I stated, "The panic must come from knowing that it is your penis that you want to cut off." He crossed his legs tightly and a long, tense silence ensued. I wondered aloud, "What were the words you wished me to hear which were drowned out by your scream on the phone?" As if a raw nerve had been touched, David abruptly sat up on the couch and choked out the words, "I want to be your penis." Then as tears coursed down his cheeks he collapsed into uncontrollable sobs, rolling onto his side and curling up like a small child on the couch.

When the tears subsided, I asked David which hand the severed pinky was from—"The right hand," he said. After further inquiry, he remarked, "That would mean I couldn't write—I couldn't work." Thus, severing the pinky was a metaphor, and David realized in horror that his own active cutting off of the capacity for both love and work meant the possibility of his own freedom was about to be forever frozen out of his existence. Indeed, he associated the "two ice cubes which had melted together," alone inhabiting the freezer, to the "cold" and "hopeless" stalemate within the analytic relationship, as well as his submission to the "icy stare" of his father. His previous inability to bring into language his wish to be my penis had been captured in the wordless scream. This was why he awoke with the conviction that "something was much worse" than had heretofore been imagined.

In subsequent analysis of the dream David was able to consider his relationship with his father from a fresh perspective. He had the sobering insight that he had lived as if he were "just an appendage," chronically unable to realize his own worth and autonomy. This led him to admit the perverse delight he gained from being the source of another's pleasure or the agency of another's frustration. Behind the imaginary facade of ineffectualness, he acknowledged a secret fantasy of immense power, believing he had the means of providing utter fulfillment as well as the means of inducing impotence in another. Eventually he was grateful to me for resisting his demands that I deny his autonomy and allow him to become *my* appendage. He thought it was only my willingness to risk losing him as a patient that had forced him to confront the true nature of his life-and-death struggle. This had then allowed him to dream his dream and thereby gain some recognition of his own mortality and the necessity of assuming responsibility for his life.

David's impressive capacity to engage in analytic work following the dream led rather quickly to a mobilization of interest and energy outside the office. Alarmed at the state of his marriage, he decided to "work at it" by entering marital therapy with his wife. Acknowledging that he was both bored and on the verge of bankruptcy, he secured a job in a law office. By the end of the analysis he had fathered a son and gone into independent law practice.

The two years of analysis subsequent to the dream were not always smoothly productive or devoid of major conflict. Yet, there was a clear sense that an irreversible turning point had been reached, full engagement in the analytic work itself having become a sustaining and reliable source of nourishment and gratification. Efforts to understand the paternal roots of recurrent transference struggles continued until the termination phase. However, in the context of a recrudescence of symptoms following the setting of a termination date, the fundamental maternal aspect of the transference finally emerged. David's passionate turning toward his father had followed a lengthy separation from his mother when she had been hospitalized for a postpartum depression at the end of his second year. Memories emerged that linked David's turning toward his father with the abrupt loss of the mother.

This final revelation in the work was liberating and David could now understand how the father's loneliness had led him to demand total devotion. Not surprisingly, David then began to reflect on his relationship with me, fleshing me out for the first time as a real person. Toward the end of our last session he remarked, as if he had not quite noticed it before, that we were rather close in age and were both at roughly similar stages in our professional careers. With obvious relish he told me that he continued to think that my taste in clothes was disconcerting, but now this was the case because he was certain that he dressed far better than I. As for the money he paid me, he claimed he no longer begrudged it, since it was likely that he would soon have a handsome income that would in all probability exceed mine. With this he caught himself, chuckled, and said, "I'm really sick of defining myself in terms of you. We don't have to be the same to be equals." With that he arose from the couch, we shook hands warmly, and the analysis was terminated.

Case Analysis

The psychoanalytic literature on impasse has focused exclusively on the "negative therapeutic reaction," most often assumed to derive from preexisting intrapsychic pathology solely within the patient, leading him to defeat a benevolent and competent analyst. Such patients, generally characterized as having "weak egos," have often been deemed unsuitable for analytic work. A review of this literature (Gorney, 1979) suggests a reformulation in which impasse is regarded as a malignant form of interactional resistance, a specific type of "interactional syndrome" (Langs, 1978–1979, pp. 93–94), with emphasis placed on complementarity of conscious and unconscious exchange between the two analytic participants. This framework highlights the dialectic of mutually objectifying empty words sustaining impasse, as well as the emergence of the signifier of desire that is the harbinger of impasse resolution. This interactional conception of impasse is now amplified by examining the analysis of David from the perspective of the master–slave dialectic and the relationship of the imaginary and symbolic orders.

Throughout David's development and during the impasse phase of analysis, his primary identification was clearly with the posture of the slave. David's hunger for recognition, his joyless, unproductive laboring for others, his idealization of powerful figures, and his paralyzing fear of retribution all sustained his fearful bondage. Yet David's objectifying, slavish consciousness was not, in our view, an indication that he suffered from "ego weakness."

Rather, he had become rigidified in a highly defended ego apparatus in which he lived according to images of becoming the fulfillment of the desire of others.

For example, David's adolescent repression of his own sexual desire, as well as his subservience in school and work, seemed directly connected to the enticing image of his father's recognition when an "icy stare" might give way to a "look of love." The rigidity of this ego configuration accounted for David's turmoil at age sixteen on learning of his father's mistress. He viewed the mistress as now being the object of his father's desire, experiencing her as phallus to the father. David's response was immediate. He began to masturbate for the first time (perhaps in an attempt to be the phallus for himself or some fantasized being) and to play the secret role of con man or trickster. He then engineered his public refusal of a scholarship precisely so that he might evoke and see the tears that eventually came to his father's eyes. With this sight of the tears, as the visual mode remained pervasive, David could once again imagine himself to be the complete object of his father's desire, that he could be "just an appendage." Thus he could once again work for his father, this time in the college of his father's choice.

The father's despair during the crisis of his middle age recalls Hegel's characterization of the dead end of the master who cannot receive true recognition from others and who must depend on the work of others for satisfaction. The father's affair, quest for lost youth, and alienation from wife and son all indicate that his ego's victory in the struggle for domination was eventually experienced as hollow and unproductive. The father's mounting depletion was not entirely lost on David and was no doubt a factor in his abortive experiments with autonomy as he took a job with a law firm and got married. Yet, his essential image remained unchanged. It was not surprising that the crisis that led him to analysis was precipitated primarily by the expectation that he father a child, and secondarily by a struggle for recognition at work. In response, he became impotent and a garbage man, reacting perhaps to the fear that he would soon lose his newly won position as phallus to his wife, imagining that the child would replace him as completion of her desire. Fearing this competition with the child, he retreated massively into a slavish posture, as he often had done with his father, rather than once again risk a murderous struggle for recognition.

At the beginning of analysis David was the slave who labors joylessly. But who now was the master? The master at that point could be understood as the paternal function whose promise of a child had come to dominate David's fears and led to the imaginary castration manifest in his sexual impotence. For David, this imaginary castration became a necessary symptom because of the importance for him of *being* the phallus, rather than *having* the phallus. In other words, the impotence represented his ego's identification with the imaginary fulfillment of the other's desire as well as the relinquishment of his own autonomy.

The paternal function readily shifted from the father to the analyst in the transference, facilitated by the structural aspects of times, fees, and use of the couch. These dimensions were immediately experienced as an erotic arena for competition, conformity, and captivation. It was not surprising that the patient articulated in the second session the leit-motiv of the eventual transferential struggle when he fantasized being "screwed in the ass" by the analyst. This fantasy not only expressed a passive longing, but announced his intention to compel the analyst into a master–slave struggle. In this struggle David ostensibly worked for the analyst's pleasure, attempting to become the imaginary completion of his desire. The powerful and seductive nature of this transference led to an impasse in which the discourse between analyst and patient locked them into a dual ego-to-ego struggle from which any mediating third dimension, the discourse of "the Other," was excluded. Demands by both participants substituted for and prevented the expression of desire. The resulting discourse consisted of the "empty words" of an objectifying ego, which Lacan views as the locus of misunderstanding.

As impasse deepened, the analyst became enmeshed in his own imaginary struggle. Robbed of his usual powers of interpretation, his comments to the patient expressed his own anxiety at not being permitted to be the customary "good analyst" of his ego ideal. The empty words of the analyst, which David correctly observed were suitable for a tea bag label, reflected his therapeutic despair at approaching a dead end—the dead end of the master evoked in the countertransference. Unable to receive equal recognition from the patient, and unable to derive any direct satisfaction from the work, the analyst became vicariously dependent on the slavish, joyless labor of the analysand. The impasse was thus interactionally and dialectically sustained within the empty words of the transference–countertransference.

It is our contention that the psychoanalytic impasse, in a manner which parallels the master–slave dialectic, is an unstable configuration containing the seeds of its own resolution. David's nightmare constituted the breakthrough in his treatment, but this dream was preceded by an escalating series of imaginary demands, culminating in his demand for a fee reduction. This was his last-ditch effort to receive some concrete proof of being the object of the analyst's desire. The dream followed David's admission that he was too much of a coward to risk killing himself. By resisting the patient's demands, the analyst permitted some revelation of the patient's fear of death, which could be viewed retrospectively as the beginning of the transformative labor accomplished in genuine discourse. Yet, that conscious discourse achieved a limit by virtue of David's admission of his death-threat hoax. This set the stage for another dimension of discourse, the symbolic discourse of the Other previously absent in the treatment, not on the level of the ego and not captivated by aggressivity. The countertransference implications of the dream can be restated in terms of the dream's message to the analyst. Caught up in the aggressivity of the struggle to be recognized, resorting to the empty speech of the analysis of resistances, the analytic discourse was closed to the patient's signifier: the imaginary order governed what went on, and the only way the patient could be heard is by a wordless scream. This forced the analyst to listen in a new way, to drop the analysis of resistances, to go beyond the prolonged struggle for recognition as masterful ego.

If impasse is viewed as congruent with that stage in the master–slave dialectic when the slave has not yet fully recognized the impact of the fear of death and imagines that he labors only for the master's enjoyment, then a way out of impasse can occur through an affective experience of personal mortality that dissolves the rigid structure of resistance. The nightmare, and its accompanying wordless scream, provided the necessary breakthrough out of imaginary capture and into the symbolic order. The two linguistic axes of combination and selection can be seen as operative in the dream in the mode of metonymy or displacement as well as the mode of metaphor or condensation. An auditory, metonymic contiguity guides the associative displacement from "pinky" to "pinkle," "tinkle" to "penis." Here the word "pinky" has been provided by the dream as a signifier, making possible symbolic discourse and revealing the source of unconscious desire. The metaphoric mode is found in the ice cubes, signifying the frozen impasse, as well as by the letter opener, signifying a means of unlocking the discourse. The letter opener (the *p* leading from *p*inky to *p*enis) also exposes symbolically the patient's imaginary identification with the phallus, that is, his *not having* the phallus in order to *be* the phallus. Indeed, by virtue of the dreamwork, this wish was now finally capable of being experienced by the patient as life threatening. The conclusion of David's dream, in which his pinky was placed in the freezer just prior to a wordless scream, can be understood as a symbolic communication of the impasse dilemma. The signifier, the medium of symbolic exchange, was frozen out of the stalemated analytic exchange and could only emerge subsequent to an articulation of the fear of death.

The symbolic and communicative structure of David's nightmare functioned in the treatment as the transformative labor of the slave through which he began to release himself from bondage. The dream served to negate the immediacy of the imaginary transference–countertransference struggle; it established the presence of an "other scene," the dimension of the unconscious, where desire is operative in a linguistic mode. The dream itself was therefore a kind of death, putting an end to the rigidity, aggressivity, and resistance of the ego-to-ego struggle. The symbol, Lacan tells us (following Hegel), is the murder of the thing: that is, in language the physical presence of objects is negated, transformed into a symbolic presence that enables us to talk about anything in its absence. In David's dream the symbol can also be seen as murder of imaginary identification, negating the immediacy of captivation, seduction, and aggressivity by allowing previously repressed desire to be articulated and be present in the chain of signifiers. By obtaining recognition of this desire as articulated in the symbolic discourse of his dream, the patient no longer had to enact an imaginary struggle for recognition.

Can we say anything more about the joint function of death and work in resolving impasse? The work of Pascal, Kierkegaard, Heidegger, and many others is richly suggestive here. In Heidegger (1927), for example, anxiety about one's own death transforms everyday existence into authentic resoluteness, clearing the way for the active realization of one's own potentialities. There are other ways of talking about this familiar experience. What is central is that the patient, face-to-face with his own mortality, somehow becomes free to seize his own life and work at making a go of it, freed up from being identified with others' desires and free to take action to realize his own desire.

For Hegel death is the negation of all particularity and therefore a kind of correlative to the subject as negativity, the subject as desire who transcends given nature in work. The fear of death dissolves all particularity, all defensive postures, all dependency on particular objects—including imaginary ones. But the fear of death in the absence of work is sterile; conversely, work without fear of death remains caught up in the deceptive structures of self-will and oppositionalism and reflects at best a partial grasp of oneself as self-consciousness. In the final analysis, the slave must come to realize that, as Hegel says, death is the sovereign master, standing behind every imaginary master, who opens up our gap of desire and reveals ourselves to ourselves as radically finite negativity.

Conclusion

David's analysis culminated in an expanded understanding of his wish to become the father's penis. This was ultimately understood to be itself a derivative of a traumatic early separation from the mother. As Lacan has observed, the signifiers of desire come to proliferate metonymically through language with the phallus becoming the symbol of the impossible longing to regain the fantasy of a once blissful perfect union. That David was able to articulate the phallus as signifier in such a direct fashion is no doubt unusual. Nevertheless, it is well known in analytic practice that the final working through of the transference involves the evocation of fully symbolic speech, which optimally enables the patient to express his wish to return to a lost maternal paradise.

In conclusion, we shall summarize some of the ways in which Lacan's elaboration of the master–slave paradigm enriches an understanding of the transference–countertransference relationship in psychoanalysis. Lacan asserts that "it is in the disintegration of the imaginary unity constituted by the ego that the subject finds the signifying material of his symptoms" (Lacan, 1966, p. 137). This "imaginary unity" is constituted by a fabric of distortions, misunderstandings, reflected images, and identifications that over time has succeeded in alienating the patient from his subjectivity. Indeed, it is precisely this imaginary unity that is then offered up to the analyst in the unfolding of the transference. It is therefore essential that the analyst not respond to the transferential demands of the patient as if they were equivalent to the symbolic articulation of desire. The patient characteristically asserts a defensive, distorted image of himself in order to lure the analyst into an ego-to-ego struggle for recognition. Since the psychoanalytic situation is itself structured, as Greenacre has noted (1954, p. 674), in the form of an unequal "tilted relationship," countertransference–transference phenomena generally become patterned according to the master–slave paradigm. The analyst must recognize that this paradigm is an imaginary configuration within which neither participant can grant true recognition to the other and in which productive work cannot occur.

When the master–slave relationship persists over time during treatment, therapeutic discourse becomes a two-way litany of empty words. It is at this point that impasse is likely to occur. Just as in the master–slave paradigm, the psychoanalytic impasse contains within itself the seeds of its own dialectical resolution. Resolution can occur when the analyst becomes finally able to facilitate the patient in the production of a signifier, making possible an entry out of the imaginary into the symbolic order. In the treatment that has been reported, such a facilitating moment occurred in the analyst's refusal of a demand, which then enabled David to dream his dream, confront the limits of his mortality, and articulate a signifier. It is only through disengaging himself from the imaginary identifications of his own countertransferential struggle with the patient that the analyst can make room for an Other, a symbolic third dimension that can transform the frozen discourse of impasse. In the words of Lacan, "In order to free the subject's speech, we introduce him into the language of his desire, that is to say, into the *primary language* in which, beyond what he tells us of himself, he is already talking to us unknown to himself, and in the first place, in the symbols of the symptom" (Lacan, 1966, p. 81).

References

Freud, S. (1900-1901), The Interpretation of Dreams. *Standard Edition*, 4 & 5. London: Hogarth Press, 1953.

Gorney, J. E. (1979), The negative therapeutic interaction. *Contemp. Psychoanal.*, 15(2):288–335.

Greenacre, P. (1954), The role of transference: Practical considerations in relation to psycho-analytic therapy. *J. Amer. Psychoanal. Assn.*, 2:671–684.

Hegel, G. W. F. (1807), *The Phenomenology of Mind*, 2nd. ed., trans. J. B. Baillie. London: George Allen & Unwin, 1964.

Heidegger, M. (1927), *Being and Time*. New York: Harper, 1962.

Jakobson, R. (1956), Two aspects of language and two types of aphasic disturbances. In: *Fundamentals of Language*, eds. R. Jakobson & M. Halle. The Hague: Mouton, pp. 53–82.

Kojève, A. (1947), Introduction to the reading of Hegel. *Lectures on the Phenomenology of Spirit*, assembled by R. Queneau, ed. A. Bloom. Trans. James H. Nichols, Jr. New York: Basic Books, 1969.

Lacan, J. (1951), Some reflections on the ego. *Internat. J. Psychoanal.*, 34:11–17, 1953.

———— (1964), *The Four Fundamental Concepts of Psycho-Analysis*, ed. J. A. Miller, trans. A. Sheridan. New York: W.W. Norton, 1978.

———— (1966), *Ecrits: A Selection*, trans. A. Sheridan. New York: W.W. Norton, 1977.

Langs, R. (1978–1979), Some communicative properties of the bipersonal field. *Internat. J. Psychoanal. Psychother.*, 7:87–135.

Levenson, E. (1978), Psychoanalysis—Cure or persuasion? In: *Interpersonal Psychoanalysis: New Directions*, ed. E. Witenberg. New York: Gardner Press, pp. 47–63.

Muller, J. P., & Richardson, W. J. (1978), Toward reading Lacan: Pages for a workbook. *Psychoanal. & Contemp. Thought*, 1(3):323–372.

IV

Transference,
Countertransference, and
the Holding Environment

11

Masochism in the Analyst

Ann C. Greif, Ph.D.

Too little attention has been given to the emotional price paid by psychoanalysts in the pursuit of remediating the suffering of their patients. Abstinence, delay, and inhibition of even indirect instinctual gratification at the expense of the patient have all been accepted as necessary requirements of the analytic frame. While as helping professionals we are rightly concerned with the potential for exploitation and victimization of those individuals who come to us with pain (Menaker, 1942), it cannot be ignored that a heavy toll is imposed on the analyst, especially in the treatment of severely disturbed individuals.

The motives, talents, and skills that converge to bring someone to such a profession are complex and varied. Yet, it is relatively common among analysts to find underlying the wish to cure the patient a deep and abiding wish not only to cure the self but also to heal the suffering of their parents. As such, the motivation of the analyst mirrors one of the hidden dynamics in the patient's life. Nowhere is this equivalency more noticeable and noteworthy than in the treatment of those severely disturbed individuals who seem to cling tenaciously and masochistically to the very "bad object" that has been the source of their suffering in the past. For this reason, treatment of this type of patient places special demands on the analyst to observe, manage, and resolve his or her countertransference.

The following clinical material briefly illustrates how the analyst's therapeutic aim can become intertwined with the patient's masochism. It will be suggested that the analyst's ability to present himself as alive, active, and potent (that is nondead, nonpassive, and noncastrated) in the treatment setting, and thereby to overcome the pull toward a masochistic surrender to the patient's pathology and to the patient's persecutory inner objects, facilitates the patient's recovery.

Clinical Example

The patient was a twenty-nine-year-old woman who had been in treatment with me for nearly three years. Prior to her admission to the open hospital setting where I have been seeing her, she had been in and out of other hospitals for the preceding six years. Her father had died five years before and she was quite clingy and dependent on her mother. Primary symptoms included a severe eating disorder, cutting, and suicidal gestures. When I first began working with her, the patient felt controlled and overwhelmed by her self-destructive impulses and would spend sessions engaged in seemingly endless litanies about either her eating habits or her depression. Just as she seemed to keep track of the food she ate ritualistically, she treated her own affective experiences as if they were substances to be counted, measured, and categorized. In the early phase of working with this patient, I often found myself feeling bored and tired. I had trouble not responding out of frustration in an effort to break her free of her symptoms and so seemed to vacillate to the other extreme of feeling immobilized. It would seem that this countertransference problem mirrored the patient's experience of me as the abandoning, rejecting mother and the dead father as well as my own overdetermined wish to be helpful. Gradually, she began to make some tentative steps toward forming an alliance, but at the same time there were hints of her feeling pushed into this new attachment by external forces, particularly the departure of her mother for an extended trip to Europe. She became more depressed, looked haggard and disheveled, and complained about her problems with a former analyst upon whom she had become "too dependent." Finally, in one session not long before her mother was due to depart and shortly before the anniversary of her father's death, the patient, who had been going on and on about some obscure problem with another patient and some difficulty with getting herself to eat enough food, suddenly let slip that she had mentioned to another patient that she was feeling suicidal. I felt startled and jolted out of my inertia, although I had for some time been aware of the countertransference problem I was having and it was not atypical for this patient to refer to feeling depressed and to speak of suicide as an option. What in retrospect seemed different was the manner of presentation; instead of directly presenting this as a symptom to be inspected and eliminated by the analyst, she brought up these feelings almost casually, unconnected with any affect. I then inquired about what she had been feeling or still was feeling. While the content that had preceded this supposedly "accidental" disclosure now seems highly meaningful in terms of how this patient felt unable to get her needs met by me or anybody, I was out of touch empathically with this dynamic until I realized that she was presenting me with an opportunity unconsciously to either repeat a trauma or to respond differently. Her own indifference to

what she was speaking of seemed to reflect better than anything the fused relationship with the inner persecutory object. While on this occasion I simply
interpreted back to the patient what I felt she was struggling with and did not
share my own feelings and did not actively confront her with how she was
going to manage these impulses, on subsequent occasions this is what I have
done with increasing regularity and success in terms of both diminishing symptomatology and promoting insight and personality reconstruction. This particular incident was followed that evening by a minor cutting episode.

My interpretive approach was not enough for this patient who, on the
one hand, seemed capable of understanding interpretations intellectually but,
on the other hand, could not emotionally make use of them to curb her own
self-destructive impulses. With this patient and others like her I have become
increasingly impressed by the tenuousness of their self-preservative instincts,
and the need for the analyst to be continually on the watch for any passivity or withdrawal that might mark a giving in to the patient's own hopelessness and defeatism. Yet it is very easy with such a patient to feel beleaguered
and battered down by the stubbornness with which they cling to their symptoms, and to be fooled into believing that simply assuming an interpretive
stance ensures one against acting out countertransference problems.

Discussion

The importance to the patient of experiencing the analyst's liveliness, vitality, and interest has been recognized before (Berman, 1949; Little, 1951;
Reich, 1966), but I believe it is of special importance to patients who waver
on the edge of surrendering either to attacking sadistic inner objects or to falling into an empty aloneness that feels limitless and engulfing (Green, 1975).
The word "surrender" is used here quite deliberately to indicate that these patients are caught up in a continual struggle to hold onto reality, and that it is
only with tremendous effort and cost to their enjoyment in life that they usually manage to present a reasonably intact facade of functioning. Like many
patients, one of the core problems for the self-injuring, masochistic patient
is a genuine terror of their own affective experience, and as such they tend
to shy away from contact with reality that might engender a depth of feeling
and challenge the original libidinal tie (Khan, 1968). For long stretches of
time, particularly early on in the treatment, if all is going well, these patients
lean up against the analyst's vitality (Spitz, 1956) without it being acknowledged or needing to be acknowledged by anybody. If all goes well this lean-
ing up against the analyst's vitality and coming to know its strength and reliability is what may eventually stimulate the patient's hope for recovery and

his own interest in objective reality, especially as this is presented in the person of the analyst. The analyst's ability to convey a sense of aliveness should not, however, be confused with an inclination to act on feelings of frustration and impatience with the patient, who may at times seem to be inextricably wedded to his own inner world. This is not to say that at some point in a treatment it might not be advantageous or even imperative to let these patients know of some of the difficulties in working with them (Winnicott, 1947; Little, 1951; Benedek, 1953).

Menaker (1942) has cautioned analysts about the potential for the analytic setting to reinforce rather than to dislodge a masochistic adjustment. In addition, to the tendency to encourage helplessness and submission, I would include certain other features of the analytic setting and technique that mirror the original "real" trauma. By this I mean there are certain features of the analytic setting that give rise to pain and that the patient is expected to endure for the sake of his treatment, and most importantly from the patient's perspective, for the sake of the relationship with the analyst. For example, by his or her very presence, the analyst challenges the patient's original bond to the parents, and by the interpretive technique calls forth in the patient a reexamination and therefore a reexperiencing to some degree of the old dilemmas from which relief is being sought in the first place. Further, once established, the new attachment to the analyst threatens the patient with the possibility of again failing to achieve the long sought after mutuality and yet separateness in an important relationship. This is what Balint (1932) first recognized in his paper "Character Analysis and New Beginning," and what Anna Ornstein (1974) later referred to more specifically as the patient's "dread to repeat." These necessarily cruel or unfeeling aspects of the analytic setting may take the patient somewhat by surprise, although on some level he is always seeking a better experience than what he has known before. More paranoid patients may believe these factors have been manufactured specifically for them to either remediate or exacerbate their pain. The following dream from a young woman in her first year of treatment exemplifies some of the feelings of outrage and submission engendered by the treatment process. In the dream, the patient is in a dentist's chair about to have some teeth extracted. The dentist says he will be giving no painkiller because if the procedure is done properly there will be no pain. The dentist then goes off in the middle of the procedure leaving her in pain and wondering when it will be over. While there are many levels to this dream, the patient did seem to be communicating rather directly her sense that treatment ought to proceed without inducing pain, and her suspicion that the analyst would repeat either through ineptitude or malice the alternation of abandonment and intrusion that she had known as a child. In fact, the experience of intrusion alternating with withdrawal seems to be a rather common occurrence in the therapy of more severely disturbed individuals whose fragile ego boundaries and tenuous object constancy do not allow for a sense of continuity between periods of activity and inactivity on the analyst's part.

At the same time that the patient is being subjected to some of these difficult realities about the treatment setting so too is the analyst, who must not only live within the strictures of his method but must also repetitively affirm these and give witness to their necessity with the patient. Some aspects of the self-denial required of the analyst by the treatment process are obvious: the physical inactivity, the abstinence from acting out in relation to the patient and what he or she might evoke, the social isolation, the delay required to formulate relevant and cogent interpretations are only a few examples. Greenson (1966) in his paper "The Impossible Profession" noted the constant assault on the analyst's narcissism caused by the patient's projections and resistance to change, as well as the depressive pull to identify with patients in the process of empathic listening. Annie Reich (1951) came to the conclusion that "the slow cumbersome process of analysis makes high demands on the analyst's patience and narcissistic equilibrium" (p. 144). Being an analyst, like being a parent, can severely test the integrity and cohesiveness of the sense of self (Saretsky, 1980), since the effort to care for another human being entails joining with that person and venturing with them through a maturational process that always holds the potential for anxiety-provoking confrontations with the self and the other.

Because of the deep personal satisfactions that can also be part of this work, analysts have perhaps not so quickly and keenly perceived the more restrictive and demanding aspects of what they do, or at least this is not mentioned as frequently in the literature as are the dangers involved in gratifying oneself at the expense of the patient. While I do not wish to be in the position of saying that every sublimation ought to be defined as masochistic, although some have extended the concept of masochism almost to this extreme (de Monchy, 1950), it does seem that there are certain features of the analytic setting, when taken together with the stresses imposed by treating a certain kind of patient, that can lead quite regularly to countertransference problems involving the analyst's own masochism. Such problems commonly take the form of discouragement with the self or the entire enterprise of psychotherapy, boredom, suspiciousness and envy of colleagues, guilty over-involvement alternating with resentment of the patient, and sometimes the conscious sense of avoiding the patient's rage. Of course, any such difficulties for the analyst can be exacerbated by lingering omnipotent strivings (Searles, 1966) and the insufficient dissolution of idealization (Saretsky, 1980) of parental figures. Lest the analyst's effectiveness be compromised and the treatment degenerate into a setting where fantasies of guilt, punishment, and expiation are lived out by both participants, it would seem important for the analyst to tolerate and recognize his or her own masochism (Racker, 1958). Just as analysts have come to appreciate the importance of acknowledging their own sadistic impulses toward patients and of sometimes informing patients of their occurrence (Winnicott, 1947; Little, 1957), masochistic responses to either the patient's self-defeating or more overtly hostile behavior must be noted and understood. As Lucia Tower (1956) argues in her paper on countertransference, such vicissitudes in the analyst's response to the patient indicate the presence of a very real and potentially growth-promoting affective exchange.

While many have noted the importance of the analyst deriving some gratification from his work in order for the treatment to proceed optimally (Balint and Balint, 1939; Berman, 1949; Cohen, 1952), ultimately, whether the treatment succeeds or fails, enhances the analyst's self-esteem, and confirms his professional identity, depends on the complicated mix-up of the dyad, a two-person group in which both persons are very real active participants. This interdependence is another obvious parallel between the analytic setting and the early environment that for the masochistic patient originally engendered a sense that his own well-being had to be sacrificed or compromised in order to secure the love of the parent. Thus, these patients are ready to use their interdependence with the analyst as the arena for enacting their transference problems, and it is here where the analyst joins the patient with his countertransference. While different patients pose different challenges, these patients regularly behave in ways that seem to ask such questions as: "Do you care for me or for how I perform (or don't perform)?" "Do you care for me enough to accept my not changing?" "Can I get you to change and to care for me in the ways I want, if I won't change or I get worse?" Likewise the analyst brings his own deep-rooted personal concerns to the process in the form of those motives that initially compelled the choice of career. While typically manifested and experienced in a highly attenuated and sublimated form, the reparative drive or wish to cure the parent and the accompanying sense of interlocking interdependence and mutuality between people are what frequently lies at the heart of the analyst's commitment to the work (Cohen, 1952; Winnicott, 1954–1955; Money-Kyrle, 1956; Searles, 1966). Searles (1975) has gone so far as to contend that all humans have an innate psychotherapeutic striving, and while that seems probable to me, it also seems likely that those individuals who either choose psychotherapy as a profession or come to it for help, have likely had some particular troubles or concerns having to do with curing and being cured by others in less artificial surroundings. This reparative motive in the analyst can make him a prime target for countertransference struggles with the patient, as he can easily become locked into an identification with the patient's suffering or can come to feel guilty when united with the patient's "bad object." Both types of countertransference, identification with the patient and identification with the negative parental imago, can, I think, be understood as reactions to threats to the analyst's own inner sense of goodness, of having something to offer that is helpful and nurturing. Olinick (1969) has described the potential for a regressive revival of the urgency to rescue the depressive mother. Greenson (1960), in likening good empathizers to depressives who search for the lost love object, seems also to recognize the potential countertransference problems involving the reparative drive of the analyst.

As has already been mentioned, self-defeating and self-destructive behaviors represent resistance to giving up a sadomasochistic relatedness to an inner persecutory object from whom it is still hoped love can be extracted. Put in other words, the masochistic patient is defended against the pain and mourning associated with giving up the struggle with the early parent. These patients can be said to have only managed to achieve "unit status" (Winnicott, 1954–1955) at the expense of a masochistic adjustment that bypassed the normal mourning and reparative work associated with the depressive position. Consequently, these patients are not typically inclined to trust symbolic abstract modes of communication, that is, verbal discourse. Instead, they remain inwardly preoccupied much like schizoid patients and often communicate their predicament through the use or abuse of their bodies. Khan (1976) has described masochism as a special variant of manic defense. Thus, these patients by being walled off and inaccessible frustrate the analyst's wish to be eaten as described by Winnicott (1954–1955) in the following passage:

> What do we want [as analysts]? We want to be eaten. . . there is no masochism in this. To be eaten is the wish and indeed the need of a mother at a very early stage in the care of an infant. This means that whoever is not cannibalistically attacked tends to feel outside the range of people's reparative and restitutive activities, and so outside society [p. 276].

Masochism for the analyst is not in wanting to be incorporated but in how he or she handles the frustration of this goal. To be taken in is rather part of the analyst's reparative and restitutive activities.

Technical Considerations

Menaker (1942) has suggested avoiding transference interpretations in working with masochistic patients, and focusing attention instead on the "real" relationship in order to avoid a regressive reenactment of the earlier object relation. While it seems unnecessary to exclude any type of intervention, it does seem tremendously important with these patients to keep in mind how our own personalities within the analytic situation shape both the real relationship and the transference. Racker (1958) has made the observation that just as the patient may be said to create the analyst's countertransference, so too the analyst can be said to create the transference. Benedek (1953) also emphasized the importance for the analyst of tolerating the reflected image of the self in the patient's transference. With these patients who begin treatment withdrawn and inwardly preoccupied, it would seem especially important to welcome those instances when they do recognize the analyst as a separate entity even if it is in a somewhat distorted form. At the same time that such an intervention makes for positive change in the patient, it also ameliorates the analyst's sense of growing frustration and invisibility, decreases feelings of guilt and anxiety related to suppressed negative feelings toward the patient, and renews interest (Racker, 1958) and commitment (both intellectual and affective) to the work. Further, by helping patients articulate their perceptions of the analyst and by explicitly or implicitly acknowledging the accuracy of these perceptions, the analyst will facilitate the freeing up of the patient's empathic capabilities and stifled reparative strivings.

As well as helping patients articulate their view of the analyst without resorting too quickly to transference interpretations, the analyst should be ready to withstand the onslaught of the patient's rage, as the past is relived in the therapy. Lucia Tower (1956) describes how she temporarily adopted a masochistic stance vis-à-vis the patient's sadism. She writes: "There developed in me, on a transient basis, an amount of masochism sufficient to absorb the sadism which he was now unloading, and which had terrified him throughout his life." She goes on: "The other ingredient of my affective response was, I believe, a joining with him and a supporting of him, through identification, in a true unconscious grief reaction" (p. 248). This is another element in the analyst's successfully dealing with the patient's masochism, namely, tolerating first the conscious recognition of the grief and sadness the patient is still defending against. By both absorbing the patient's rage and being available to experience the hidden grief, the analyst moves out from under the struggle with the patient over who will change and who will feel, and accepts temporary submission at the hands of the patient's pathology in the service of ultimate conflict resolution and working through. Eisenbud (1967) has noted the critical importance of such interventions for restoring a sense of efficacy to the masochistic patient. The analyst must be able to step back from the patient's pathology and to tolerate the patient's resistances without feeling defeated, emptied, or castrated and without detaching emotionally from the patient. On the other hand, when the patient's resistances take the form of self-destructive impulses, the analyst has to be ready to challenge the transference distortions, and to refuse to participate in the patient's pathology. In this way, the analyst readily concedes that his therapeutic aim can be easily thwarted by the patient, and that the patient, rather than being helpless, is in an important way determining the course of the analytic enterprise.

References

Balint, A., & Balint, M. (1939), On transference and countertransference. *Internat. J. Psycho-Anal.*, 20:223–230.

Balint, M. (1932), Character analysis and new beginning. In: *Primary Love and Psycho-Analytic Technique*. New York: Liveright Publishing, 1965, pp.151–164.

Benedek, L. (1953), Dynamics of countertransference. *Bull. Menn. Clin.*, 17:201–208.

Berman, L. (1949), Countertransference and attitudes of the analyst in the therapeutic process. *Psychiatry*, 12:159–166.

Cohen, M. (1952), Countertransference and anxiety. *Psychiatry*, 15:231–243.

de Monchy, R. (1950), Masochism as a pathological and as a normal phenomenon in the human mind. *Internat. J. Psycho-Anal.*, 31:95–97.

Eisenbud, R. J. (1967), Masochism revisited. *Psychoanal. Rev.*, 54:561–582.

Green, A. (1975), The analyst, symbolization and absence in the analytic setting (on changes in analytic practice and analytic experience). *Internat. J. Psycho-Anal.*, 56:1–22.

Greenson, R. R. (1960), Empathy and its vicissitudes. *Internat. J. Psycho-Anal.*, 41:418–424.

———— (1966), That "impossible" profession. *J. Amer. Psychoanal.*, 14:9–27.

Khan, M. (1968), Reparation to the self as an idolized internal object: A contribution to the theory of perversion-formation. In: *Alienation in Perversions*. New York: International Universities Press, 1979, pp. 11–17.

———— (1976), From masochism to psychic pain. In: *Alienation in Perversions*. New York: International Universities Press, 1979, pp. 210–218.

Little, M. (1951), Countertransference and the patient's response to it. *Internat. J. Psycho-Anal.*, 32:32–40.

———— (1957), "R"—The analyst's total response to his patient's needs. *Internat. J. Psycho-Anal.*, 38:240–254.

Menaker, E. (1942), The masochistic factor in the psychoanalytic situation. *Psychoanal. Quart.*, 9:171–186.

Money-Kyrle, R. E. (1956), Normal countertransference and some of its deviations. *Internat. J. Psycho-Anal.*, 37:360–366.

Olinick, S. L. (1969), On empathy and regression in the service of the other. *Brit. J. Med. Psychol.*, 42:41–49.

Ornstein, A. (1974), The dread to repeat and the new beginning: A contribution to psychoanalysis. In: *Annual of Psychoanalysis*, Vol. 2, ed. Chicago Institute for Psychoanalysis. New York: International Universities Press, pp. 231–248.

Racker, H. (1958), Psychoanalytic technique and the analyst's unconscious masochism. *Psychoanal. Quart.*, 27:555–562.

Reich, A. (1951), On countertransference. *Internat. J. Psycho-Anal.*, 32:25–31.

———— (1966), Empathy and countertransference. In: *Psychoanalytic Contributions*. New York: International Universities Press, 1973, pp. 344–360.

Saretsky, T. (1980), The analyst's narcissistic vulnerability: Its effect on the treatment situation. *Contemp. Psychoanal.*, 16:82–89.

Searles, H. (1966), Feelings of guilt in the psychoanalyst. *Psychiatry*, 29:319–323.

——— (1975), The patient as therapist to the analyst. In: *Countertransference and Related Subjects*. New York: International Universities Press, 1979, pp. 380–459.

Spitz, R. (1956), Countertransference. *J. Amer. Psychoanal Assn.*, 4:256–265.

Tower, L. (1956), Countertransference. *J. Amer. Psychoanal. Assn.*, 4:224–255.

Winnicott, D. W. (1947), Hate in the countertransference. *Internat. J. Psycho-Anal.*, 30:102–110.

——— (1954–1955), The depressive position. In: *Through Paediatrics to Psychoanalysis*. New York: Basic Books, 1975, pp. 262–277.

12

Countertransference Identification

Jill D. Montgomery, Ph.D.

This chapter begins with two assumptions: the first is that the psychoanalytic relationship is usefully described as an "intersubjective field." That is, "a system of differently organized, interacting subjective worlds" (Atwood and Stolorow, 1984, p. 119). Each word in the above sentence is important for our purpose, which is to understand what happens in a meeting involving two whole personalities—the patient's and the analyst's—(Racker, 1957) within an institution defined as therapeutic that results in change. The language with which we describe this relationship will structure our perceptions of it. We should therefore pause to examine the language more closely. "Inter" suggests a location that is neither "inside" nor "outside." We are organisms who psychologically differentiate developmentally by constructing boundaries. We carve out our self-consciousness divisively, dividing experience into organizing dualities. We exist in a linguistic world that captures our experience of duality—inside–outside, self–other, subject–object, mind–body, etc. We are in turn captured by our language. It is difficult for us to even begin describing psychological processes without using the inherited dualistic vocabulary of our discipline. Fantasy–reality, internalized–externalized, introjection–projection, even transference–countertransference, all reflect this division. Even the positing of such dualities that are then said to be "dialectically related" does not truly serve to overcome the dilemma of dualistic relations. (Possibly it is dissatisfaction with this theoretical vocabulary that accounts for the current popularity of such boundary dissolving images as "mirror.") Although we have been told (Shafer, 1976) that the psychological universe does not exist concretely, it is still necessary to remind ourselves at the outset of this inquiry that the boundaries of a subjectivity are constructed arbitrarily as punctuations in a fluctuating experiential universe of meaning and activity. In the psychoanalytic relationship action and meaning happen "in between." But "in between" is not to be understood as the negative space separating two enclosed consciousnesses who are objects to each other. "In between" must be understood as an "inside–outside" or an interacting "among."

"Subjective" positions us within the mind. Our interest is in the experiencing, meaning-giving subject (Atwood and Stolorow, 1984), the individual to whom all mental representations or operations are attributed, the thinking or cognizing agent, the locus of sensation and perception. For this inquiry, truth value, then, resides in the mind rather than in "things" as somehow "external" to mind. But it will be misleading to think of this "subjectivity" as correlative to an "objectivity" to which it is opposed. Our subjectivity will fill the imaginary space marked off in the encounter of the analytic participants subjugating things to the dominion of personally organized meaning giving shapes and patterns. This space is what is meant by "field."

Field offers an agile metaphor with meanings borrowed from optics, physics, mathematics, athletics, and everyday life. It delimits a circumscribed range in which objects are visible to the eye or mind (optics), yet invisibly organized under the influence of some agent or principle (physics), where logical operations and transformations can be performed (mathematics), suggestive of activity, contest, interaction, intention, and encounter (athletics). Like "mirror," field as a psychological space has boundaries that are capable of dissolving or commenting on themselves as illusory. Within its bounds actions can be understood as real, imaginary, and symbolic; as happening in the past and in the present; and as "transitional" (Winnicott, 1951), participating in this and not-this simultaneously. The field under examination in this paper is the therapeutic field formed by the intersection (Atwood and Stolorow, 1984) of three subjectivities—those of the patient, the analyst, and the institution.

The second assumption is that masochistic patients, individuals trapped in long-standing situations of self-inflicted suffering, have given meaning and continuity to their lives through the structuralization of cumulative, passively endured experiences of victimization. They bring to their treatment a subjectivity that rigidly organizes phenomena into preexisting dyadic configurations of master–slave.

"Structuralization" presents us with the idea of consciousness as an active organizing process that builds or constructs itself and its world by way of structural "residue"; that is, relatively stable, limited, and slow changing principles and patterns. These structures are derived in part from experience and are also the means by and through which experience is perceivable, understandable, and negotiable. This of course would be a dead end, with new experience understood only in terms of old rules, and old rules the only tools for negotiating new experience, if not for the fact that psychological structures are modifiable through processes that allow the individual to encounter new experience, recognizing it as the same and contiguous with a past, yet novel, opening toward a future that is different but likewise contiguous. In other words, structures are modifiable in ways and by functions that allow change while maintaining the coherence and continuity essential for the organism to maintain itself without undue distress.

This modification becomes possible through the functioning of two general principles—organization and accommodation/assimilation (Piaget, 1950, 1952, 1954). Organization is the means by which structures interact and are integrated into systems of greater complexity and subtlety; assimilation involves the person in dealing with the environment in terms of his or her old structures, and accommodation involves the transformation of his or her structures in response to the environment (Ginsburg and Opper, 1969). Assimilation and accommodation are simultaneous and present in every act. Experience—psychosexual and psychosocial, physiological and psychological, affective and cognitive, personal and cultural—is organized and assimilated/ accommodated over time in relation to a developing individual who seeks to perpetuate and preserve his or her unity, integrity, and coherence (Klein, 1976). Change can and does occur. It is not, however, inevitable, nor is it "synonymous with what is adaptationally effective" (Klein, 1976, p. 284), enlivening, fulfilling, or forward moving.

The meeting between patient and analyst is in the service of change. This can be argued in great complexity from any number of points of view, but change, nonetheless, remains the reason for the meeting and its justification as a treatment. For the hospitalized patient the meeting occurs within the greater context of an institution defined as therapeutic by its healing administrations. Even if all the clinical terms are translated into nonmedical ones there is still an individual in distress seeking someone (and some place) to alleviate the suffering, someone (and some place) to accomplish a change. It becomes rapidly evident to us when working with masochistic patients, however, that change will not easily be the outcome of the therapeutic encounter, and that in some cases change begins to seem unlikely. The patient efficiently organizes and assimilates/accommodates new experience to a limited repertoire of old structures that "resist" modification with a monothematic attachment to old rules, images, and accompanying affects. This subjectivity swallows us, along with our insight, optimism, and good will, in its powerfully defining configurations of meaning. Despite the intensity of their self-induced pain, despite the desperation and pleas for help, slave and master are locked together in perpetuity. Within their masochistic subjectivity there appears to be no exit for patient, and no entrance for analyst.

Case Example

A particular patient, a pathologically entrenched, masochistic woman, came to our hospital after ten years of unsuccessful treatment.* She brought with her a subjectivity built from a life of radical discontinuity. She had developed a flat, chinalike exterior that resembled a death mask. Certainly, as she stated, she had been dead for ten years beginning with her first hospitalization at age nineteen. Her repertoire of behaviors included life-threatening anorexia and bulimia, massive anxiety, depression of psychotic proportions with immobility and mutism, suicidal obsessions, and dangerous suicide attempts—overdoses and car accidents. She mutilated herself, cutting herself with razor blades, burning herself with cigarettes, injuring herself by jumping off ledges. She was unable to live on her own, to hold a job, or to go to school. She spoke of herself in a bland, disinterested way, as if she were talking about someone else, and seemed diffusely angry, discouraged, and reluctant to accept any responsibility for her difficulties. She appeared to her analyst to be stubborn, clinging to her symptoms and patient identity. She displayed a tremendous inertia. After ten years of previous treatment, this intelligent woman showed little understanding of "what was wrong." She displayed no sense of a past that she was moving away from, or a future toward which she could move with some sense of personal agency, but was stubbornly ahistorical, as if frozen in a deathlike present. In a poem that she wrote early in her treatment at the hospital she stated "my self-created coffin of destructively designed despair deepens and destroys all that could be me." She was enthralled by the self-generated structures that gave coherence to her life. Although she "wanted to get better," change was feared as catastrophic and persecutory. It had no part in her system, which functioned efficiently to negate change.

After three and a half years of further treatment, she left our hospital. Something had occurred. By then she was attending college, where she earned outstanding grades and was preparing for a professional career with a sense of optimism. She had a steady boyfriend who treated her with respect and concern; they planned to get married, and she looked forward to eventually having a baby. She had a small circle of friends. Her weight was stable. She believed that the biggest change was that she felt things, that she was aware of things that she was never aware of before, such as "fear." She could do things without inviting her mother to spoil them with her own definitions, and she could keep things to herself. She saw and felt with greater dimensionality and was able to tolerate complex ambivalent emotional states. Although

*The iatrogenic element in this woman's consolidation as a chronic patient, and the specific clinical method used in addressing this in her treatment is presented in detail elsewhere (Montgomery, 1988).

she was often frightened and sad she was never blank and dead. How did change occur?

Identity, Change, and the Making of a Self

How are we to pursue this question? From the outset the language chosen will begin to organize the experience. The subjectivity of the inquirer shapes perception, suggesting the questions and limiting the answers to its particular universe of meaning. Classical drive theory uses the materialist language of determinism with powerful defining structures of "cause," "motive," and "force" to explore the question of a patient's inability to change in terms of "resistance" and "the compulsion to repeat." The adaptational and developmental vocabulary of ego-psychology organizes information in terms of functional strengths and deficiencies in relation to a facilitating or obstructing environment that results in "ego weakness," "synthetic-integrative incapacities," and "arrested" or "uneven development." Using the vocabulary chosen for this study, change (or the lack of it) must be viewed as an event that takes on a particular meaning in relation to a particular subject. Change must be understood from within the subjectivity of the meaning-giving subject. A particular subjectivity is understood as the outcome of the organization of personal historical experience into cohesive configurations. Change exists as a shift in the organization of experience.

Experience is organized and sorted in a variety of ways. Similarity and difference mediate the structuring of a world from the simple, merged, passive, and unfocused toward the complex, differentiated, active, and focused. Individuality emerges from its context, drawing into itself segments of a progressively receding field of impersonal things and closed surfaces which remains "outside." The modern western consciousness is a highly articulated "self-consciousness" or a consciousness of a "self," with clear notions of inside versus outside, self versus other, activity versus passivity. This thinking, acting subject makes distinctions, draws lines, and appropriates a self as "me," "I" and "mine" out of the communal experiential field. This self-system allows the subject to move through diversity maintaining a sense of cohesion and continuity, as an agent, as a subject, and as a locus (Klein, 1976).

The self is a coalescing structure present as background or foreground. Its illusory determinacy is nonetheless haunted by the annihilating specter of change. The very structures of the self have developed over time through repeated confrontations with change—with difference and discontinuity (Klein, 1976). Selfhood is challenged to repeatedly remake itself as it moves from past to future, from moment to moment, from developmental stage to developmental stage. In the course of development the individual is continually required to maintain his or her selfhood in the face of profound internal and environmental changes that challenge the enduring self schema (Klein, 1976). As we have seen with our patients the integrative outcome of this confrontation does not necessarily have to be in the direction of an enlarged, more differentiated self-conception. Individuals greet change by positioning themselves in relation to its threat of meaninglessness, discontinuity, and disunity in highly diverse ways. Three aspects of this encounter might be isolated. They are the previous structures brought to the change; the degree of discontinuity represented by the change; and the subject's experience of activity or passivity in relation to the change.

In the case of the woman patient mentioned previously, her self schema developed out of disruptive change that was radically redefining, cumulative, and passively experienced. She was born in the Orient to a family in which the father worked for a multinational corporation and moved back and forth between countries. Whenever the patient attempted to separate from home, home would literally disappear as the family once again moved. Repeatedly, any attempt to establish continuity was destroyed. With every move possessions were jettisoned and ties were severed. A harsh lack of sentimentality was imposed on the children. No tearful goodbyes were allowed. Pets were given away; letter writing and holding onto old friends was strongly discouraged.

The patient's family had little if any sense of continuity between generations. Both parents had severed their ties with their families. The family never mentioned the grandparents who remained hidden and unnameable. The patient, along with her brothers and sisters, felt a heightened sense of insecurity and dependence on the family unit, which was intensified by living in dangerous foreign countries. In addition, there was considerable marital conflict and the father was frequently absent. His homecomings were brief, happy events that would rapidly fade as he withdrew into an alcoholic, irritable silence.

The patient's mother was a grimly forebearing, Catholic woman of nononsense asceticism and rigidity. She believed that heaven and hell were very real possibilities, the outcome of bad or good behavior. The mother maintained herself as separate from and superior to the foreigners with whom she was forced to live. Her sense of racial superiority, however, was compromised by having had a Japanese grandmother, a fact that she had tried unsuccessfully to keep buried. The patient's own Asian blood became a source of deep shame. Both the patient's parents had been interned by the Japanese in prison camps for four years during World War II.

The home atmosphere was tense and uncomfortable with a tremendous emphasis on conformity, surface compliance, and obedience. The patient was an accommodating, rather passive infant raised by a succession of Chinese nursemaids during her early years. This caretaking was inconsistent and unstable, alternately overindulging and severe. Rather than becoming rebellious like her other siblings, the patient became withdrawn, clinging, and shy.

The family moved from the Orient to Scotland when the patient was five. This was a tremendous uprooting for her, leaving her with a chronic feeling of difference and alienation from her peers. She remembers being teased about her accent and misunderstood. She felt unable to communicate and once helplessly wet her pants in school. Humiliated, she was scolded and made to stand apart as an example to the other children of "infantile behavior." There seems to have been little recognition or support within her family of the painful effect of this move.

Upon the family's later return to the Orient when the patient was thirteen, there was a repetition of this traumatic separation, complicated and exacerbated by the patient's own transition into adolescence. At the age of fifteen, the patient fled the family in an effort to secure some psychological distance, to establish, if possible, a more coherent sense of her own identity, and to escape the impingements and overstimulation she experienced at home. In addition, by attending a boarding school in America, she seemed to have been searching for allegiance to a cultural group. At boarding school the patient gradually began to make friends and found that many of the students had similar backgrounds to her own. However, she began struggling with her developing female sexual identity as one more uncontrollable and disruptive change forced upon her. She was late developing physically compared to her peers; by the age of sixteen she had not yet menstruated and still had quite an immature figure. It was decided by her physician to try to put her on a course of hormones. Either the hormones or natural development resulted in menstruation and sudden growth. In less than a year she grew several inches, developed large breasts, and put on considerable weight. She felt a pronounced need to diet, and began a pattern of overeating alternating with desperate dieting. The patient came to experience the rapid onset of puberty and her female sexual identity as an out-of-control, alien transforming force imposed on her from outside by doctors.

Upon finishing high school, the patient spent the summer with her parents who had again moved, this time back to Europe. In the fall she decided to attend a large American university in yet another part of the country, where she knew no one. The patient later said that she was unable to identify even to herself how scared she was of yet another change. She found life at the huge American university overwhelming, with its imposed curriculum and lack of attention. She rapidly faded into a progressive isolation and finally a paralyzed suicidally depressed state. Her family was advised by a physician that she needed treatment. They chose, however, to go on a vacation, a tour of Europe, taking their now severely troubled daughter with them. The sudden death of her father shortly afterward when he was away on a business trip had a violently disrupting effect. The patient did not see him again; there was no funeral, only his cremated ashes, which the mother kept in her possession and later alone scattered "somewhere in the North Atlantic."

What began at that point was a ten-year treatment history that followed the patient through hospitals in four different countries and at least six diagnoses. All that seemed to be noted in her files was a progressive elaboration of more profoundly self-destructive symptoms and a stubborn "resistance" to improvement, treatment, and change.

The patient encountered change with a self structure, a complex system of meanings, which in itself was the integrative achievement and sum total of previous change. Erikson describes this gradually established configuration as the outcome of successive syntheses and resyntheses "integrating constitutional givens, idiosyncratic libidinal needs, favored capacities, significant identifications, effective defenses, successful sublimations, and consistent roles" (1956, p. 116). Out of this the patient worked to establish her idiosyncratic self, grounded in the communal meanings of a family, a culture, and a biology. It is important to keep in mind that this self is a configuration, not a unitary agency or reified mechanism, and that it is "real" in its historicity, that is, as the outcome of real events. To not do this is to collude with the masochistic patient's belief that the self is without historical reality, and "real" only in the frozen present as an object, thinglike and fixed.

The patient developed within the historical reality of family and place. Within this context change took on a particular meaning and was met in characteristic ways. The family's experience of passively endured, repeated radical discontinuity was thematized as "victimization" with an accompanying affect of shame. They were a family of victims. Life forced on them new identities and stripped them of what they were. Throughout the generations of this family people were abruptly redefined by the impress of external events—the father orphaned, the mother abandoned, the mother against her will defined by her Asian blood. Their nationality was neither this nor that as moves were imposed on them. They lost position, possessions, status, and country. During World War II they were imprisoned and reduced by the Japanese. At home the family became a microcosm with the parents enacting on the children the victimization–shame experience. Self-definition was to be imposed by outside authority, the adults. The children must conform. Obedience and passivity were rewarded. Within her own history, the patient's repeated encounter with potentially disruptive and redefining change took on structure and meaning in relation to this victimization and shame theme. She came to experience herself as the shameful victim of events beyond her control and was held prisoner by the imposed definitions she passively received. The Catholicism added a further layer of significance, allowing her to suffer change within a world of sufferers, awaiting some ultimate deliverance.

The patient was held to this limited pattern by the intensely dyadic nature of her subjectivity. The attachment to her mother, the father's absence, the repeated moves, the lack of peer relations, and the dependence on the family isolated from any larger community, all contributed to her limited range of experience and the rigidity of her dyadic structures. There was only a child and a mother, a family and a world, children and adults, sinners and God, patients and doctors, us and them. The totality of this binary system pervaded all thought and experience. All units were actually dyads, and the dyads were constructed as master–slave—body to mind, morning to night, desire to its object, self to other, motion to rest—dysjunctive oppositions, one surrendering to the redefining impress of the other. Experience was sorted into a relational pattern that had become an integral part of her selfhood. Her masochism lay in this total ordering of the fluctuating temporal field in terms of passive surrender to the redefining impress of change. In the process the indeterminant self became reified and thinglike existing as an object in relation to a defining other. The implications would have been catastrophic for personal psychological survival if not for the fact that hidden in the nucleus of this surrender was a reversal, a powerful ''no'' that established her subjectivity as a perpetual negation.

Psychological survival, the cohesion of selfhood in a world experienced as cohesive, depends on maintaining relatedness and meaning while simultaneously maintaining autonomy. The self can be thought of as embedded within a matrix of relationships and connections that are understood to function by a certain set of rules and principles. Information is organized in such a manner as to preserve the central sense of personal agency, while preserving attachment and meaning. Passively endured, self-dystonic experience severely threatens this order. The self is forced to secure its position within the matrix of its intersubjective ties, ties to others, and ties to reality, by some form of acceptance of the event. George Klein (1976) suggests that children use identification to assimilate and accept such information. Identification preserves self agency by extending the circumference of the self to include the imposed experience. In this act of identification the self, through a reversal of roles, actively becomes the agent of what it was forced to passively endure.

The patient was forced repeatedly to endure what she experienced as the annihilating force of change. Change always meant a passive giving in before a powerful new definition. This was supported by the family as outlined above. Life presented shameful blows to the self that must be endured, worth was measured by the quality of one's endurance in the face of the inevitable. Even death was but one more change, more frightening in its hiddenness, a sudden relocation to hell or heaven, a redefinition as blessed or damned. Change understood from within this subjectivity had nothing to do with self-initiated progress, something unfolding from within a developing individual, nor was it seen as a beckoning opportunity toward which to move. Change for this patient was rather understood as a random, crass, destructive erasure of what was.

The patient survived in much the same way prisoners survive—by holding on to an active part of herself (Bettelheim, 1943). She began early in her life to build a self around a hidden nucleus of power and negation. Her earliest childhood memory was of carrying her valued toy china tea set into a hidden spot and "for no reason" impassively smashing a cup. In this act *she* became the agent of destruction. She organized the randomness of experience in this reversal of voice. Identifying with the negating force that had worked against her, she became both victim and destroyer. All the movements of a self developing within the experiential temporal field—affect and desire, hope and memory, curiosity and experimentation—were erased in her self-negating acts. As the agent of her own destruction she tore down what she internally built up. The organization of meaning was complete, she had secured her psychological survival, maintaining her attachments within the structures of her family, as she greeted her own unfolding change with a powerful negating act that was paradoxically a self-assertion.

Identification in the Countertransference

The analyst likewise brings to the psychoanalytic situation a complex subjectivity, a personal system of ordering and establishing meaning, the outcome of his or her history. Racker (1957) described the psychoanalytic situation as "an interaction between two personalities, . . . each personality has its internal and external dependencies, anxieties, pathological defenses; each is also a child with its internal parents; and each of these whole personalities— that of the analysand and that of the analyst—respond to every event of the analytic situation" (p. 308). The analyst and patient are both constituted within their structures of meaning, their differently organized subjective worlds (Atwood and Stolorow, 1984). What occurs in the interaction—the intersubjective field—can be punctuated in a manageable way with either patient or analyst as locus. The transference then is "all the ways in which the patient's experience of the analytic relationship becomes organized according to the configurations of self and object that unconsciously structure his or her subjective universe,'' and the countertransference is ''how the structures of the analyst's subjectivity shape his or her experience of the analytic relationship and in particular of the patient's transference'' (Atwood and Stolorow, 1984, p. 47).

Both patient and analyst seek to maintain their personal psychological survival, a sense of continuity and meaning, an experience of personal cohesion inextricably linked to a world experienced as cohesive. The frequency of countertransference reactions in our work with troubled patients (Searles, 1959) reflects the very real difficulty with which such cohesion is maintained. As an analyst constructed within the structures of the patient's subjectivity, we receive within the transference violently dysjunctive and fluctuating identifications and find ourselves reconstructed maddeningly askew. The patients' experience of themselves reconstructed within the analyst's subjectivity as alien, with new meaning and new identity, is likewise potentially maddening. Such mutual identifications, misidentifications, and reidentifications might be conceptualized as an act of identification that establishes and locates the other ''as.'' The as then positions the other as an object known and defined, related to a self who knows and defines. In this regard such constructions as ''you are a patient'' can be understood to mean ''I who know, identify you as patient.'' Likewise, ''you are angry'' is ''I who know, identify you as angry.'' Within the countertransference this type of identification structures the analyst as ''knower'' and the patient as ''known.'' The patient exists in the analyst's identifications, spoken or unspoken constructions, that know the patient ''as.'' These identifications are the patient's meaning as object and as information known and organized within the analyst's world. For some patients these identifications seemingly rise up as impingements, alien presences on the sudden horizon of what previously was the horizonless field of their own subjectivity.

In the intersubjective field both patient and analyst search for a connection, an entrance into the alien world of the other, an entrance that will allow them to preserve a sense of cohesion, unity, and integrity and yet establish a connection. Personal subjectivity is a nexus of relationships since meaning always takes form in relation to a central self, the spider at the center of the web. Definitions emanate from and are in relationship to the meaning-giving subject. They provide, in a sense, slots or spaces in the world of the subject. By accepting these definitions the object of the definition takes on a relationship to the subject and most importantly is allowed admittance to its world. When the patient accepts the analyst's identification ''I who know identify you as patient'' he or she finds a vacant space within the world of the other in the form of ''I am patient to you who knows me.'' The patient may accept the identification in the service of relatedness and attachment to find a place and be held in the subjective world of the other. The importance of this mutual search for a place in the alien subjectivity of the other cannot be overestimated.

The masochistic patient described here had encountered herself as different and redefined within her previous treatments. Interventions of the type that provided her with "new information," "insights," about herself located her once again as a passive object alien to herself modified by an active knowing other. This information was masochistically assimilated/accommodated and organized within her subjectivity where she remained the victim of powerful redefining forces while violently negating herself. The patient had come to experience herself as a set of totally false yet thoroughly defining relationships imposed by the defining external other. She accepted the definitions of self with a surface compliance as a necessary condition of relatedness, organizing around first her family's and then medically offered definitions and meanings. She became consolidated "as" patient; and after ten years of well-intentioned treatment "as" chronic patient. New information was assimilated by old patterns. Identifications of self and other were masochistically organized as master–definer to slave–defined. The vicious cycle continued.

Identification, however, has a second meaning that might be conceptualized as identification with. While the first type of identification, "identification as," establishes meaning as a link between an object separated from its subject, "identification with" establishes meaning by the consubstantiality of subject and object. Identification as organizes experience divisively, analytically, establishing boundaries, maintaining connections by cognitive acts. Identification with participates in an imaginary world of subjects through correspondence and the fantasy of merger. Identification as announces itself entering boldly through the front door; identification with disguises itself, entering surreptitiously through the back.

It is the analyst's empathic understanding of the material presented by the patient that encourages identification with in the countertransference. Racker distinguishes two types of countertransference identification—concordant identification and complementary identification. Both may be considered as varieties of identification with:

> 1. *Concordant Identification* is based on introjection and projection, or in other terms on the resonance of the exterior and the interior, on the recognition of what belongs to another as one's own ("this part of you is I") and on the equation of what is one's own with what belongs to another ("this part of me is you").
>
> 2. *Complementary Identifications* are produced by the fact that the patient treats the analyst as an internal (projected) object, and in consequence the analyst feels treated as such; that is he identifies himself with this object [1957, p. 312].

In the treatment of the masochistic patient presented here, concordant and complementary countertransference identifications functioned to obscure the boundaries between patient and analyst. The illusion of sameness that this provided concealed the threat of difference from the patient and allowed the analyst to enter the patient's world as a double. The information brought to her in this manner seemed to develop from the inside and was accommodated and assimilated by the patient without the threat of a self-negating discontinuity. But also the analyst introduced modifications since the identifications were based on the analyst's empathically created simulacrum, an imitation of the patient and her world, built from the material available in the analyst's own subjectivity, based on the analyst's own history and experience, populated with characters from the analyst's life. There was a transposition of characters, themes, and places within this reproduction, which for the most part functioned unconsciously as a basis of comprehension, and the transposition included flaws and differences. It was only in retrospect that the analyst understood how her unconscious countertransference identifications with the patient in the recreation of imperfect substitutions functioned advantageously to offer the patient an exit from her perpetually self-negating structures.

Institutional Countertransference Identification

The therapeutic field for the hospitalized patient includes a third subjectivity—that of the institution. The therapeutic hospital, as world, theater, and other takes on observable roles and has an observable interactive impact on the treatment. The situation is very different for an outpatient treatment where the many-voiced reality context is present but is not an active, reflective participant with a voice in the dialogue capable of modifying its actions in response to the psychotherapeutic situation. The institution as superordinate context is a powerful active defining force, not just the passive recipient of projections. Its formative subjectivity shapes the progress, regress, and outcome of the treatment as it holds the analyst and patient within its meaning-giving structures. The institution is continually understanding analyst and patient, is interpreting behavior and defining experience in relation to its own system of meaning. The institutional subjectivity is a conglomerate, a metasubjectivity, the outcome of the institution's history and the history of its individual members. What has been said previously about the subjectivity of patient and analyst can also be said about the institution: that the institution exists in and through the organization of meaning and activity in relation to an institutional self structure or identity; that this institutional self structure is a gradually established configuration, the outcome of a series of syntheses and resyntheses, idiosyncratic but grounded in communal meanings; and that the institution organizes and assimilates/accommodates new experience and change over time in relation to this institutional self schema or identity that seeks to perpetuate and preserve its unity, integrity, and coherence. The institutional subjectivity exists as a nexus of relationships, definitions, self–other representations, images, values, ideals, and ideas. In accepting its definitions analyst and patient take on a relationship within this third subjectivity and are allowed admittance to its world.

If the psychoanalytic field is the intersection of these three subjectivities, something very curious might happen at the points of overlap where analyst, patient, and institution see themselves reconstructed, redefined, and reidentified within two alien subjectivities. This redefinition was described above as the transference and countertransference. It was said that when a patient reidentifies the analyst within the patient's subjectivity in terms of the patient's structures and meaning, this was the patient's transference to the analyst. The analyst's response when running into him- or herself redefined in such alien shape was the analyst's countertransference response. The analyst can also reshape the patient in terms of the analyst's own structures and this again is another type of countertransference restructuring or response. It is important to realize that the institution also has these countertransference reactions to both patient and analyst. The institution finds itself redefined and given new meaning in relation to either analyst or patient in terms of each of their subjectivities. The institution is capable of experiencing reactions to the continual flux of these redefinitions and reidentifications. The checks and balances built into the therapeutic hospital, the forums for institutional self-scrutiny, are necessary precautions monitoring such formative and potentially disruptive reactions. The institution has its characteristic pathological and healthy defenses, its periods of depression and elation, its bouts of unwarranted optimism and pessimism. The institution can be pathologically anxious, guilty, or ashamed in relation to its internalized ideals, irrational fears, and degraded or inflated self-images. In short, the institution has a complex subjectivity, a whole personality that responds to every event of the analytic situation.

The institution's countertransference identifications include the two types mentioned above, "identification as" and "identification with." In the act of identification as the institution establishes and locates analyst and patient "as," positioning them as objects known and defined in relation to an institutional self that knows and defines. This type of identification is a particularly powerful and binding act on the part of the institution, most often unexamined and unacknowledged. From the moment the patient is accepted by the institution, the idiosyncratic individual, now patient, has in a sense passed over into the alien subjectivity of the institution and is continually struggling against the subsuming identification as patient. This works for and against the treatment. It works for the treatment in that it consolidates and organizes the often fragmented and disavowed aspects of the troubled individual into a particular, cohesive identity "as" patient. This can be a necessary, temporary, curative procedure. Much as the shaman and patient come together to shape experience around an agreed on imaginary disease object or cause that is later banished, the institution's identification of the troubled individual "as" patient functions to give form to a formless turbulence. The identification as patient works against the treatment in several ways, but most importantly for this inquiry it functions to impose an external definition, an iatrogenic sense of self or identity, on an individual who is powerless to resist since the very existence of the patient as patient within the institution is proof of the definition. Within the institution there is seemingly no space within which to not be "patient." The masochistic patient found herself once again in a familiar world of defining masters and defined slaves. From within the patient's subjectivity this one act of the institution—its power to define her "as"—was a resonant link between their subjectivities allowing her to assimilate rigidly the new experience to the old structures. She saw herself once again imprisoned within the shameful definitions of external others, asserting her resistance in her self-negating acts of chronic despair and destructive immobility.

Another aspect of an institutional subjectivity or metasubjectivity is that it is extremely slow-changing and conservative. Like the "spirit of an age" or "Weltanschauung" or "culture," it is a difficult to locate but nonetheless operative current organizing the group experience. Its conservative nature is expressed in the tenacity of its images and beliefs and is possibly due to the sheer mass of the conglomerate. The identifications of a group subjectivity stick. As any school child knows, the "sissy" stays identified as "sissy" in the group's conglomerate mind with all the meanings and stigma. To escape from the bonds of that structure is no mean feat, requiring impressive acts of heroics that appear to exist with some frequency in movies but rarely in life. The therapeutic institution is continually challenged to examine its identifications and modify its images of self and other. The institutional resistance, disequilibrium, and distress that this causes should not be underestimated just because change is the manifest goal of the treatment. All the participants in the therapeutic hospital "want the patient to get better." Nonetheless freedom and a release from the pathological definitions of "patienthood," "diagnosis," and theory, is never given. It is probably more accurate to say that freedom is not really theirs to give. The intersubjective field is after all an inside–outside where all participants find themselves rewoven on the looms of the other. To undo an "identification as" requires an assertion of separateness, an unraveling of a relationship with its securing attachment. The violence of this act of individuation—the fight to escape the structures of the other—can be understood in relation to the strength, ambivalence, and embedded nature of the attachment. Everyone is familiar with the turbulent revolutions of adolescence. The adolescent fights to break the inside–outside shackles of family/culture/class, the organizing structures that exist in the intermediate space within which the individual is constituted. No one is given this type of freedom; it has to be fought for and won. There are very real casualties in this intra- and interpsychic fight as the statistics for adolescent death testify. There is no release from the organizing definitions of the other without intense emotion, struggle, and inevitable feelings of guilt, loss, anxiety, and a sense of personal ruthlessness.

The masochistic patient discussed in this chapter developed within a family that insisted on dependence on a family unit that saw itself as the only safe harbor in a paranoid sea of hostile foreign others. Although the mother was inconsistently present, her very inconsistency made the dyadic tie even greater. The family strongly discouraged the patient's attempts at individuation. Things were understood and seen "their way." As a family they had their own language, their own jokes, their own exclusive history. They taunted the patient when she experimented timidly with trying on bits and pieces of friends outside of the family. When she "talked like her teacher at school" or acted like someone else it was immediately spotted, laughed at, and discouraged. Further, the intense affects associated with separation, the aggression, personal ruthlessness, guilt, loss, and anxiety were intolerable. Conformity and solidarity were the only feasible solutions. The father's absence, the repeated moves, the continual experience of alienation in relation to the world of social reality augmented the dependency. After all, does one really fight to leave a family only to attain a frightening exile? That was the patient's understanding of freedom lived out now in her contented internment as a patient. She had found a familiar home in the subjectivity of the institution and had no plans to leave.

The institution's countertransference identifications include the tendency to "identify with" aspects of the patient's subjectivity. In the intersubjective field of patient, analyst, and institution there is a resonance of sameness, a recognition that what belongs to another is one's own (Racker, 1957). The institution also finds itself treated by the patient according to the patient's structures and meanings, treated as an internal (projected) object (Racker, 1957), and as such identifies with the object and behaves like that object. The patient formed an intense dyadic attachment to the institution, which she perceived as an authoritarian, punitive, safe, defining parent. This was the patient's transference to the institution. The institution knew all, protected her, demanded nothing of her but compliance, saw the world as dangerous but inferior, saw her as vulnerable and at risk, would discourage attempts at separation, and so on. In the institution's countertransference identification with the internal structures of the patient it behaved as such. Just as a psychotherapeutic dyad functions as a circumscribed space where enactments allow for the potential of knowing (Khan, 1969), the institutional space is also a powerful medium for potential enactments. The ability, however, to understand, intervene, and interpret institutionally is severely limited. The potential for a vicious cycle of enactments at the institutional level is a continual problem for the treatment, since such unconscious mutual resonant identifications support the masochistic solution and the status quo.

The institutional tendency to conserve what is and the patient's need to maintain self cohesion through enactments that recreate familiar structures perpetuate rigid dyadic configurations by excluding the third. The ability of the dyad to collapse the third into its binary patterns of meaning is an expression of the stabilizing weight of the past as it presses on dangerous disorganizing future possibilities. If a world is constructed solely out of dyads, master to slave, self to other, us to them, the third exists as an absent possibility. The problem of the missing third is everywhere apparent in the developmental history of the patient and in the history of the treatment. Most simply understood the third is the agent of separation. As the "father" of separation–individuation, the third facilitates the movement of the child out of the mother–child dyad toward the triadic world of separation, agency, and distance. The third is the advocate of change and dimensionality. The third offers a vista as opposed to a lap. The third opens a door, and therein lies the possibility and the threat. In the masochistically constructed subjectivity it is exceedingly difficult to introduce the presence of an active third. It is always being collapsed into existing structures of master or slave, self or other. The triad, patient–analyst–institution, becomes dyad—patient–analyst to institution, or patient to analyst–institution, or analyst to institution–patient. In other words, in the patient's transference the analyst and institution are one. They are the definer, the enslaver, the one who knows, and the patient is victim, defined, known. The institutional countertransference tends to collapse analyst into patient addressing the analyst as patient in a way that closely parallels and duplicates the dyad established in the analytic situation of analyst and patient. The analyst receiving this identification easily slips into the role of patient in his relationship with the institution, acting out of his countertransference identification with the patient a masochistic relationship with the institution as victim. The institution, however, can also identify with the patient's anxiety and become the vulnerable victim in relation to the analyst seen as the powerful disruptive representative of change.

The question "how does change occur?" can be restated as "how does one introduce a third into a dyadic universe without becoming immediately assimilated into an existing dyadic structure?" How do you open a door? How do you modify a structure without becoming a part of that structure in ways that simply perpetuate its old rules? How can the therapeutic participants function within the intersubjective field maintaining the efficacy, cohesion, and integrity of their own structures in the presence of alien projections and resonant counteridentifications? The answer in the case of this treatment is somewhat surprising since it appears to have used the confusion of the countertransference identifications and misidentifications to advantage. The confusion in identities seems to have allowed the analyst to function somewhat like a double agent moving between the subjectivity of institution and patient, past and present, cloaked in the misidentifications. Disguised as a double the analyst introduced subtle variations into the structure, modifications in the enactments that gradually lead to change.

Identification, Substitution, and Change:
A Countertransference Fantasy

When a countertransference position (Racker, 1957) passes into an articulated countertransference fantasy something in the nature of the therapeutic situation has already changed. The embedded nature of the intersubjective structuring of experience has passed from unconscious enactment or empathic, intuitive participation into the symbolic and recollectable. The empathic identification with, which in itself implied the unconscious fantasy of merger, has begun to give way to conscious experiences of difference and strangeness. The patient who seemed so familiar and understandable, now seems "different," "three dimensional," "her own person" in ways that seemingly have nothing to do with analyst or treatment. By the time the analyst reported the following countertransference fantasy the patient had successfully left the hospital after three and a half years of inpatient treatment. She held a job, attended college, lived in her own apartment, had a boyfriend, and continued her treatment as an outpatient.

Analyst and institution must accommodate to change even as the patient must accommodate to change. As the treatment moves toward termination, change redefines all participants, raising personal questions about meaning, actions, and self definitions in the face of loss. This requires a working through for institution and analyst, which is rarely talked about. The remembering that accompanies any loss, the review of the history of a relationship, is part of the attempted restructuring of a world with one of its previous members now missing. The analyst's countertransference fantasy was her retrospective review of the treatment. It was her attempt to solve something. For our purpose, it suggests an answer to the question "how did change occur."

During a session the analyst had the fantasy that, disguised as the patient, she had taken her place within the institution. Disguised as the patient but with the knowledge of an analyst, she had forced the institution to release her. This fantasy had happened after the patient had already been discharged from the hospital, and the analyst was puzzled about its meaning. She realized in her retelling of this fantasy that it was actually based on a Hasidic tale that she had read some time ago and only later remembered. Since it is so relevant to the treatment the actual story will be quoted in full and is as follows:

Why the Rabbi Learned to Dance
    The Spoler grandfather told the following experience of his youth:
    Once he arrived in a small town and learned that a nearby Polish Count had jailed a Jew for debt. He learned also that it was the Count's custom to compel his victims to dance at a ball he held on his birthday. If the prisoner danced satisfactorily, he was freed; otherwise he was returned to the dungeon. The Rabbi resolved to free the Jew, securing a dancing instructor, and soon became very proficient. On the night of the ball, he crept to the dungeon and succeeded in entering the basement. Soon he heard the groans of the poor Jew and prevailed upon him to change clothes when the opportunity came. The Rabbi carefully enlarged the hole through which food was passed to the prisoner and thus the exchange was made.
    When the Count's servants arrived to take the prisoner to the ball, the real victim walked out into the basement, and the Rabbi stepped forward. The deception was unnoticed in the dim light. The Rabbi was brought to the ball, where he was ordered to don a dried bear skin. He was told that if he failed to perform the correct steps he would be beaten. . .the Rabbi danced masterfully and was released.
    The grandfather remained an excellent dancer his whole life [Newman, 1963, p. 66].

The story itself is exceedingly interesting. It comes out of the masochistically organized world of victims and powerful masters, the climate of desperation and misery, of mideighteenth century Polish Hasidic Jews. As an enigmatic religious parable of inner and outer power relations, it teaches the release of prisoners, the hopeless and defined, through substitution—identifications that are actually self transcendent self modifications within unmodifiable relationships, and the use of what we would call the manic defense. The self modification (prisoner now dancing Rabbi) accounts for the change, a change that is enacted within the dyad master–slave, a change in defensive style, a change in the relationship of the internal objects, self to other, a change that permits the slave seemingly to accept the misidentification of the other while knowing inside he is not that at all. We might question the integrity of such a freedom that leaves the worldly inequality in the power structure unchanged. But a religious solution, although lacking the satisfaction of the Hegelian, or Marxist political solution to the master–slave dilemma, might in fact be more relevant to psychological structures than we might like to admit.

   In the fantasy the analyst sees herself as the rescuer, as the agent of change. She also understands that change is an event in a dramatic field of players that must happen from within that field. She must find an entrance. She does not lead a cavalry charge to rescue the prisoner from outside, nor does she appear as herself or as an alien rescuer to negotiate the release. Such activity would obviously be doomed. Disguised as the prisoner, cloaked in the transference–countertransference identifications she instead substitutes herself in the dyad of master–slave. She brings her new information into the old structures through her identification with the patient. Through a variation rather than a new theme she changes the patient's relationship to the activity of self-identification.

   When the patient began treatment at our hospital she was rigidly self-negating and immobilized. All new information seen as alien to the self was experienced as persecutory impingements that she rapidly negated. She began working with a young female analyst who, like the patient, was also from a large, Catholic family. The similarities between patient and analyst were in some ways striking. The countertransference concordant identifications appeared to help organize and give continuity to the patient's precarious sense of self. The analyst was a gentle, calm woman who seemed totally at ease with the patient's refusals and comfortable in her own relationship with the institution. She was in no hurry and quietly bore witness to the patient's need to "just be." It was a new relationship for the patient, a new way of being with one's self that was nonanxious, accepting, compassionate, utterly consistent, and nonimpinging. It was the identification with the unconscious resonance between patient and analyst that allowed the patient to assimilate and accommodate the new experience as nonpersecutory. In the therapeutic dyad the structural deficit of her early object ties was slowly being reworked as she developed her own internally arising self-definitions through the consonant mutual identifications of and with her analyst. Through the addition of something new, simple variations began to enlarge the range and complexity of the patient's self structure. The patient later referred to this therapy as "a house" within which to safely dwell. Two and a half years into the treatment the patient's analyst became pregnant and later took a maternity leave of absence. This was an exceedingly difficult time for the patient, a potentially destructive redefining change over which she had no control. But by this time she had sufficiently developed to allow a new response to this unanticipated change.

   The patient responded by choosing to transfer to another analyst permanently rather than waiting masochistically for hers to return. The option to change analysts in consultation with the Director of Psychotherapy is open to all patients at our hospital. In this way a repeat of a masochistic scenario was not inevitable, there were choices and options. The patient felt vaguely that there were things that *she* wanted to work on, her own agenda, and although she could not articulate exactly what they might be, *she* had chosen a new analyst whom she felt could best help her locate them. She was angry and hurt by her previous analyst's pregnancy, but aside from that was able to state clearly in her consultation that the pregnancy imposed a theme on her treatment and she wanted desperately to discover her own themes. She said that she was not just empty and envious, but she did not know whatever was inside of her that was hers and special. Like an adolescent she was trying now to separate by looking outside of the family for new identifications. Unlike her own family, which obstructed all attempts at identification outside the family, the institution allowed her this freedom.

The patient had chosen to work with a second female analyst, one who was quite different from her previous analyst, and seemingly quite different from the patient herself. Their defensive styles, strategies, attitudes, how they defined and negotiated power relationships, their historical backgrounds, their physical presence were all manifestly different. There was, however, a similarity between patient and analyst, a similarity later expressed in the analyst's countertransference fantasy of being the patient's rescuing double. Patient and analyst both organized experience in terms of masochistic structures in characteristic patterns of oppressors and oppressed, masters and slaves. The analyst's relation to the defining other, however, was different from the patient's and had developed within the subjectivity of a Jewish family that had structured the destructive events of its history in terms of victimization, but with a different response. Where the patient met the destructive misidentifications of the powerful other with a depressive–paranoid compliance, immobility, and self-erasure, the analyst, on the other hand, responded with a manic optimism, motion, self affirmation, and overt oppositionalism. While concordant countertransference identifications were important in the patient's treatment with her first analyst, complementary countertransference identifications functioned with the second.

For example, when the second analyst began working with the patient, the patient would have long periods of grim, deathlike muteness. The patient would sit frozen during her sessions with a heavy depressive paralysis. In the silence the analyst had the notion that the patient was duplicating in the transference a way of being with her internal objects. The patient was structuring her experience in terms of characteristic shapes and patterns, the old rules that organized her world. The patient was treating the analyst like a projected internal object, and in consequence the analyst identified with that object. The analyst suspected that she was receiving the projected self representation of the patient herself and that the patient was treating her the way she had been treated by her grim, irritable, silent father. The analyst did, however, choose not to interpret this. Rather, she readily accepted the projected role of victim and abandoned daughter but unconciously shaped it based on the material of her own subjectivity. The analyst, now merged as victim–daughter, did not

merely passively accept the silent father–daughter relationship. Speaking
as the projected self representation, the analyst presented the patient with
a new way of relating to one's abandoning objects. The analyst, acting in
the countertransference, told the patient that maybe she thought the analyst
was interested in death, but that she was not. Actually the analyst was more
interested in life, and if the patient did not have something to say maybe
she should leave and come back when she did. The analyst said that she
was not going to be held hostage by the patient's silence.

And in relation to the institution: when the patient began working with
her new analyst she had not only left an analyst but had also recently made
the decision to move across the courtyard from the patients' hospital
residence to a small, minimally supervised patient group home. This was
a self-initiated, redefining change that she immediately regretted. She once
again experienced an internally arising impulse for separation and change
as an external persecutory redefining annihilation of what was. She became quite anxious and inconsolable in a public way, began actively
speaking and worrying about suicide, and severely cut her legs with a razor
blade.

The patient's new analyst, who was in favor of the patient's desire
to move, found herself suddenly as the only one who thought it possible.
Through the institution's contact with the patient (through nursing staff
who reported daily on the patient's anxiety and preoccupation with suicide,
and through the analyst's supervision) the institution was becoming enlisted in an enactment that would support the patient's masochistic solutions. The enactment was prompted by the potentially disorganizing loss
of her familiar structures and would give cohesion to both self and other
and reinstate the status quo. The fact that the movement toward change
and the concomitant anxiety were originally located within the patient
herself was forgotten as analyst and institution identified with various
aspects of the patient's dyadic world, aspects that unconsciously reso-
nated with their own system of beliefs and images. The patient in the
meantime had seemingly absented herself from the conflict as others now
enacted in the countertransference the struggle for her.

In the daily morning conference the clinical administration expressed
the opinion that the patient should return to the twenty-four-hour hospital
facility. The analyst opposed that opinion and informed the staff why she
thought this to be an error. The analyst in her unconscious countertransference identification with the patient as victim spoke to an institution
whom she misidentified as an oppressor. She spoke for the patient in the
voice of the victim but a different victim, an advocate of change, a dancer
who knew the required steps, who collided head-on with the definitions
she felt were being imposed on her. The analyst was aware that she felt
the institution to be misidentifying the patient's pathology. She was aware
of a distorted intensity of emotion around her desire to ''release the
patient,'' but also felt the institution was overly anxious and rigidly

focused on symptomatology and genetic reconstruction, which only supported an encrusted chronic patient identity from which the patient "needed to be freed." The patient in her transference to the institution treated the institution as a powerful defining conservative parental other to which she was passive. The institution now spoke out of this countertransference identification with the internal objects of the patient's world. Speaking out of this role the institution felt that the patient "was vulnerable and at risk," that there was "no need to hurry," that there was "more slow and interpretive work still to be done," that the institution needed to protect the patient. Various members of the staff interpreted that the analyst was "colluding with the patient and enacting a ruthless destruction of the previous analyst and therapy." They said that "this could only lead to guilt and thus the suicidality of the patient." The analyst accepted this and said that she "supported and acknowledged to them and to the patient the necessary ruthlessness and inevitable guilt that is part of any healthy separation and movement of any sort, especially for a patient whose mother had appropriated her body." The outcome of this complex dialogue was that the patient remained in the halfway house and did not return to the twenty-four-hour facility.

This is but one example of the ongoing dialogue between the participants. The dialogue functioned on many levels simultaneously, conscious and unconscious, and was based on distortions as well as accurate clinical judgments. The participants maintained their integrity and their identities while simultaneously acting within the dyadic unconscious countertransference identifications. In this case it worked to the advantage of the treatment. Certainly in others it can work to its disadvantage. It does, however, suggest that modifications in a patient's subjectivity occur in a complex fashion over time in relation to important transference and countertransference identifications. Subtle variations and new behaviors were allowed to enter the system as a resonant identity with the existing structure. The impressive changes this masochistic patient accomplished in the restructuring of her life had to do with the slow modifications introduced through the interaction of institution, analyst, and patient as they struggled to see and adjust to each other within the identifications of overlapping worlds.

The patient's sense of self was embedded in a frozen universe of meaning. The cohesion of self and other was maintained at the expense of change and motion, structuring the experiential field of flux into rigid patterns of victimization. Self affirmation was expressed through the reversal that borrowed the destructive power of the other to define, to erase, and to negate. The analyst introduced movement from another universe of meaning into this system. She taught the patient a self affirmation in relation to the imprisoning definitions of the other by denying the power of the identifications while seemingly acting from within them.

References

Atwood, G., & Stolorow, R. (1984), *Structures of Subjectivity: Explorations in Psychoanalytic Phenomenology*. Hillsdale, N.J.: Analytic Press.

Bettelheim, B. (1943), Individual and mass behavior in extreme situations. *J. Abnorm. Soc. Psychol.*, 38:417–452.

Erikson, E. H. (1956), Identity and the life cycle. *Psychological Issues*, Monograph 1, Vol.1, No.1. New York: International Universities Press.

Ginsburg, H., & Opper, S. (1969), *Piaget's Theory of Intellectual Development, An Introduction*. Englewood Cliffs, N.J.: Prentice-Hall.

Khan, M. (1969), Vicissitudes of being, knowing, and experiencing in the therapeutic situation. In: *The Privacy of the Self*. New York: International Universities Press, 1978, pp. 203–218.

Klein, G. (1976), *Psychoanalytic Theory—An Exploration of Essentials*. New York: International Universities Press.

Montgomery, J. (1988), Chronic patienthood as an iatrogenic false self. In: *The Facilitating Environment: Clinical Applications of Winnicott's Theory*, eds. M. G. Fromm & B. L. Smith. New York: International Universities Press.

Newman, L. I. (1963), *Hasidic Anthology*. New York: Schocken Books.

Piaget, J. (1950), *The Psychology of Intelligence*, trans. M. Percy & D. E. Berlyne. London: Routledge & Kegan Paul.

——— (1952), *The Origins of Intelligence in Children*, trans. M. Cook. New York: International Universities Press.

——— (1954), *The Construction of Reality in the Child*, trans. M. Cook. New York: Basic Books.

Racker, H. (1957), The meaning and uses of countertransference. *Psychoanal. Quart.*, 26:303–357.

Searles, H. F. (1959), The effort to drive the other person crazy—An element in the aetiology and psychotherapy of schizophrenia. In: *Collected Papers on Schizophrenia and Related Subjects*. New York: International Universities Press, 1965, pp. 254–283.

Shafer, R. (1976), *A New Language for Psychoanalysis*. New Haven & London: Yale University Press.

Winnicott, D. W. (1951), Transitional objects in transitional phenomena. In: *Through Paediatrics to Psychoanalysis*. New York: Basic Books, 1975, pp. 229–242.

13

Challenges to the Holding Environment: Treatment Crises in the Psychoanalytic Hospital

Jill D. Montgomery, Ph.D.

The clinical work presented in this volume took place within a particular context—an open, long-term, inpatient psychoanalytic hospital. The hospital is located in a rather picturesque rural setting. It is open in that there are no passes, no locked wards or seclusion rooms, no privileges to be earned, or hierarchy of levels of functioning. All patients have the same rights and privileges, come and go as they please, and participate as equal members in a democratic, patient-run community. They may also, however, choose not to participate, since attendance and participation are not imposed. The dimensions of this environment are interpersonal and psychological as well as material. Its structures exist in space (the old attractive buildings, the large trees, and mountain vistas), and as images, mental representations, notions, and ideas held in mind by patients and staff. All aspects of this complex setting of people and things participate in the treatment in that they have meaning and organize and communicate to the patient a certain sense of being. They are the "holding environment" (Winnicott, 1960; Modell, 1976). Although the treat-

Acknowledgments. This study was conducted with the assistance of my colleague Dr. Ann Greif. The author also wishes to acknowledge Dr. Daniel P. Schwartz, Dr. Martin Cooperman, and Dr. Ess A. White, whose clinical philosophy and leadership was expressed in the data from which this study was drawn.

ment philosophy stresses the centrality of the analyst–patient dyad as the agent of change—patient and analyst meet four or five times a week—the therapeutic hospital (clinicians, clinical administrators, nurses, and patient community) forms a superordinate context. Psychopathology as well as the possibility for change exist in the actions—external behaviors and internal representations—that unfold over time within the multiplicity of these interrelationships.

The patients presented in this book all had long histories of previous treatment and long-standing problems in living. They brought to the hospital their masochistically organized representational worlds (Sandler and Rosenblatt, 1962), the patterns that unconsciously organized and gave meaning to their perceptions and within which they were constituted. The hospital offered a potential space for the examination of that which was being prereflectively (Atwood and Stolorow, 1984) lived out by the patients. Since the masochistic organization of their lives was made up of archaic self–other configurations involving brutality, victimization, violence, destruction, pain, despair, bondage, and hopelessness, enactments within the hospital would also potentially involve these elements. The possibility of life-threatening and lethal behavior, stagnation and stalemate, the destruction of the patient's own treatment and the treatment of others were very real problems. These treatments were difficult and crises were inevitable.

The reasons for the crises were manifold, but for the analyst the fact that one was in a crisis was impossible to ignore. The call for a review of the treatment most often came from outside the analyst–patient dyad. Someone else within the hospital would call a crisis, and often the analyst, so immersed in the transference–countertransference ebb and flow, felt caught unaware, accused or attacked or intruded upon by that fact. It appeared that by the very nature of the therapeutic process with these masochistically organized patients those things that could not yet be integrated in words in the analytic relationship were extruded and occurred first in a chaotic and destructive manner in the outside world (Daniel P. Schwartz, personal communication). They were then brought into the therapeutic interaction by external forces. These external forces had to overcome the resistance of analyst and patient. This is a different understanding of the term *acting out* than is usually implied.

The crises occurred as complex states marked by external behaviors and internal experiences. Either the disintegration of the treatment frame spread circles of chaotic behavior throughout the therapeutic community or there was impasse and stagnation. The personal experience was one of isolation, confusion, hopelessness, and rage. Although for the analyst there was a distinct sense of alienation, in truth all the therapeutic participants shared in the turmoil and distress.

Treatment Crises

Jeannine

Jeannine was a tall, ungainly, prim, young schizophrenic woman. Long-suffering, she postured in a saintlike martyrdom. Self-effacing, rigid, plain, and retiring, she was a peripheral figure to the patient community. She did not provoke envy or competition; her psychosis was so quiet, her rituals so private, that she avoided staff concern and patient provocations. She presented herself in and out of therapy as a "nice," devoutly Christian woman. There was little direct expression of sexual or aggressive feelings, wishes, desires, anxiety, fantasy, or conflict. There had been much evidence, however, from her psychological test records and past overtly delusional states, of an interior experience of much confusion and emotional dedifferentiation. Her therapist was a tall, soft-spoken, middle-aged married man. An experienced clinician and researcher, he was a quiet and thoughtful man who was not given to speaking in open forums. In the treatment he was beginning to feel some frustration around Jeannine's stilted façade of compliance and "niceness." In contrast his two other patients were turbulent schizophrenics, often in trouble with the hospital, one an obstreperous alcoholic male, and the other a young, sexually provocative woman.

A year or so into the treatment at the hospital, Jeannine became the focus of attention, an added burden to her therapist who was already overburdened with two publicly problematic patients. Jeannine began making morning reports—the daily assembly of nurses, therapists, and clinical administrators, including the Medical Director, Assistant Medical Director, and so on. Jeannine was disorganized. She was loud and public, now overtly psychotic, and needed to be watched constantly. The patients and nursing staff took turns "specialing" her. Jeannine, however, was ungrateful. The biggest problem, the thing that seemed hardest to bear, was her new, flagrant sexuality. She repeatedly threatened to expose her naked body in public; she was preoccupied by sex, taunting other patients; and in what seemed to be her least tolerable behavior she openly exposed the secret sexual liaisons within the hospital between different patients.

In the Morning Conference the nurses asked for direction. The clinical administration began to ask the therapist to comment on the treatment. The patient community meanwhile in their forums began to complain and then to insist that something be done. Jeannine was suddenly being talked about—patient to patient, patients to their therapists, therapist to therapist—and people began to develop their own theories. While Jeannine was alienating herself from the patient community and becoming a focus for scapegoating and pressures towards extrusion, her therapist found himself the target of more questions. The patient–analyst dyad was simultaneously more exposed and more alienated. Within this context theories and suggested interventions multiplied.

Jeannine's behavior continued to escalate over a six-week period, exhausting the usual avenues of support, until finally she set fire to a pile of tampons and papers at the foot of her bed.

Donald

Donald was a schizophrenic patient. Although he was a large, handsome young man he managed to present himself as an object to be scorned and mocked. He had come into treatment with many grandiose delusions about becoming president of the United States and outdoing his powerful, upper-class father, despite his apparent inability to work at anything for any length of time. He was preoccupied with what he considered to be his defective penis, which he believed had been permanently damaged by a previous physician. He was a sad young man whose vestigial boarding school "preppy" identity was giving way progressively to the stereopathy of schizophrenia. Time was running out for him. He verged on a deteriorated appearance that did not quite fit. He was provocative, a snob, a bigot, and "a sexist" in the midst of a female-dominated patient community. Needless to say he remained relatively isolated except for a few male friends. For the most part he stayed away from the women in the community.

According to Donald, he was always getting "fucked" and "shafted." He took no personal responsibility for his problems but saw himself as the victim of circumstances. In his treatment he had been recalcitrant and argumentative with his therapist. As the treatment progressed Donald became quite fond of his young therapist, a large, powerfully built Midwestern man. Donald grew a beard similar to his therapist's and in many ways displayed his growing attachment.

One day, two years into the treatment, Donald physically attacked an older psychotic female patient. He had no history of physical assaultiveness prior to coming to the hospital, being most often the object of attack himself. On the day of the attack he had made an unsuccessful attempt to get the patient community to move a television out of a common room and have it replaced by a piano, which he enjoyed playing. This thwarting of his rarely seen initiative seemed to lead directly to the incident with the female patient, a chronic, schizophrenic woman who had been at the hospital for many years. Donald had gone to this patient's room to ask her to lower the volume on her television set. When he had asked her to turn the television down, she said something about "not catering to your neuroses" and slammed the door. Donald then kicked her door several times, breaking his wooden clog on it. He returned to his own room. The female patient burst from her room yelling and screaming that she would refer him to Task, a patient community judicial group that handles social problems within the community. Donald stood inarticulate and then charged her, in his words "like charging the pitcher's mound." He pushed her to the floor. A male nurse was on the scene and separated Donald from the screaming woman patient who was not physically hurt.

The female patients were uncharacteristically united now in their moral outrage. The incident seemed to crystallize the male–female split in the patient community with the healthier articulate females against the more regressed inarticulate males. The women demanded Donald's immediate discharge. The nurses were anxious and voiced their concern about the "appropriateness of this patient." An assault by a psychotic male patient within an open setting is viewed as an ominous occurrence in the therapy. A growing threat of assaultiveness is an indication that a treatment may not be able to continue in an open setting. Positive change and a growing attachment elicit turbulent affects that it is hoped are containable within the patient–analyst relationship. For the therapist the experience was that something of terrible importance was about to be destroyed and that an action needed to occur rapidly if the treatment was to be salvaged and this precarious patient spared another treatment failure.

Janet

Janet, a young woman diagnosed as borderline, considered herself to be an incurable mess with suicide as the only remedy. She hated herself and hated her therapist who had "trapped" her for several years now in a turbulent therapy from which she felt there was no escape. She had had several psychotherapies prior to her admission, all of which had proved unsuccessful in alleviating her anxiety, abandonment fears, recurrent hypochondriacal concerns about her body, and commitment to patienthood as an identity. Her most intense attachments had been to male therapists by whom she felt chronically abused and to whom she was chronically abusing. Janet's treatment had foundered repeatedly around her therapist's vacations. Her therapist, an attractive, recently married man, weathered her repeated assaults in connection with his comings and goings, her vitriolic attacks questioning his sanity, training, and motives, her suicidal gestures—dramatic but not life threatening, her demands for a change of therapist, and her public declarations of his incompetence. But the treatment seemed to survive and all of the above seemed more or less predictable, not indicative of crisis, understandable, and part of their ongoing work, since she continued to make significant change. During nonvacation periods Janet felt quite safe in her working attachment to her therapist.

However, during and immediately following a vacation two years into the treatment Janet appeared to "up the ante." While her therapist was away she sought consultation with a very prominent psychiatrist who was also her referring doctor to the hospital. She did not inform anyone at the hospital that she was having this consultation. Janet presented herself to this doctor once again as the abused victim both of her current therapist and of the prestigious doctor's own bad referral. She vividly described her unimproved state, and to her surprise after their brief interview he agreed and also denied that he had ever recommended referral to the hospital, now advising her to seek treatment in a different setting. In her first session after her therapist's return, she reported the consultation and a dream in which she found her favorite teddy bear shredded into pieces because her mother had failed to protect it adequately.

The day after reporting this dream Janet broke into her therapist's office and took from his desk her own folder containing his therapy notes. In explaining her actions, Janet said her plan was to prove true her fantasy that the record would contain hatred and ridicule, and then commit suicide. Janet was surprised to discover neither hatred nor ridicule but thoughtful reflections on her therapy and a sense that her therapist cared for her.

The therapist was very angry with Janet and declared a suspension "of their therapeutic contract" despite continuing to meet with her. He declared that the treatment was in crisis and that it had received "a major assault." In this crisis, it was atypically the therapist who requested a staff Clinical Review of the treatment. He was forthright about feeling very angry and told Janet "that it was up to each of them to decide whether they wished to continue the therapy and whether this continuation was possible." Janet in the meantime continued to work at a job she held outside of the hospital and dated several young men from town, but developed a new eating symptom of self-induced vomiting.

Lillian

Lillian, a voluptuous, tall, strikingly attractive, twenty-six-year-old woman who was diagnosed as a histrionic personality disorder, was "cranking up again," but this time her behavior was affecting the entire community in and out of the hospital. A sure indication of trouble for the therapist occurred when members of the staff at Morning Conference mistakenly called Lillian's female therapist by Lillian's name instead of her own. Lillian was a problem, but a well-liked one. People became attached to her, despite the seemingly foolish antics that left her in dangerous situations, despite the blatant advertisement of her perverse masochistic sexuality, and even despite her cruelty and provocations of psychotic male patients. Her ideal, she explained, was to live as Zelda and F. Scott Fitzgerald had lived. She also thought that she might become a *Playboy* centerfold. In any event she expected she "would die young, probably in a violent and sexual way." Lillian was a binge drinker and therefore she believed "not an alcoholic." Her attachments were stormy as she went from college to college, repeatedly rescued financially by her emotionally uninvolved father.

Her last binge found Lillian dressed in her mother's skintight, low-cut, electric blue jumpsuit creating a commotion in our small, conservative, New England town. She fell down a flight of stairs, made scenes in quiet local restaurants, crashed her sports car on Main Street, and was found in the evening in the patient's common room passionately embracing the toothbrush of a young schizophrenic male patient who had locked himself in his bathroom and was screaming. Her behavior was not only endangering her own treatment but that of several other patients who were becoming psychotically agitated in relation to her.

Paradoxically, almost everyone felt that the treatment of this turbulent and uncontainable woman had been going well. Lillian valued her new attachments, especially her therapist. She considered the hospital a home, and she longed to be able to make a life for herself. But the community had come to the end of its rope. The focus of the outrage was more on Lillian's sexuality than her obvious alcoholism. This led the therapist, who felt that she had to maintain control of the treatment, to state angrily that the issue was more "the hospital's countertransferential response to the disturbing impact of Lillian's sexuality and female sexuality in general rather than a more disinterested concern for the treatment." The therapist added that she noticed that the "delinquent and sexual behavior of male patients did not cause as much administrative concern." People fought about Lillian. The staff now insisted that her behavior was "no longer tolerable."

Jeffrey

Jeffrey always announced his psychotherapy sessions. A southern Californian, an identity not easily missed by others, he roller-skated down the hallway to his female therapist's office singing loudly. He was a late adolescent in love. Jeffrey's long history of abuse and neglect had the additional malignant feature of heavy illicit drug use beginning at the age of eleven. His street life was marked by violence, prostitution, and suicide attempts. His explosive violence alternated with suicidal states of despair. One year into his treatment he began using street drugs in an overt and destructive way. He formed an alliance with a regressed, paranoid, schizophrenic male patient and started sharing his street drugs with him. Jeffrey had managed to make some friends in the patient community, although he remained in an oppositional and isolated position trying primarily to win friends through his car and illicit drugs. He flaunted his "badness." He formed an "outlaw" group of male patients, boycotting the patient community and their judicial groups. He set himself apart as a powerful leader defined by his opposition.

During this period, at Morning Conference his therapist expressed her growing anxiety over his seductive and menacing behavior in her office. He had brought in his guitar to sing to her, and she responded with an interpretation that suggested that his amorous attachment had a defensive function. He was instantly enraged, threatened to kill her, and exploded out of the office. Things rapidly deteriorated. He requested a change of therapist but never took the initiative to do anything about this. The patient community requested his car keys, because they were concerned about his driving. He refused medication and was approached by his therapist about his treatment being in jeopardy. He stated that he felt murderous toward her and that he wanted her to assume responsibility for his feelings. After several sessions in which he was agitated and volatile, he stopped coming and began to be more threatening and hateful with both staff and patients. He was acutely psychotic and, although he reluctantly agreed to begin taking antipsychotic medication, his behavior continued to be agitated.

Edward

Edward's near fatal suicide attempt was not anticipated. It was only in the Clinical Review of Edward's treatment that the appearance of his inexorable, relentless movement to suicide as the only remaining option was retrospectively discussed. The treatment impasse had gone unnoticed and unnamed. The struggle between therapist and patient, so painfully intense and hidden, had contracted to include only the space of the office in which both parties fought daily to survive psychologically the 50-minute hour. Edward was a tall, tortured, schizophrenic man. He believed he was both vampire and victim. He had a grayish-pale complexion and dark-ringed eyes frozen in a stare. He did not sleep at night. He would, however, appear regularly for his treatment hours.

For the therapist the experience of sitting with Edward was profoundly disturbing. Edward aroused a primitive anxiety of sadomasochistic surrender. To engage with Edward required courage. Edward's treatment seemed to demand privacy, seemed to ask the therapist to hold within himself the psychotic anxiety of Edward's self-dissolution, and Edward's therapist was by nature a quiet, private man.

After a protracted period of depressive withdrawal, isolation, and hopelessness, Edward returned from a visit of several days with his family. Not long after his parents had returned him to the hospital Edward took a lethal overdose of medication and quietly went to sleep. He was discovered by the nursing staff at 4:00 A.M. on their rounds. He was transferred immediately by ambulance to the local hospital. When he was no longer in medical danger the center had to decide whether Edward was to return and if his treatment could continue.

    The following study is an attempt at a systematic and detailed examina-
tion of such inevitable crises and is based on the assumption that it is not the
presence of an upset that marks how a treatment is going, so much as how
the upset is weathered and survived.

Method

Crises are an obvious fact of hospital life within the treatments conducted by
experienced senior clinicians as well as their less experienced junior colleagues. Retrospective examination and the literature (in particular Atwood
and Stolorow, 1984) provide compelling ideas about what precipitates a crisis and its meaning in intensive psychoanalytic treatment. There is, however,
no clear delineation, no experience near analysis of what a crisis is. What
behaviors and experiences constitute its domain? What underlying structure
might give coherence to the manifestly chaotic behaviors and inform the hospital's interventions? The seemingly disordered behaviors, interventions, and
intense affects associated with these treatment crises seem a far cry from any
model of systematic, let alone rational, intervention. Treatment crises and the
interventions around them appear to exist somehow outside of the hospital's
usual image of itself—a departure from the usual psychoanalytic mode of treatment. A simultaneous concern and an inseparable aspect of the study then was
to examine how the hospital functioned to intervene. What if any were the
processes and principles by which the crises were resolved? Were these principles systematic? Most importantly, what was their relationship to the overall psychoanalytic model of the hospital?
    For this study crisis was defined simply as any case-specific treatment
occurrence that was referred to a special meeting called the Clinical Review.
A clinical review is not called casually. Behaviors prevalent in the psychoanalytic work with masochistic patients are at times regressive, threatening,
and potentially self-destructive. A clinical review is not simply called because
of a particular type of behavior, but when a behavior is felt to be a threat to
the treatment. The emphasis is not on managing the patient but on managing the treatment. This meeting can be called by any member of the staff, on
any level, and in any relationship to the patient and the treatment. The patient is usually although not necessarily informed that a clinical review has
been called and is later told of its recommendations. All the facets of the hospital are represented: the psychotherapist, Medical Director, Assistant Medical
Director, and Director of Psychotherapy, Medications Director, Chief Psycholo-
gist, Community Director, Clinical Director, heads of Nursing, the patient's
primary nurse, and the Social Worker. Other therapists and interested mem-

bers of the staff are also invited to participate. It is a serious working meeting led by the Clinical Director, with a prescribed, efficient format. It lasts for only one hour. At the conclusion of the clinical review, the therapist is responsible for recording his or her detailed notes of the proceeding—who was present, the background of the crisis, the pooling of information, the discussion, the recommendations, and guidelines—which are then transcribed and filed in the patient's chart and in a separate file with the Clinical Director. The Director of Psychotherapy reports on the clinical review at the following Morning Conference.

The data for this study were drawn from the transcription of these clinical reviews. Thirty-five transcripts were chosen. Eliminated from the data pool were transcripts lacking in complete information; also eliminated were meetings that were not related to treatment crises (e.g., disagreement around discharge plans, transfers, and medication).

Data Analysis

The method of data analysis was based on the systematic procedures outlined by Giorgi (1975) and Becker (1978) involving two general operations: dissection and articulation. This is a method of qualitative data analysis that proceeds by labeling thematic nonredundant meaning units, moving them by way of structural summaries to progressively more abstract levels, and in the process uncovering relationships between thematic units. It presents redescriptions and reworkings of the information, with a shift of conceptual organization or vantage point by which information is subsumed under some other term (Shafer, 1976). It does not propose to test hypotheses, control variables, or proceed by statistical procedures. It seeks rather to generate theory, to uncover structures, and to suggest principles of functioning.

The outcome of this method of analysis is different from that of other methods, and this difference is most obvious in the manner of presentation of its results. The difference is not only in the absence of quantitative expressions but also in the idea of "explication," that is, the presentation and elucidation of results. The results of a statistical analysis are presented in two distinct parts—the presentation of the outcome of the statistical operations followed by an elucidation of their meaning. In these analyses, the outcome *and* the elucidation of its meaning are one and the same. The results unfold their meaning over a span of pages where the data are presented at various levels of abstraction.

Outline of Data Analysis

Before an initial reading of the data the researcher first had to become as aware as possible of her preconceptions. This was done in discussion with colleagues and then in a written formulation of the researcher's assumptions, preconceptions, and point of view. The data analysis then proceeded as follows:

1. There was an initial reading of data. The researcher noted what was emphasized for each crisis situation and the particular style of the participants in relating and constructing the experience.

2. The researcher then transcribed each of the thirty-five crises individually, noting who the therapist was and summarizing—with very little reduction and using the original words of the clinical review—the history of the crisis, the crisis behavior, the discussion of the group, its interpretation of the crisis, and the guidelines or recommendations suggested by the group. Further, the researcher coded the crisis as to male or female patient, male or female therapist, level of experience of therapist, and diagnosis of patient. Each line of the text of this first summary was numbered for reference. None of the material was rearranged, none of the words were changed.

3. The transcripts were then divided and grouped by type of crisis. Nine types of crisis were noted: (a) sexual acting out; (b) psychotic disorganization—nonassaultive; (c) psychotic disorganization—assaultive, menacing, or hostile; (d) self-destructive behavior in nonpsychotic patients (e.g., self-mutilation, suicide threats, laxative abuse); (e) self-destructive behavior in psychotic patients; (f) alcohol and drug abuse; (g) acting out against the institution and patient community (e.g., theft, fire setting, vandalism, assaults against patients); (h) withdrawal (e.g., schizoid withdrawal from the community, mutism, withdrawal from treatment); (i) nutritional crisis in any diagnostic group.

4. The researcher then sorted the summary statements into the nine types of crisis. Each of the nine categories was then summarized at a more abstract level. At that point in the analysis the data in each category showed no differentiation in the recommended approach to the crisis.

5. The same procedure was then repeated, grouping the crises by other criteria, such as sex of patient, diagnosis of patient, sex of therapist, and level of experience of therapist. Again, recommendations for each crisis were not differentiated by any of these factors but were consistent across groups.

6. The categories were then collapsed for a reexamination of the summaries of the thirty-five discussions and the thirty-five recommendations. To do this the researcher studied the individual sentences, each of which was sorted into one or more thematic categories. The researcher had to find the thematic meaning units and reorganize the data around these nonredundant themes.

7. These thematic units were once again reexamined and reorganized and rewritten into a more coherent statement, still in the original words of the clinical review. Meaningful thematic relationships were further illuminated. The

categories and key terms employed were developed through contact with the data and not before (Giorgi, 1972).

8. At the final step of data analysis the researcher attempted to articulate the structure of the experience as revealed by the above step. This formulation of the coherent underlying structure was the analysis at its most abstract and generalized level, which was nevertheless grounded in the relationship between concrete particulars.

Results*

In a crisis the ongoing therapeutic activity of the hospital has been interrupted. The collectively held image of the hospital—its way of understanding and defining itself, its ability to empathize, to "hold," to master conflicts, to modulate tension—has been threatened. There is a pull to participate in the inner masochistically organized world of the patient. One or all of the therapeutic participants feels overwhelmed, misunderstood, unheard, or unsupported. There is a state of fragmentation and anger, often unacknowledged.

During crises there is a tendency to be reductionistic, to point to this or that or them as the problem; and also a tendency to "take action," to "do something," to "get control." This is often expressed as "getting tougher" and/ or "giving more." In opposition to this, the clinical review as the first intervention of the analytic hospital strives for a tolerance of ambiguity rather than reductionism and strives to reinstate the method of interpretive understanding rather than action.

With the call for a clinical review the first intervention has taken place. Formally the clinical review functions in direct opposition to reductionist thinking and precipitous action. It is as if in the middle of battle the hospital takes time to regroup. The hospital begins to reinstate order by the very nature of the anticipated meeting. Since the meetings themselves are scheduled for only one particular day a week there is a delay. Although this delay is felt as imposed and is criticized, it is important in face of the felt urgency to act. The meeting is hierarchical with all groups and directors represented. The order of presentation and the areas covered are ritualistically prescribed. There are many ideas, often contradictory. The clinical review enforces through its variety of voices the tolerance for ambiguity in a context of order. The clinical review reinstates the central activity of the psychoanalytic hospital, the interpretive function of the analyst. The clinical review's manifest purpose is to understand. It is not so much a question of "what should we do," but rather "what does this mean," and "how are we to understand this behavior."

---

*All quotations are taken directly from the original clinical review transcripts.

In terms of the content of the clinical review itself, the data analysis reveals a coherent unifying structure, a treatment approach or method for the management of crises. The type of crisis does not differentiate the approach, which operates according to four principles. The principles operate in concert, in a particular order, and represent four realms of action. These actions are not just congruent with the overall treatment philosophy of the hospital. They are in fact an inseparable manifestation of the clinical theory that informs them and are familiar to psychoanalysis as an interpretive science. Each principle is designated by its most salient feature "re-membering," "holding," "understanding," and "reckoning."

1. Restoring Order by Re-membering

The structure of the open hospital exists, in part, through the meaning-giving actions of its members. All the members of the therapeutic hospital have an identity and a place defined by their actions. Actions mean more than a set of behaviors; they include a mode of experiencing a complex set of interrelationships based on values, responsibilities, limits, power, and powerlessness. Part of the crisis involves a breakdown of this order. In the formal assembly of the clinical review the hospital "re-members" itself. The hospital reexperiences its members in the presence of all its members. It is, in a sense, the body of the hospital standing in front of a mirror.

Through its formal process and its verbal dialogue, the clinical review re-members each segment of the hospital:

a. The Clinical Administration. The clinical administration provides a greater context, a law. This includes the law they represent and the actual physical presence of the senior administrative clinicians, an authority whose presence is visible to the entire hospital community. The authoritative presence of a functioning clinical administration places the therapeutic dyad in a greater context. The intensely dyadic nature of the analytic relationship needs the modulating presence of a clinical administrative authority. This implies safety to the members of the therapeutic dyad who at times find themselves isolated, endangered by the intensity of their mutual relatedness, at odds with the community and administration, at odds with each other. The analyst and the patient may experience this authority in many ways. The importance, however, is that it be there to be pushed against or reconciled with.

The clinical administrative authority re-members making itself through its injunctions:

> The patient is encouraged to discuss his treatment with the Clinical Director who will inform him of the staff's understanding of the treatment.
> The clinical review cannot condone the patient's violent behavior.

The patient is to be informed how seriously the institution takes these behaviors, that radical changes in her therapy plan may follow should they continue.

b. The Nursing Staff. All are reminded of the deprivations and boundaries of the nursing role. The nurses are protected from voicelessly absorbing assault through this acknowledgment. The nurses, as frontline troops, experience at times the full impact of the assault, chaos, anxiety, and intense affect of the masochistically organized patient. They are asked on a day-to-day basis to absorb without retaliation and with absolute reliability the rageful and lustful behaviors of the patients. Their position in relation to the patient–analyst dyad places them as next-closest observer to the psychotherapy. But because of their role definition they have less power, less voice, and feel encouraged to absorb and endure masochistically. The nurses often precipitate indirectly the convening of the clinical review by naming a limit: "We are asked to go beyond the definition of nursing in an open hospital as we understand it."

The hospital re-members the nurses. Acknowledgment of their presence can protect them at times from what feels like unacknowledged abuse. All members must be seen and continually held in mind.

c. The Patient Community. In re-membering the patient community, behavior is witnessed as part of a community system of interacting patient participants. Within the patient community context, crises are beyond the personal and intrapsychic. There are "extrusion processes," "scapegoating processes," "delinquent attempts at community self-definition," and "symbolic murder, guilt, and restitution." There is the repeated tension around the most psychotic and most sociopathic members who are often extruded in pairs after periods of tension as the community tries to define itself. The community must be remembered as a force to be worked with, heard from, and understood. It is often noted that the patient community in its treatment of the patient mirrors the clinical staff's treatment of the analyst.

d. The Analyst. In re-membering the therapist, it is seen that what is absent from the therapy appears in a public and problematic way in other contexts. The injunction to the analyst is to "get the behavior back in the psychotherapy." This is an interpretation of acting out that implies that there is an unacknowledged collusion between patient and analyst to not address or name an important issue within the treatment dyad. Appropriate communications belong to appropriate places and often, when unheard, appear in other ways as lived-out actions. Often the patient and analyst are seen to be colluding to protect the therapeutic dyad at the expense of the treatment. What the patient feels cannot be safely communicated to the analyst is communicated to other segments of the therapeutic community. The communicative value of this behavior disappears with the danger of the actions, as well as appearing in areas (nursing staff, patient community) whose functions are not to interpret behavior. The responsibility of interpretation is that of the analyst. The symbolic, metaphorical, and fantasy modes of wishing and being belong to the space defined by the therapeutic dyad. The analyst is directed to attend to what is not being named.

e. The Patient. The therapeutic hospital includes the membership and full participation of the patient. The patient must take responsibility for the maintenance of his or her own treatment. Such responsibility balances the regressive pull of individual treatment. In a crisis there has been an emptying process through which the patient externalizes his or her anxiety, hopelessness, fear, or confusion. Chaotic situations are created in which others start feeling that somebody must do something. The seemingly passive position of the patient is unmasked. The dysphoric affect must be relocated in the patient, as well as the necessary controlling actions. "The therapy can only continue if the patient can adequately work to create a therapeutic atmosphere." "The anxiety for the maintenance of the treatment must be put back into the patient."

2. Intervening by "Holding" the Treatment in Time

In the treatment, the therapeutic hospital is always mindful of the dimension of time—mindful of the past, the present, and the future, mindful of continuity, movement, and flux. The hospital holds the treatment in the dimension of time since these patients are stubbornly ahistorical, freezing time in the deadening stereotypy of master–slave, attacking continuity, and sabotaging change. Affect states become an unending present, a "no exit" of growing hopelessness and desperation.

In a crisis, this function has been compromised. Time contracts for one or more of the participants. It appears that the hospital itself has no memory and no hope. The clinical review intervenes by reinstating this dimension— by waiting, by reviewing, and by predicting. The clinical review remembers the history of the treatment of the specific patient and also the treatment of other similar patients. There is a necessary working tension between a particular crisis, and the generalized history of other such crises. This places the immediate behavior in a greater context. There is an overall assessment of progress versus impasse.

The clinical review "holds" the possibility of change. This is often expressed as "a second chance." A statement is made that implies that something has *not* been destroyed by an assault or by default, but rather that something is being built, in time, possibly even through such assaults and survivals. This understanding delineates a space which the hospital, in a sense, holds in mind, a space that holds the participants in the treatment.

3. Reinstating Interpretive Understanding as the Central Activity of the Psychoanalytic Hospital

Interpretative understanding, the explication of personal meaning, is the central activity of the psychoanalytic hospital. According to this principle a crisis is a failure in understanding. Something went unheard or misheard. In this sense, in a crisis it is the patient who gives the hospital a second chance to "get it right." The crisis behavior is a communication with the sound turned up and full of distortion and static.

The clinical review proceeds by way of inquiry: "What are the potential merits of the current crisis behavior?" "Was there a precrisis error?" "Has each incidence of the acting out been judged on its own merits?" "What is the patient's assessment of the crisis, and what is his 'cure'?" "Does the behavior merely replicate something or is it analyzable if we do not unwittingly participate in the replication?" "What is being communicated?" "What is the function of the crisis behavior intrapsychically?" "What does it supply to the patient that is otherwise lacking?" The clinical review understands that "psychoses can populate an empty world or allow something to come to awareness that couldn't be talked about or thought about before," that "death can be a love relationship," and that "pain can be necessary for maintaining the integrity of a self."

Understanding, however, is not sufficient unto itself, for in the communication of this understanding there are further possibilities for failure. The precipitous unmasking of an unfolding fantasy or a secret desire might be experienced as an assault; to be understood too well, too soon, might be experienced as a dangerous merger. Timing and tact, how and when, are understandings about understanding.

Meaning is ambiguous; behavior serves many functions. Understanding, however, tends to search for the one answer, a rule of thumb or a theory to cling to. In opposition to this, the many voices of the clinical review enforce the tolerance for ambiguity. The consensus typically appears as an alignment of multiple meanings rather than an autocratic elimination of meanings.

4. Restoring the Framework by "Reckoning"

Actions are real and are acknowledged as such by reckoning. Reckoning settles accounts, either by repairing, surrendering, or limiting. Reckoning is practical and straightforward. It proceeds by straight lines, the integrity of which ultimately become a framework that supports the treatment.

a. Repairing. The clinical review believes in the impact of actions real and symbolic. The institution and the patient engage in killing as well as healing actions. It is therefore necessary at times to make reparation for wounds inflicted and received. The possibility for reparation must be taught and cannot be taken for granted. It can be experienced as a crucial occurrence. The ability to make reparation on the part of all participants is a healing option—to be sorry that someone was hurt out of a lack of understanding, out of fear, out of anger, through oversight, through human limitation—analyst to patient, patient to community, administration to patient, patient to analyst, and so on.

b. Surrendering. When psychotherapy turns into a battle, the very real desire to defeat and destroy is named. The defeating process is often named by those not immediately engaged in the struggle. This creates a bracketing of the experience, allowing the analyst and the hospital to work toward clarifying the meaning of defeat to the patient without getting caught up unaware in the cycle of being defeated. Rather than resist, the hospital and analyst surrender. "I suppose that if you want to defeat me, that is of course an achievable goal." When caught in the struggle it is difficult not to try harder.

c. Limiting. Implicit in the open hospital are invisible but known limits that are not to be transgressed. When these limits are crossed something can be irreparably broken. The clinical review affirms that behavior has consequences and that boundaries can be crossed in uninterpretable ways. When wishes are made actual, treatment becomes a replication from which the participants cannot extricate themselves. There is a moment when saying no, when calling an end, becomes the most powerful interpretation. Understanding gains its force and function through knowing the limits of its realm.

Discussion

Each crisis presented in the first part of this chapter was brought to a clinical review. The following discussions and recommendations are taken directly from the recorded notes of the clinical reviews and illustrate the principles discussed above:

Jeannine (see p.205)

Discussion. The nursing staff felt that a staff person had to be with the patient at all times to prevent the risk of a fire. Such specialing felt to them more like guarding than working with the patient. It was observed that Jean-

nine was in a hypomanic episode, and that the problem was one of containment.

Several possibilities were seen to exist: (1) to transfer her to a closed hospital for a period of time while concomitantly keeping open her place at our
hospital; (2) to continue the nursing and patient specialing; (3) to hire special nurses on a private basis; (4) to medicate her. The problem of medication was complicated since the family's religious beliefs forbade the use of
medication.

It was observed that since Jeannine was in a hypomanic state, affect and
not idea determined her behavior. Therefore, a pact or a contract with her
would not be effective. Further, it was observed that over a period of time
Jeannine would on her own come out of this hypomanic episode.

As the options were reviewed it was clear that the hospital could offer
her transfer to a closed hospital for a period of time and also that the current
pattern of nursing specialing could not continue, as the nurses were being
taken beyond their limits. The hospital was also prepared to offer Jeannine
the resource of medication, but whether her family would accept the use of
medication would be left up to them. The introduction of special, privately
paid nurses was discussed, but it was felt that it was not wise to go beyond
the normal limits of our structure.

In terms of the meaning of the behavior, it was felt that Jeannine now
showed through her actions what she had been aware of all along, but that
she had to become psychotic in order to share that awareness. It was felt that
it had taken enormous control on her part to keep these experiences, particularly the sexualized ones, out of awareness. Now, anticipating her therapist's
upcoming vacation, she would no longer keep private what had been felt in
relation to her therapist.

Recommendations. The therapist would offer the patient the options of
a closed hospital for a period, or the use of medication, which the patient may
choose or turn down. The clinical review felt that we could keep this patient
if we "stick with her." In doing that it was particularly important to work with
the patient community since their reactions to the grossly psychotic behavior
of this formerly prim and proper young lady were extremely important in this
case. In relation to Jeannine, it was important that we did not ask her to refrain from doing things, but rather approached her as someone who was having a rough time, inviting her to stick around with the patients and the staff.
We were to present things in which she might join us, activities that might
"make her more comfortable." A nursing plan was established.

Outcome. Jeannine chose medication and continued treatment in the hospital.

Donald (see p. 206)

Discussion. It was noted that this incident was not handled by the usual community process of patient-run committees. The incident seemed to be blown out of proportion and was being used for other purposes by the community. One understanding of the behavior was that Donald felt upset by the female patient's chronicity since he saw himself in her. Further, the female patient, an angry and irritable older woman, also reminded him of his mother.

Recommendations. The clinical review decided to leave the situation open as regards the patient's treatability in an open setting. If he could not refrain from physical violence then his treatability in an open setting would be called into question. The patient was to be informed by the clinical director that his future behavior would dictate his course, adding that the clinical review could not condone knocking people down. It was suggested that the two patients would be brought together to discuss the situation. It should be pointed out to Donald that he seemed repeatedly to get himself in these untenable situations and he should be made curious about this pattern.

It was also felt by the clinical review that the female patient's therapist should apologize to her for this occurrence since in her psychotic state she might not understand the issues involved without her therapist's support.

Outcome. Donald continued his treatment in the hospital with no further assaultive incidents.

Janet (see p. 207)

Discussion. All present agreed that the therapy had been attacked in a serious way but that its viability was a possibility if adequate reparations were made. Clearly, more therapeutic work had to be done, but it was up to the patient to decide whether she could engage in an effort to create a therapeutic atmosphere. The meaning of this behavior was highlighted by the fact that it occurred at a new point in her treatment when the new issue of separation was beginning to emerge. Janet herself commented that before the theft of the folder the idea of leaving the hospital was a threat she used to torture her doctor. Subsequent to the theft it became something she feared. Concern was voiced about the emergence of sexual issues following this incident, noting that Janet had a great capacity to "trash" herself through her sexual behavior. One discussant cited several reasons why he was not sanguine about the therapy after this incident. These included Janet's expectation that her therapist might send her to jail for the theft and his sense that Janet's offer of love and new symptoms (vomiting) reflected insincerity.

Recommendations. The patient would be informed that the therapy should continue if she could adequately work to create a collaborative atmosphere. The patient was to be asked to do a careful and lengthy review of what she had gotten out of her treatment thus far, in that it is not enough to look at her doctor's record of the therapy, she must discover and internalize her own record of therapy. Adequate reparations would be needed to make up for the damage done. These would include a follow-up meeting with the Director of Psychotherapy to explain Janet's decision if she chooses to continue her therapy with her doctor. Janet must also have some communication with the prestigious consultant to explain and repair her abuse of him as a consultant. None of this should be presented to her as an ultimatum. The clinical review stressed that the therapist must avoid making himself hostage to some specific time-table of repair, suggesting instead that this be presented simply as a necessary task if the treatment was to continue.

Outcome. Janet followed the recommendations outlined and continued her treatment.

Lillian (see p. 208)

Discussion. Although the therapy was seen to be heading in the right direction, it was felt that there was a chronic and recurrent problem. Two interpretations of the drinking were expressed: (1) that it was a rapprochement crisis and that the patient had difficulty reconnecting with the therapist after vacation; (2) that the patient had a recurrent, "negative therapeutic reaction" to change. Any move forward was felt with much anxiety and she immediately destroyed any progress. In any case, it was felt by the clinical review that something was being left out or split off from the therapy, and that the patient and the therapist were protecting the therapeutic dyad at the expense of the treatment. The patient's drinking was understood as a way of draining her intense transference feelings. Further, the therapist was replicating the family's unseeing and rescuing behavior rather than interpreting it. The community context for this behavior was also discussed. It was seen that Lillian enlisted male patients to protect her from the nursing staff, while flaunting her desirability in a way to not provoke their envy.

Recommendations. It was felt that an active collaboration of the nursing staff and the patient community members around alcoholism was necessary. Lillian was told that she could in fact destroy her treatment with her drinking, but that her therapist would continue to work with her if she first went to a twenty-one-day detoxification program. At the end of this detoxification program another clinical review would be called to determine the necessary conditions for her participation in treatment at our hospital. Further, she was given an ultimatum by her therapist about her sexual acting out with psychotic male patients. The therapist told Lillian that what could be tolerated in an individual therapy in a large urban, metropolitan area would not be tolerated in an open hospital. That her behavior in fact could get her thrown out of the hospital since the patient community and the administration found it intolerable and destructive to the welfare of the other patients.

Outcome. The patient chose to go to a twenty-one-day detoxification program at the end of which a clinical review was reconvened, and she was readmitted to the hospital under the conditions that she maintain her sobriety and continue as an active participant in AA. The patient continued her treatment and maintained her sobriety.

Jeffrey (see p. 209)

Discussion 1. The discussion focused on the discrepancies in the staff's perception of the patient. One impression was that the patient had been making significant progress in his treatment; however, another perception of the patient was that Jeffrey's behavior pattern of acting out had remained relatively constant throughout his stay at the hospital. It was seen that both perceptions were accurate, reflecting simultaneously Jeffrey's growing attachment to his therapy and the continuing fragility of his defenses in the face of minor disruptions and empathic failures.

One understanding of the behavior was that Jeffrey had primarily been engaged in a seduction of his female therapist, and when he felt rebuffed by her precipitous interpretation of this seductive action, he had willfully destroyed the treatment. This was seen as a retaliation for his dashed hopes. In the same vein, another discussant felt that Jeffrey repetitively punished himself for his wishes and longings for intimacy and nurturance, and that guilt seemed to motivate much of his behavior.

Recommendations 1. Another clinical review was to be held the following week to closely monitor this patient's behavior.

Discussion 2. Jeffrey's behavior was seen to become progressively more threatening, hostile, and unapproachable. His self-medication and use of illicit drugs was discussed in terms of how he made it difficult for the hospital to determine how he might respond to any of our interventions since he was so unpredictable.

Recommendations 2. The final consensus was that Jeffrey needed to be informed that his treatment was in jeopardy. Jeffrey needed to be included as much as possible in determining whether he could remain at the hospital. It was recommended that he be encouraged to take an increased amount of antipsychotic medication although he was quite resistant to this. He was advised to consult immediately with the Director of Medications for a discussion of this. It was also recommended that he consult the Director of Psychotherapy to evaluate whether a change of therapist would be advisable. Given his continuing attachment to his current therapist, it seemed that if he managed to contain his behavior in the short run, he might usefully explore in consultation with the Director of Psychotherapy whether he wished to switch therapists or work it out with his current therapist with the support of the hospital. Finally it was decided that if he was unable to work with the staff around the issues listed above, it was recommended that the patient be transferred to a closed hospital setting.

Outcome. The patient was transferred to a closed hospital setting where he once again interrupted his treatment and was discharged against the hospital's advice.

Edward (see p. 210)

Discussion. Edward's inexorable, relentless movement to suicide, which he felt was the only remaining option for him, was discussed. The focus was to decide whether Edward, who was now in a medical unit at a local hospital recovering from his overdose, would be allowed to come back to the hospital and continue his treatment. It was felt that Edward saw himself as a terminally ill person who was waiting to die. It was felt that there were no objective means to assess the risk of suicide accurately in this patient. What was obvious was that the attempt directly followed his visit with his family. The question of what was different about this particular meeting with his family needed to be carefully explored. The Clinical Director, in a consultation with the patient at the medical hospital, tried to locate what had been different about this family visit. Edward had read an article about aspirin overdose and had his parents stop at a pharmacy where he surreptitiously bought the aspirin. His mother followed him into the store, she did not pursue him despite her suspicions, nor did she share her concern with any staff. The mother's wish for the death of this child was discussed; also his desire to cure the family through his martyrdom.

It was noted that his withdrawal from the community and the isolation of the treatment struggle reflected a treatment impasse.

Recommendations. If a dialogue could be initiated to explore the issues that had resulted in an impasse between the patient and his therapist, it was then felt that it would be possible to continue the psychotherapeutic work. The clinical review stressed the patient's murderous wishes, which were seen in the malignancy of his attack against the therapist and the treatment, and in his lying and withholding. Edward's level of functioning was described as primitive, infantile, and merged. Crucial to Edward's possible continuation of treatment would be the successful undoing of his need to defeat his therapist. The clinical review stressed the necessity of getting back to the hurt that initially resulted in the patient's decision to withdraw from treatment altogether.

Outcome. The patient returned to the hospital and continued his treatment.

Conclusion

Crises are inevitable in the treatment of vulnerable and masochistically organized patients. Surviving these crises requires a restoration of the treatment's structure. Structures are created by theories, values, and identities, an idea commonly accepted in individual psychoanalytic treatment. This study describes how hospital treatment, like individual treatment also functions in relation to the integrity of its structural framework. Within the day-to-day work of the institution this is not easily seen because of the many voices of leadership, the diverse needs and anxieties of the participants, and the fracturing nature of the psychopathology. The underlying psychoanalytic principles at an institutional level, although they are not as recognized in the literature, nevertheless inform the work and are vital to its success. The study of crises presents an opportunity to delineate the structure, to elucidate the underlying principles. By approaching a crisis in this manner we can see what we do, what we cannot do, and what we have done wrong. When we are clear about who we are and what we do and then do it, the work is able to continue.

References

Atwood, G., & Stolorow, R. (1984), *Structures of Subjectivity and Explorations in Psychoanalytic Phenomenology*. Hillsdale, N.J.: Analytic Press.

Becker, C. (1978), *Phenomenology: An Overview of Theoretical and Methodological Issues.* Unpublished manuscript. California State University, Hayward, CA.

Giorgi, A. (1972), An application of phenomenological method in psychology. In: *Duquesne Studies in Phenomenological Psychology*, Vol. 2, eds. A. Giorgi, C. Fisher, & E. Murray. Pittsburgh: Duquesne University Press.

——— (1975), Convergence and divergence of qualitative and quantitative methods in psychology. In: *Duquesne Studies in Phenomenological Psychology*, Vol. 2, eds. A. Giorgi, C. Fisher, & E. Murray. Pittsburgh: Duquesne University Press.

Modell, A. (1976), The "holding environment" and the therapeutic action of psychoanalysis. *J. Amer. Psychoanal. Assn.*, 24:285–307.

Sandler, J., & Rosenblatt, B. (1962), The concept of the representational word. *The Psycho-analytic Study of the Child*, 17:128–145. New York: International Universities Press.

Shafer, R. (1976), *A New Language for Psychoanalysis*. New Haven and London: Yale University Press.

Winnicott, D. W. (1960), The theory of the parent-infant relationship. In: *The Maturational Processes and the Facilitating Environment*. New York: International Universities Press, pp. 37–55, 1965.

Afterword:
A Note to the Reader

Our project from the beginning was a communication from clinician to clinician. We felt, therefore, that something further should be said but resisted the temptation of writing a conclusion that might artificially distort our material in some final summing-up. From the outset our goal was to present the complexity of experience that constitutes living a life without forcing homogeneity by eliminating information. This afterword then is rather a lingering with our readers, and a statement of completion—what we have done and what we have not done.

Otto Will, in his paper on the uniqueness of the psychotherapeutic relationship, stated that the analyst acquires a range of tolerances not easily maintained: "involved, he is detached; alone, he is close; expert and experienced, he accepts the limitations of these terms; with change he is constant; and seeking to mold another, he is to an extent molded" (1971, p. 43). We have attempted to communicate something of this experience to our readers without doing violence to the privacy and unique reality delimited by the patient–analyst bond. The paradoxical states outlined by Will, states which are so much a part of the psychotherapeutic relationship, are not easily revealed to a third party. For very real reasons, we are, as Winnicott suggests, a profession of isolates. We work in private, in a space marked off by different rules than those that govern everyday relations, that allows for and protects the unique attachment we speak of as therapeutic. There is something in this attachment that defies communication, that cannot easily be labeled or named. In fact, the analyst verges on betrayal when he or she takes the position of the other, joining with the audience by articulating the experience in the language of the witness rather than that of the participant. Nonetheless, because in this relationship to our patient, we remain analyst, not parent, friend, teacher, or lover, we have organized our experience in the language of our discipline and joined it with the discourse of our profession.

In our work, we have come back again and again to the concept of psychoanalytic treatment as a developmental process. We have seen how very difficult it is for these patients to make their first steps at revealing themselves to their therapists. Typically, the symptoms presented early in the treatment are designed to obscure more than to communicate. Yet they reveal much about the patient's adaptation, whether it be schizoid withdrawal or flamboyant self-mutilation. The therapy works toward a state of attachment and communication with the masochistic patient. These patients have spent a lifetime feeling objectified, frozen, and unconnected; and, a subjective self has never quite been attained. During the period of engagement, the analyst acts as a container structuring and limiting, while at the same time providing glimpses of new expanses yet to be charted and traveled. What follows is often a time of overt and covert exchange, in which the enactment of the transference begins to unfold. The transference must be met with an openness and delight, akin to how we greet the playfulness of young children elaborating in fantasy their desires, disappointments, and conflicts. The elaboration and examination of the concurrent countertransference fantasies is no less crucial. Often it has seemed to us that this phase involves a mutually regulated exchange of projections based on past relationships, the history of the treatment, and the assessment of the probable future outcome of the work together.

Our patients bring with them a fractured sense of their own identities and of their capacities. In the course of the treatment, a mending seems to occur to the extent that they discover a feeling of self-initiated action, of being someone who acts. For the analyst, the treatment is also always a learning process in which there is a rediscovery of limits, both personal flaws and limitations and the limits of influence. While the patient's experience of greater expansiveness and freedom often seems the converse of the analyst's limited scope of influence and mirroring appreciation of the patient's changes, both experience a kind of liberation in the fullness of their dialogue with one another.

We have presented a group of patients and our attempts to understand and intervene in their lives. In this we have come to appreciate the complex meanings and functions of their self-inflicted suffering. We have noted an equivalent complexity in our responses that required an ongoing self-scrutiny and the support of our colleagues. We have not drawn tight conclusions, offered a new theory, or developed fully the implications of our narratives. We speak rather broadly of developmental processes, and the creative syntheses of a history, a biology, and a culture of necessary attachments. And we speak of personhood.

Our lives are an interplay of fragmentation and integration. Time repeatedly challenges the meaning and stability of what is, subjecting us to random experiences of loss and pain. We have written about individuals who have woven long-standing situations of pain into personhood. The personhood of the analyst is likewise a synthesis of personal experience. It is the opportunity of our profession that turns the pain in the personhood of the healer into clinical understanding; and it is the reweaving of the patient's pain that brings new meaning and creates an artifact of the therapeutic bond.

Reference

Will, O. (1971), The patient and the psychotherapist: Comments on the "uniqueness" of their relationship. In: *In the Name of Life; Essays in Honor of Erich Fromm*, eds. B. Landis & E. Tauber. New York: Holt, Rinehart & Winston, pp. 15–43.

Name Index

Subject Index

Abandonment
  hospitalization of child and, 55-56
negative identity and, 117
pregnancy of analyst and, 96
Abuse, substance, 116
  alcohol, 119
    binge and, 33
    loneliness and, 118
Accident
  automobile, 119
  burn as, 41, 45
Accommodation/assimilation, 181
Acting out, 136
Admiration, 87
Adolescence
  negative identity and, 106, 117-119
  traumatic separation and, 185
Aesthetics, 66
  Agoraphobia, 67
Alcohol abuse, 119
  binge and, 33
  loneliness and, 118
Alienation of body, 20, 21
  psyche and, 37–49
Analyst
  absence of, 29–36
  intense relationship with, 155
  masochistic patient and, 10–13, 169–178
  Menaker's position on, 52–53
  pregnancy of, 95–103
  public and private relationship with, 137
  refusal to recognize, 156, 161
  re-membering and, 216–217
Anger
  family's reaction to, 60
  father not allowing, 138
  at mother, 130
Annihilation, 51

Anorexia nervosa, 22, 25, 37–49
  pregnancy of analyst and, 99
Anxiety
  depressive, 70
  external regulator of, 67
Appendage, son as, 158, 160
Art, 66
  collage and, 134
  painting of man and mother, 130–131
  schizophrenic patient and, 69–70
  sculpture by patient, 59–60
Artist, hunger, 48
Assault
  physical, 206
  pregnancy as, 101–102
Assimilation, 181
Automobile accident, 119

Beating
  fantasies about, 7–9
  as image of father, 143
  male patient and, 125
Bedwetting, 112–113
Binge
  alcoholic, 33
  bulimia and, 53
Birth, delayed, 84–85
Body
  anorexia patient and, 37–49
  hero as victim and, 88–92
  mother's relationship with, 33
Bonding
  mother–daughter, 5
  mother–infant, 20
Breast, mother's hatred of, 45
Brother
  cruelty of, 114–115
  death of, 39
  dream of violence by, 35–36
  heart attack and, 133